EXPERT

Intensive training. Intensive practice. Be an Expert.

Contents

Contents

Reading (Note and table completion)

> COURSEBOOK pages 8–9 and 18–19

Before you read

1a Read the title of the reading passage. What information do you think the passage will contain?

  1 how the monarch butterfly solves problems
  2 threats to the monarch butterfly's survival

 b Read the passage. Was your answer to the question in Exercise 1a correct?

2 Consider the words in italics in the reading passage: *migration, navigational, genetic, compass.* If you don't know the meaning, try to guess it, then check in your dictionary.

Predict language; Scan for information

3a Read around the gaps in the test task in Exercise 4. What class of word (noun, adjective, verb, etc.) are you looking for?

  1 *a noun/adjective*
  2 _____
  3 _____
  4 _____
  5 _____
  6 _____

 b Find words/phrases in the reading passage that correspond to the following sub-headings in the notes in Exercise 4.

  1 Habitats   _____
  2 Reasons for migration _____
  3 Scientific interest   _____
  4 New findings   _____

Test practice

4 Read the strategy and complete the test tasks.

> **TEST STRATEGY**
>
> In note- and table-completion tasks, the information may not follow the same order as the information in the reading passage.

Questions 1–6

Complete the notes below.

*Choose **NO MORE THAN TWO WORDS** from the passage for each answer.*

> **Monarch Butterflies**
>
> <u>Habitats</u>
> Summer – eastern US and south-eastern Canada
> Winter – central Mexico
> The monarch's dependence on wintering in a
> 1 _____ → highly endangered.
>
> <u>Reasons for migration</u>
> Southwards → to escape 2 _____
> Northwards → to lay eggs near 3 _____
>
> <u>Scientific interest</u>
> Individuals live for less than one year, so cannot
> 4 _____ a route.
> The butterflies' 5 _____ skills seem to be genetic.
>
> <u>New findings</u>
> Scientists have discovered how the butterflies
> determine 6 _____ while flying.

> HELP

1 The missing word must be an adjective or a countable noun beginning with a consonant.

Inside the brain of the monarch butterfly

The annual *migration* of monarch butterflies is considered to be one of the most remarkable natural phenomena on the planet. The insects are typically found in the eastern US and south-eastern Canada, where they spend the summer months before flying south to a single spot in central Mexico (on top of the Michoacán Mountains) for the winter. The journey can involve travelling up to 3,000 miles. At these wintering sites they cluster on top of trees in their millions, and the air is full of the sound of their wings. Their reliance on this single spot to spend the winter has led to the monarch butterfly being rated as one of the most endangered creatures in the world.

Monarch butterflies migrate for two reasons. Firstly, they cannot withstand the freezing temperatures in northern and central climates. Secondly, the milkweed plants, which are the food that their larvae prefer, do not grow in their overwintering sites, so the spring generation must fly back northwards to lay their eggs in places where the plants are plentiful.

This ability to continue travelling in the same direction to the same spot year after year has been the subject of scientific interest for decades. The butterflies have a relatively short lifespan: individuals live between two and eight months. Some butterflies make the whole trip, but others lay eggs and die on the way, leaving offspring to complete the journey. It follows from this that the butterflies do not learn their route; instead their *navigational* abilities appear to be part of a *genetic* programme that enables them to make the journey. Their migration is repeated instinctively by generations, and has continued even as monarch numbers have plummeted due to loss of their main food source.

Now at last, scientists believe they have cracked the secret of how the monarch butterfly's brain works to establish the direction of flight during migration. It is hoped this discovery will help scientists understand how they navigate and locate their food.

Dr Eli Shlizerman, lead author of the study, joined with colleagues at the University of Michigan and the University of Massachusetts to show how the monarch's internal *compass* works. Dr Shlizerman, who is an assistant professor at the University of Washington in the US, said: "Their brain, which contains a compass, integrates two pieces of information – the time of day and the sun's position on the horizon – to find the southerly direction. We wanted to understand how the monarch is processing these different types of information to yield this constant behaviour – flying south-west each autumn."

Monarchs use their large, complex eyes to monitor where the sun is in the sky, but this information alone is not enough to determine direction. Each butterfly must combine that information with the time of day to know where to go. Like most animals, including humans, monarchs possess an internal clock based on the rhythmic expression of key genes. This clock maintains a daily pattern of physiology and behaviour and in the monarch butterfly, it is centred in the antennae.

Dr Shlizerman added: "We created a computer model that incorporated this information – how the antennae and eyes send this information to the brain. Our goal was to model what type of control mechanism would be at work within the brain, and then asked whether our model could guarantee sustained navigation in the south-westerly direction."

Their model also shows that when they make a mistake, monarchs do not simply make the shortest turn to get back on route. The model includes a unique feature – a 'separation point' that controls whether the monarch turns right or left to make a course correction.

Dr Shlizerman explained: "The location of this point in the monarch butterfly's visual field changes throughout the day, and our model predicts that the monarch will not cross this point when it makes a course correction. In experiments with living monarchs at different times of the day, it is evident that there are occasions where their turns in course corrections are unusually long, slow, or meandering. These could be cases where they can't do a shorter turn, because that would require crossing the separation point. And when that happens, their compass points north-east instead of south-west. It's a simple, robust system to explain how these butterflies – generation after generation – make this remarkable migration."

Questions 7–10

Complete the table below.

*Choose **NO MORE THAN TWO WORDS AND/OR A NUMBER** from the passage for each answer.*

How the monarch butterfly finds its way

Part of the body	Characteristics	Function
eyes	big and 7 _____	check the position of the 8 _____
9 _____	contain the internal clock	register the time of day
brain	has a 10 _____	combines two pieces of information

EXPERT LANGUAGE

Function is a very common word in written English, especially academic English. The noun and the verb have the same form, while the adjective is *functional*.

Task analysis

5   Answer the questions.

1   Do any of your answers contain more than two words?
2   Have you copied all the words correctly?
3   Do the words you have written fit the notes/table grammatically?

Vocabulary

> **COURSEBOOK** pages 10 and 16

The language of learning

1 Choose the correct option in *italics* to complete the sentences.

1 The most effective way to *gain / acquire* a new language is to spend time in the country where it is spoken.

2 Monarch butterflies have the *method / capacity* to steer an accurate course for thousands of miles.

3 Getting a large number of people to *retain / focus* on the same problem can be an effective way of arriving at a solution.

4 Developing new medical treatments and bringing them to market can be a lengthy *method / process*.

5 The easy availability of reference materials means it is unnecessary for people to *retain / process* a large number of facts.

6 Behavioural training typically involves changing a person's normal *capacity / reaction* in a given situation.

7 During a training course, keeping a diary can help trainees to maintain *reaction / focus*.

8 One effective training *process / method* involves getting trainees to teach other people.

9 During medical training, doctors rehearse the *process / capacity* of handing patients over to new staff at the end of the day.

10 Recent *research / focus* has provided new evidence about the monarch butterfly's brain.

2 Complete the sentences below, using your own opinions and experience.

1 I find that the best method of retaining new English vocabulary is to _____ .

2 It's difficult to focus on my work if _____ .

3 When I have to process a lot of new information, my usual reaction is to _____ .

4 I recently read a newspaper article about research into _____ .

5 My capacity for _____ is improving.

6 I have acquired quite a lot of knowledge about _____ through _____ .

Collocations

3a Underline the word on the left which collocates best with the word/phrase in bold.

1	demonstrate	establish	express	**intelligence**
2	get	acquire	obtain	**a skill**
3	process	deal	stir	**information**
4	apply	collect	focus	**attention**
5	conduct	make	accomplish	**research**
6	activate	initiate	trigger	**a reaction**

b Complete the sentences with a phrase from Exercise 3a.

1 A lot of practice is necessary when attempting to _____ such as skiing.

2 Although humans often regard themselves as a superior species, a lot of animals _____ .

3 Modern scanning technology has increased scientists' capacity to _____ on the human brain.

4 Research has shown that individuals _____ in a variety of ways, so teachers need to vary their methods accordingly.

5 Images of peaceful, rural landscapes appear to _____ in most individuals.

6 It is difficult to _____ on a task when there are too many visual or auditory distractions.

Describe trends

4 Do you agree or disagree with the following statements?

1 The cost of course materials has gradually increased.

2 Tuition fees have risen steadily over the last few years.

3 The price of computers has fallen slightly in the last year or two.

4 Many students find that their concentration levels fluctuate over the course of a day.

5 Owing to new technology, our understanding of the human brain has risen sharply in the last two decades.

Dictionary skills

5 Complete the spidergram below. Use a dictionary to help you if necessary.

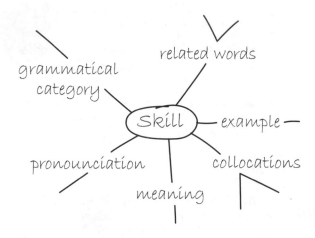

6 Choose another word from Exercise 3a and produce a spidergram.

7a Which of the following ways of recording new vocabulary do you use?

1 add it to an unordered list

2 create a spidergram

3 include it under a topic heading

4 add it to an alphabetical list

b Which way works best for you? Why?

Language development

> **COURSEBOOK** page 13, **EXPERT GRAMMAR** page 176

Synonyms

1a Complete the sentences with the phrases below. Add a pronoun if necessary.

talk through   up-to-date   top up   get in

1 If you can't find the book you are looking for, the bookshop assistant can _____ for you.
2 If you move house, you should make sure that the library has your _____ address.
3 If the online application form isn't clear, ring up and someone will _____ it.
4 If the print on your photocopies looks faded, you probably need to _____ the ink.

b Rewrite the sentences in Exercise 1a using the words below. Add a preposition if necessary.

refill   explain   current   order

1 _____
2 _____
3 _____
4 _____

Prefixes

2a Match the prefixes (1–6) with their meanings (A–E). Two have a similar meaning.

1 inter-	A not/no
2 un-	B make
3 en-	C bad/wrong
4 in-	D again
5 mis-	E between
6 re-	

b Complete the sentences with the word in brackets and the correct prefix from Exercise 2a.

1 Many new head teachers decide to _____ (organise) the staffing structure in order to improve a school's performance.
2 Unfortunately, it appears _____ (likely) that all of the UN goals for children's education will be met.
3 The collection of data on a massive scale will _____ (able) scientists to understand how certain diseases spread.
4 _____ (national) cooperation is essential for addressing issues such as universal internet access.
5 For people living in remote rural areas, higher education is often _____ (accessible).
6 Some user manuals are _____ (informative) because they lack detailed diagrams.
7 According to analysts, the main cause of student debt is financial _____ (management).

3 Complete the text with the words below. There is one extra word which you do not need.

access   enable   inadequate   informative
international   likelihood   management   reorganisation

Conference in Seattle

A major 1 _____ conference will take place in Seattle this August. The theme of the conference is financial 2 _____ . Thanks to a 3 _____ of IT resources, participants at this year's event will be able to attend either in person or by video link. This will 4 _____ busy executives to avoid spending time travelling long distances.

Last year, approximately 1,200 people attended the conference, and this year there is every 5 _____ that attendance will exceed this figure. Disability 6 _____ and catering facilities, both of which were felt to be 7 _____ at last year's conference, have been given special attention.

Word formation

4a Complete the sentences with the correct form of the words below.

digit   easy   law   value   vary

1 _____ technology has made it possible to collect and store huge amounts of information.
2 Data on a large scale ('big data') is _____ for both governments and private organisations.
3 Data is routinely collected from a wide _____ of sources.
4 Retail companies can _____ collect data about customers who shop on the internet.
5 In some countries there are _____ constraints on the storage of personal information.

Expert language

The prefix *in-* usually makes an adjective negative (e.g. *inadequate*), but in the case of *valuable* it strengthens the meaning.

b Complete the text below with the correct form of the words in Exercise 4a.

Safer cycling

Urban planners in cities around the world may soon buy data in 1 _____ form from a cycling website, to find out where and when people ride. Although it is still 2 _____ to pass on personal information without consent, now the owners of the website are hoping that they can use the popularity of 'big data' to license anonymous information on a 3 _____ of cycling-related topics. Then they can supply the information to city planners who will find it 4 _____ when trying to create a safer infrastructure for cyclists.

Writing (Task 1)

> **COURSEBOOK** page 14, **EXPERT WRITING** page 191

Understand the task

1a Read the writing task. Underline the parts of the task which tell us

1 the place indicated (definite or vague).
2 the unit of measurement.
3 the date range (which figures are definite and which are predicted?).
4 the main focus of comparisons.

The graph below shows the number of students graduating in different science subject areas in one country between 2004 and 2016 (and predicted figures for 2020).

Summarise the information by selecting and reporting the main features, and make comparisons where relevant.

Write at least 150 words.

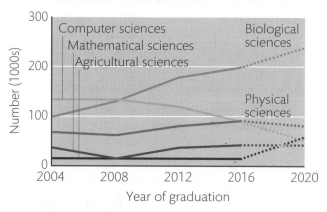

b Look at the graph in detail and answer the questions.

1 How many different subject areas are shown?
2 Which area shows the biggest increase?
3 Which shows the biggest decline?
4 Which areas remain relatively steady?
5 Which area is predicted to rise significantly in future?
6 What is the main message you take from the graph?

Structure your answer

2 Number A–D in the correct order to make a suitable structure for writing about the graph in Exercise 1b.

A Explanation of most important features (with data).
B Overview (summarising the overall message of the graph).
C Explanation of other important features (with data).
D Introductory sentences (what the graph shows, how it is measured).

Summarise features

3a Look at the writing task in Exercise 4a. Read the sentences below which come from sample answers to this task. Which one do you think gives an effective overview?

1 The graph shows five different types of courses at a given adult education college and the number of students on them.
2 The graph shows significant variation in the number of students on different courses in one adult education college over 30 years, including the predicted figures for 2025.

b Which of the following sentences describe a trend and which describe a detail?

1 In 1985 this group was only the third most popular but by 2015 it had risen to first position.
2 The most striking change was in the popularity of Employability courses.
3 In contrast the number of adults studying languages declined significantly.
4 The number rose from 500 to 650 students with this figure set to rise to 800 by 2025.

Test practice

4a Look at the task below and identify the topic and categories. Make a plan for your writing following the structure in Exercise 2.

b Write your answer in not less than 150 words. Remember to include an introductory sentence, an explanation of features with data and an overview.

The graph below shows the number of students studying different subject areas in one adult education college between 1985 and 2015 (and predicted figures for 2025).

Summarise the information by selecting and reporting the main features, and make comparisons where relevant.

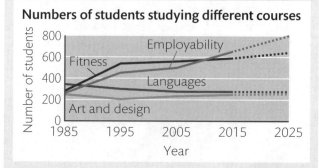

Listening (Section 2)

> COURSEBOOK pages 12 and 15

Before you listen

1   Skim the test task questions (1–4) in Exercise 3. What do you think the topic of the listening will be?

Predict alternative language

2a Look at the test task in Exercise 3. The basic elements of question 1 are shown below. Think of alternative ways of expressing the points in options A–C.

Q: Question about the history of the college

A combining two institutions
B changed courses over 20 years
C not the same location

b   Read an extract from the audio script and answer question 1 in the test task.

> 'We've been on this current site for only 20 years, but we started in London, opening our doors to students in 1857. A decision was made to make the change when student numbers on all our courses grew considerably.'

Test practice

3   ◀)) 1.1 Complete the test task.

Questions 1–4.
Choose the correct letter, **A**, **B** or **C**.

1 What does Andy say about the history of the college?
   A It was formed by combining two older institutions.
   B It has changed its courses a lot over the last 20 years.
   C It has not always been in its present location.

2 What mode of study is increasing in popularity at the college?
   A part-time study   B distance learning
   C sandwich courses

3 Students say the best thing about studying at the college is
   A the high standard of teaching.
   B the range and availability of resources.
   C the good rates of employment on graduation.

4 Which building on campus will soon be redeveloped?
   A the library   B the sports complex
   C the student support hub

4a Now look at the second part of the test task (questions 5–10). What is the main difference between questions 1–4 and questions 5–10?

b   Underline key words in the questions. Think of alternative ways of saying these.

c   ◀)) 1.2 Listen to the second part of the talk and complete the test task.

Questions 5–6
Choose **TWO** letters **A–E**.
Which **TWO** things does Andy say about campus accommodation?

A students can reserve a specific room
B students usually live on campus in their final year
C students can't choose who to share with
D students all have access to kitchen facilities
E students live in small 'village houses'

Questions 7–8
Choose **TWO** letters **A–E**.
Which **TWO** things does Andy say about ways of getting to the college?

A the bus service runs until late at night
B students are able to get special rates on bus tickets
C the train station is 10 minutes' walk away
D taking a taxi can be relatively cheap
E there is a special cycle route from the city centre

Questions 9–10
Choose **TWO** letters **A–E**.
Which **TWO** things does the speaker say many people forget to include in their application?

A a recent, passport-sized photograph
B a scanned copy of their certificates
C how they'd prefer to be contacted
D an up-to-date telephone number
E all parts of their name

TEST STRATEGY

For multiple-choice questions, avoid selecting a letter simply because one of the words heard in the audio appears in the option. This kind of word matching is deliberately put into wrong options as a distractor. Sometimes all the key words in the options are heard in in the audio but you must understand exactly what point is being made before you choose your option.

Language development

> **COURSEBOOK** page 16, **EXPERT GRAMMAR** page 176

Tense review

1 Match the underlined verbs in the sentences (1–8) with the tenses (A–H).

1 The actress <u>was training</u> as a dancer when she was offered a role in a stage play.
2 Workforce training <u>has evolved</u>, and is no longer based on traditional lectures.
3 The trainees felt that they<u>'d learnt</u> a lot of new strategies by the end of the course.
4 The tutor's <u>going to give</u> the group a task to complete before the next training session.
5 An occupational psychologist <u>is helping</u> the company to improve their recruitment procedures.
6 They<u>'ll introduce</u> new selection procedures based on the advice of a consultant.
7 While junior staff <u>attended</u> a training course, their colleagues dealt with phone calls.
8 One of the most popular forms of training across all fields <u>involves</u> role play.

A present simple
B present continuous
C present perfect
D past simple

E past continuous
F past perfect
G future with *will*
H future with *going to*

2 Rewrite the sentence below by changing the verb form to match the tense in brackets.

I study Spanish.

1 *I am studying Spanish.* (present continuous)
2 _____ (past perfect)
3 _____ (future with *going to*)
4 _____ (past simple)
5 _____ (future with *will*)
6 _____ (present perfect)
7 _____ (past continuous)

3 Complete the text with the correct form of the verbs below. Make any other necessary changes.

appear   become   fall   find   get   paint   see (x2)   talk

Good morning everyone. The subject of my lecture today is urban wildlife. We **1** _____ used to hearing bad news about wildlife – how numbers **2** _____ and species are becoming endangered and so on. But I'm going to tell you about some research findings which **3** _____ a very positive picture! Because what scientists **4** _____ is that wildlife in our cities is actually increasing.

Now, just a few years ago, if you **5** _____ an eagle on your way to the office, you would have been extremely surprised. But now, animals that we normally regard as belonging in the countryside **6** _____ in our cities. You might even **7** _____ a badger or a fox in your garden. In fact, our cities now **8** _____ the perfect natural habitat for a variety of mammals and birds. And I **9** _____ first about some of the reasons for this development.

Vocabulary

Describe trends

4 Match the descriptions (1–4) with the graphs (A–F). There are two extra graphs.

1 Spending climbed in the first three months, and then dropped again. It then remained more or less stable until October, when it soared.

2 Over the first six months of the year spending decreased slightly, after which it went up.

3 Spending increased slightly from January to June, and then it remained constant. In October it plummeted.

4 In the first few months spending declined, and then in June it grew. From August on it remained constant.

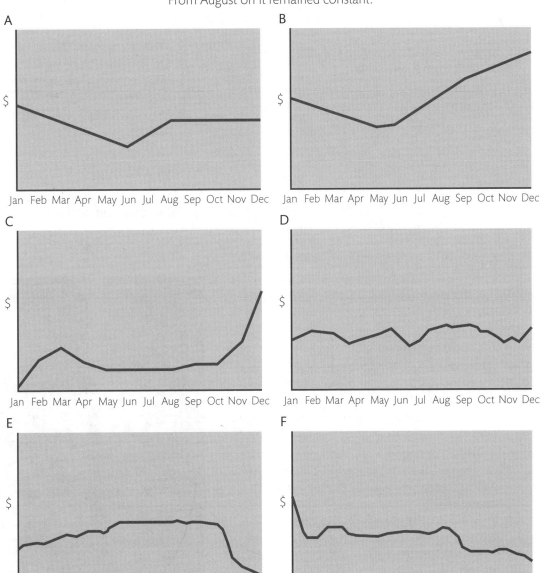

5 Describe how you might respond to the following situations.

1 Your daily expenses increase.
2 The price of plane tickets plummets.
3 The quality of service at your favourite shop declines.

Speaking (Part 1)

➤ COURSEBOOK page 17

Vocabulary development

1a Complete the table.

Noun	Verb	Adjective
ambition	X	1 _____
dedication	2 _____	3 _____
demand	4 _____	5 _____
X	dishearten	6 _____
7 _____	inspire	8 _____
9 _____	X	talented

b Complete the sentences with the correct form of the words from Exercise 1a.

1 I like watching really _____ dancers perform.
2 I'm learning to play the piano but I'm not very _____ . I just do it for enjoyment. I don't want to win any prizes or anything.
3 I've got a qualification in karate, but I wouldn't want to do it professionally – it's too _____ .
4 I was _____ to do a drama course after watching a musical called *Mamma Mia!*
5 I like gymnastics, but I'm not _____ enough to practise regularly.
6 When you've practised a lot and then you don't perform very well, you feel _____ .

2 Match the questions about skills (1–6) with the answers (A–F).

1 What are you quite good at doing?
2 How long have you been doing it?
3 Where do you usually do this activity?
4 What kind of training did you have for this skill?
5 How often do you practise?
6 How will this activity benefit you in future?

A Well, I've joined a dance group and we meet at weekends, so once a week usually.
B Oh, I'm not sure exactly … but I've probably been dancing for around eight years now. I started when I was 15.
C Well, it keeps me fit and active, because it's quite fast, so I expect it's good for my health. And I've made new friends, so it'll be good for my social life too.
D I think I'm quite good at dancing. I really enjoy it – in fact it's one of my favourite activities.
E I started going to a dance class in the evenings, but it was only two hours a week, and only in the winter. I did that for a year.
F I go to a small town about 15km away, and it's in the community hall there. It's a big room and it's very light and attractive.

3 🔊 1.3 Close your book and listen to the questions in Exercise 2. Answer them yourself.

> **TEST STRATEGY**
>
> In the Speaking exam, pay special attention to the tense of the verb in the question.

Test practice

4 🔊 1.4 Listen and answer the questions about studying English. Record your answers if possible.

1 How long have you been studying English?
2 How old were you when you started studying English?
3 Where do you usually study English?
4 Do you enjoy studying English?
5 Which do you find easier, reading in English or listening to English?
6 How will taking the IELTS test benefit you in future?

Assess and improve

5 Listen to your recordings in Exercise 4 and answer the questions.

1 Were you able to use verb tenses correctly?
2 If not, which tense do you need to practise using?

Writing (Task 1)

> COURSEBOOK pages 20–21, EXPERT WRITING page 191

Understand the task

1 Look at the charts below and answer the questions.

1 What is the key information represented in the graphs?

2 Which age group does the first graph refer to? And the second?

3 Is the location vague or specific?

3 What is the unit of measurement?

4 What time period is covered? Which period is predicted?

Numbers of 'non-traditional' students in one university: under-25s and over-25s

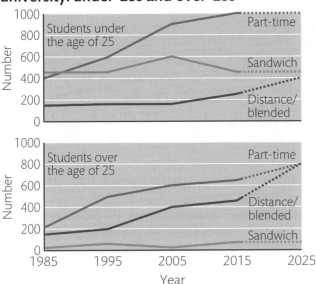

Plan the task

2a Write an introductory sentence to describe what the two graphs in Exercise 1 show.

b Reorder the following sections from a sample answer to form a coherent description.

A The number of under-25s taking sandwich courses has fluctuated over this period: this mode started as the most popular in 1985, rising to a peak of 600 in 2005 before declining back to 450 in 2015. For over-25s, numbers for all three non-traditional modes have increased.

B For younger students, the biggest increase is in figures for part-time study, which rose from 400 in 1985 to 1,000 in 2015.

C There was also a marked increase in mature students studying part time, rising from 200 in 1985 to 620 in 2015. The difference is that this mode is predicted to increase slightly in popularity (800 by 2025) for older students whereas figures for younger part-timers are set to remain steady.

c Write an overview sentence which summarises the key message(s) of the graphs.

Language and content

3a Which verb forms should be used for predictions?

b To avoid repeating words, what alternative expressions could be used for the following words?

1 students under 25   4 rise
2 students over 25   5 fall
3 predict

Write your report

4 Look at the writing task below. Plan and write your answer, using ideas from Exercises 1–3.

The graphs below show the percentage of loans in different categories, in two libraries between 1980 and 2010, with predicted figures for 2020.

Summarise the information by selecting and reporting the main features, and make comparisons where relevant.

You should write at least 150 words.

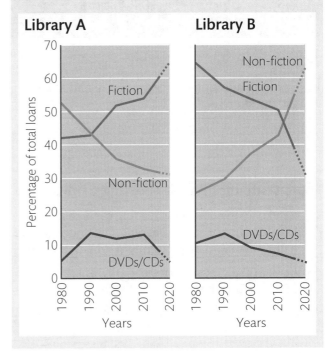

Assess and improve

5 When you have finished, leave your answer and return to it after several hours. Check your writing and answer the questions.

1 Does your answer have an introductory sentence? Is it accurate?

2 Does it contain an overview? (This can be either near the beginning or at the end.)

3 Are key comparisons identified? Do you think they are the most important points revealed by the graphs?

4 Is any important information missing?

2a Human development

Reading (*True/False/Not given*; Short-answer questions)

> **COURSEBOOK** pages 24–25 and 34–35

Before you read

1   Scan the questions in the test tasks and answer
    the questions.

   1   What do you think the reading passage will be
    about?

   2   What kind of information might the passage contain?

Topic sentences and supporting details

2a Read only the title of the reading passage and the
    first sentence of each paragraph. Will the article be
    mainly about urban problems, or urban solutions?

  b   Look at the first sentence of paragraph 2. Which
    of the following topics does it signal?

   1   the time and location of the conference
   2   the qualifications of the experts
   3   the growth of support for smart cities

  c   Look at the first sentence of the third paragraph.
    Which of the following topics does it signal?

   1   characteristics of smart cities
   2   examples of smart cities
   3   problems of smart cities

3   Read the passage. Were your predictions in
    Exercises 1 and 2 correct?

Test practice

4a Underline the key words in question 1 in the test
    task above.

  b   Scan the reading passage to find phrases which are
    similar in meaning to those you have underlined.

  c   Follow the same procedure for questions 2 to 5 in
    the test task above, then complete the test task.

> **TEST STRATEGY**
>
> Statements like these follow the same order of
> information as in the reading passage. Use this sequence
> to help you locate the right parts of the passage.

Questions 1–5

*Do the following statements agree with the
information given in the reading passage? Write*

TRUE   *if the statement agrees with the information*
FALSE   *if the statement contradicts the information*
NOT GIVEN   *if there is no information on this*

1   Figures show that in future a greater proportion
    of people will live in cities.
2   Rural areas are more economically productive
    than urban areas.
3   Smart technology will be used to facilitate some
    projects which have an impact on entire cities.
4   The cost of health care is likely to be reduced
    with the introduction of telemedicine.
5   All cars will be powered by hybrid engines by
    the middle of the century.

> **HELP**

4   The reading passage mentions health care and
    telemedicine, but does it mention cost?

Test practice

5a Tick the methods (1–6) which are appropriate for
    answering questions 6–10 on page 17.

   1   Underline key words in the questions.
   2   Predict the grammatical form of the answers.
   3   Underline matching words/phrases in the reading
    passage.
   4   Copy the answer from the reading passage.
   5   Rephrase the words in the reading passage.
   6   Check that all your answers consist of either one
    or two words.

  b   Complete the test task. Use your list from
    Exercise 5a to help you.

Smart Cities

Sustainable, smart cities are where entrepreneurs, government officials and academics come together, using shared data and digital technology to improve urban living.

At a recent conference attended by experts from emerging smart cities across the UK, it was argued that the need for cities to become smarter, more integrated and sustainable has never been greater. "Cities drive economic growth and prosperity," one speaker argued. "In 2010 more than half the world's population lived in cities. By 2050 that figure will have risen to 70 percent". In numerical terms, it is estimated that in 30 years, seven billion people will live in urban areas. It was also pointed out that 80 percent of global income is generated in cities, and as they grow, there is increasing pressure for them to become more sustainable. This means that cities need to be smart in how they communicate, plan and respond to the increasing demands on space and resources. Communication, energy, waste and transport will all need to be sustainable, and technology will be the solution.

So what is a smart city? It is one that uses digital communication to enhance services and performance. Key to this is the ability to collect, organise and share data in the public domain. That data, from public and private organisations alike, allows businesses and governments to make better decisions, and allows citizens to be better informed.

Some applications of smart technology will be vast city-wide initiatives, while others will be small and localised. For example, smart metering means that domestic heating and lighting can be controlled remotely, and only used when needed. Telemedicine will enable healthcare to be more readily available and instantaneous. Solar-powered batteries will let communities generate and store electricity, to avoid overloading the national grid during times of peak demand. Virtual barriers on roads will automatically switch hybrid cars to electric power when air quality passes a pre-set, acceptable level.

It is the pooling of data that lies behind smart innovation. In Bristol, one of the UK's leading emerging smart cities, a new app matches satellite positioning data with planning data to identify routes around the city which are suitable for wheelchair users, because they avoid steep hills and sharp kerbs. It is a small but significant innovation, and it shows how strategic collaboration can be turned into a service that enhances the lives of citizens. Many cities in the UK are running pilot projects like this, which will eventually form the basis of a fully integrated, digital smart city.

Transport systems will be key to the development of smart cities. Using data, sensors and smart technology, traffic flows, congestion and speed can all be controlled. The result will be faster movement around highly populated areas, with citizens having the real-time information they need to reduce the cost of a journey, the time it takes, and the impact that it will have on emissions. As one speaker at the conference said, "We want to get to the point where the cars themselves know about traffic flow and how to regulate it. The cars will be able to communicate with each other." Automated cars are closer than many think. London's Heathrow airport already operates driverless, laser-guided pods to carry up to four passengers and their luggage from the car park to Terminal 5.

Insurance companies also have a vested interest in smart-car technology. In the UK, insurers pay out £27m every day in motor claims. However, more than 90 percent of all accidents on the road are caused by human error, so cars without humans at the wheel should improve road safety.

However, some voices at the conference sounded a note of caution. The move towards smart city infrastructures is not without its challenges. One of these is to ensure that citizens themselves approve and actively participate in the changes. According to the head of business development for the telecoms company that is working with many authorities to provide the networking grids for sharing data, it is crucial that smart city projects have the end user in mind. "We will struggle to get user stakeholders unless the projects are user-led," she said.

Questions 6–10

Answer the questions below.

*Choose **NO MORE THAN TWO WORDS** from the passage for each answer.*

6 In future, which aspect of the environment will trigger a change to a car's power source?

7 Which group of people will benefit from an app to locate flat routes within a city?

8 What will be one fundamental aspect of smart cities?

9 Whereabouts in London are automated vehicles already in operation?

10 Which type of business will particularly benefit from the introduction of smart cars?

Task analysis

6 Answer the questions. If your answer to any of them is *No*, think about how you can improve in this area in future.

1 Did any of your answers in Exercise 5b consist of more than two words?

2 Did you copy the words from the passage correctly in Exercise 5b?

3 Were your answers to the questions in both test tasks in text order?

EXPERT LANGUAGE

The suffix *-able* in *sustainable* often means 'able to be' (able to be sustained). Other words with the same suffix include *manageable* (able to be managed), *breakable* (able to be broken) and *washable* (able to be washed).

Vocabulary

> COURSEBOOK page 26

Academic verbs

1a Match the sentence beginnings (1–6) with the correct endings (A–F).

1 Owing largely to the rise in car ownership, pedestrians have almost
2 The expansion of mobile phone infrastructure has
3 Even today, only a minority of women have
4 Many people from the smallest Pacific islands have left their homes and
5 In just a few years, certain internet-based companies have
6 Modern skyscrapers and transport systems have

A emerged as global market leaders.
B progressed to the most senior levels of industry.
C disappeared from some city streets.
D transformed the appearance of many cities across the world.
E settled on the mainland.
F enabled people in remote rural areas to run businesses.

b Complete the text with the correct form of the verbs below. There is one extra verb you do not need.

disappear emerge enable progress settle transform

China

Chinese society has been **1** _____ in recent years. More and more people are moving from the countryside and **2** _____ in cities, and traditional lifestyles are slowly **3** _____ . A new class of wealthy entrepreneurs is **4** _____ , as changes to the law have **5** _____ individuals to set up private businesses.

Written and spoken vocabulary

2a Match the words (1–4) with a less formal expression (A–D).

1 enable   A die out
2 emerge   B spring up
3 settle   C put roots down
4 disappear   D make it possible

b What do you notice about the two lists?

3 Write a short paragraph about changes in your own city or country. Use the vocabulary from Exercise 2a and the topic list below to help you.

- Buildings
- Transport
- Jobs
- Families
- Society

Process verbs

4a Rewrite the second sentence so that it means the same as the first, using the word in brackets. Make any other necessary changes.

1 Large areas of forest have been destroyed in order to meet global demand for timber. (destruction)
Global demand for timber has resulted in the _destruction of large areas of forest_ .
2 Plant diseases can be transferred from one country to another when plants are exported. (transfer)
The export of plants can result in _____ .
3 The earth's rotation around the sun takes just over 365 days. (rotates)
The earth _____ .
4 Hot weather can affect the amount of energy which solar panels produce. (heat)
The amount of energy which solar panels produce _____ .
5 People in remote parts of the world are able to run commercial businesses if they are connected to the internet. (connection)
Having _____ allows people in remote parts of the world to run commercial businesses.
6 Engineers will begin to construct a new hydro-electric power station next year. (construction)
_____ will begin next year.
7 By raising penalties for pollution, the government has succeeded in reducing factory emissions. (rise)
A _____ .
8 Natural gas is extracted from rock cavities by a process called 'fracking'. (extraction)
_____ is called 'fracking'.

EXPERT LANGUAGE

When *extract* is a noun, the stress is on the first syllable, but when it is a verb the stress is on the second syllable. The word *transfer* has a similar stress pattern.

b Complete the sentences below, using your own ideas and opinions.

1 One of the biggest improvements to the area where I live has been the construction of _____ .
2 One of the most popular tourist developments in my country is _____ .
3 In my country there's been a big rise in _____ .
4 Most people where I live use _____ to heat their _____ .
5 The main form of transport connecting the country's two biggest cities is _____ .
6 The addition of _____ improves the taste of a lot of local dishes.

Language development

> COURSEBOOK page 29 EXPERT GRAMMAR page 176

Present simple, past simple and present perfect passives

1 Choose the correct option in *italics* to complete the text.

The Eden Project

The Eden Project is a visitor attraction in the UK. The site of the attraction is a former clay pit which **1** *is / has* been converted into a living plant museum. Two massive greenhouses, called biomes, **2** *were / are* constructed in the pit. These **3** *had been / were* made from steel and plastic, as glass was considered to be too heavy and fragile. One of the biomes houses plants which have been brought from the tropics, and the other houses plants which are imported from the Mediterranean region. Another section, which **4** *was / is* added more recently, was designed to house art exhibitions and classrooms.

2 Complete the sentences with the correct passive form of the verbs below.

devastate find hold inhabit know take down

1 Singapore's first general election _____ in 1959.
2 In 1989, the wall dividing West and East Berlin _____ .
3 Today in many areas of the world, fish stocks _____ by overfishing.
4 Cuba _____ by Amerindian tribes when Europeans arrived on the island.
5 The so-called Gold Rush began in 1848, after gold _____ in California.
6 The Maldives _____ generally _____ for their beaches, lagoons and extensive reefs.

EXPERT LANGUAGE

Adverbs are positioned after the auxiliary verb in passive forms.

Other passive forms

3a Rewrite the sentences, putting the words in bold in the passive. Make any other necessary changes.

1 In 2008 the Kalka-to-Shimla railway, which **people had constructed** more than a century earlier, was granted World Heritage status.
2 By 1899, while **people were still constructing** a railway to transport gold prospectors in Canada, the Gold Rush was almost over.
3 Before work begins at the site of a new railway line in the UK, **people may allow** archaeologists time to search for evidence of earlier occupation.
4 When people visit Gleisdreieck Park in Berlin the peacefulness of this former railway junction **will impress them**.
5 In many parts of the world, **they are upgrading** rail transport in an attempt to reduce road traffic.

EXPERT LANGUAGE

When the subject of a passive verb is less important than the action described by the verb, it is often omitted.

b Which passive form did you write for each of the sentences (1–5) in Exercise 3a? Choose a form from the box for each one.

A modal passive   B future simple passive
C past perfect passive   D past continuous passive
E present continuous passive

TEST STRATEGY

The passive form is used for describing trends or describing a process. You will have to do one of these in Task 1 of the Academic Writing paper.

4 Complete the text below with the correct passive form of the verbs in brackets. Add adverbs where necessary.

The Ancient City of Petra

The ancient city of Petra, in Jordan, is one of the world's most important archaeological sites. It **1** _____ (situate) between the Red Sea and the Dead Sea, and **2** _____ (partly build) and **3** _____ (partly carve) into the soft red sandstone rock in the fourth century BCE. The city **4** _____ (surround) by mountains which **5** _____ (riddle) with caves and gorges.

Petra **6** _____ (inhabit) since prehistoric times. However, it continues **7** _____ (damage) by wind and rain. To try and arrest this process, Petra's most recent inhabitants **8** _____ (resettle) a short while ago. It is also likely that restrictions **9** _____ (place) on tourism in the future.

5 Write a short description of a historic place or building in your country. Use the passive form where possible.

Writing (Task 1)

> COURSEBOOK page 30, EXPERT WRITING page 192

Understand the task

1 Read the test task below and answer the questions.

1 What does the diagram show?
2 Where does the process start?
3 How many main stages are there in the process?
4 What is the final stage?
5 Do you need to write about all the features?

The diagram below shows the stages in the process of canning fruit.

Summarise the information by selecting and reporting the main features, and make comparisons where relevant.

You should write at least 150 words.

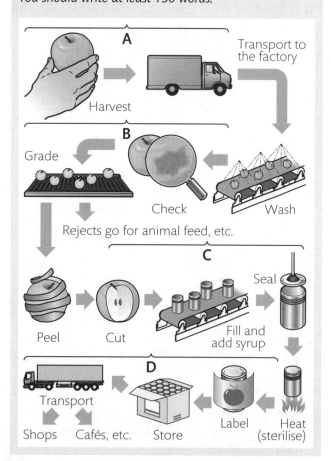

Write introductions and processes

2 Look at the diagram and match the stages of the process (A–D) with 1–4 below.

1 Preparation for sale
2 Pre-factory
3 Preparation for canning
4 Quality check

3 Which introduction best describes the process in the diagram?

1 The diagram explains how many phases there are in the sequence of canning fruit.
2 The diagram shows the different stages in the process of canning fruit.
3 The diagram shows the four main phases in processing canned fruit.

4 Complete the extract from a sample answer with the sentences (A–C.)

1 _____ To enable this to be done properly the fruit needs to be thoroughly washed: workers can only see if there are any marks or bruises when the fruit is clean. The fruit is then weighed and graded into different sizes. 2 _____ The next phase is preparation for canning. The fruit is peeled, cored and cut into pieces. 3 _____ It is only at this stage that the fruit is cooked, which also has the effect of sterilisation.

A Only fruit of the right quality and size is used for canning: rejects are sent for animal feed and other uses.
B These pieces are poured into tins, which are immediately sealed.
C In the factory the fruit undergoes stringent quality control.

Use the active and passive

5a Underline examples of the passive in the extract in Exercise 4. Can you rewrite them in the active voice? Why is this difficult?

b In the extract, a few verbs are in the active voice. What is special about these?

Test practice

6 Write your full answer to the test task in Exercise 1. You may use extracts from the sample as guidance, if you wish.

TEST STRATEGY

In Part 1, process diagrams, aim to use the passive voice for most verbs, because it is important to focus on what action is done rather than who or what does it (the agent). However, in some stages of process diagrams you should use the active voice because it is useful to know the agent.

Listening (Section 1)

➤ COURSEBOOK pages 28 and 31

Before you listen

1a Look at the instructions for questions 1–5 in the test task below. What is the maximum number of words/numbers you can use?

b For each question, predict what kind of word (name, place, number, etc.) you need to write to complete the form.

Test practice

2a 🔊 2.1 Listen and complete the test task.

Questions 1–5
Complete the form below.
Write **ONE WORD AND/OR A NUMBER** for each answer.

> **Branscombe Otter Sanctuary**
> Volunteer details
> Name: Brian 1 _____
> Date of birth: 2 _____
> Length of volunteering: Two weeks
> Country of origin: 3 _____
>
> **Contact details**
> Address in UK: Branscombe Youth Hostel
> Mobile number: 0706 549 870
>
> **Additional notes**
> Relevant experience: 4 _____
> Preferred area to work in: Visitor's Centre
> How heard about the sanctuary: 5 _____

b Check your answers. Have you made any of the following errors?

1 misspelling   3 incorrect answer
2 too many words   4 unnecessary information

Understand different ways location is expressed

3a Look at the map in the test task in Exercise 4. Try to describe the location of places A–G in relation to features shown on the map. Use the words below to write one sentence for each place.

before   in the middle   near the end   beside   behind
next to   between   in front of   to the side of
on the left/right

A is just next to the reception.
A is right next to the cub pool.

b Read the instructions for questions 6–10 in the test task below. How many places do you have to label? How many places will not be labelled?

Test practice

> **TEST STRATEGY**
> For map-labelling questions, listen carefully for the names of buildings/features already labelled because these are always used as a guide. Also, listen carefully for any distractors relating to time, for example, *It used to be there, but now it's here.*

4 🔊 2.2 Listen to the second part of the conversation and complete the test task.

Questions 6–10

*Label the map below. Write the correct letter, **A–G**, next to questions 6–10.*

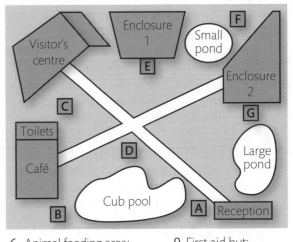

6 Animal feeding area: ___   9 First aid hut: ___
7 Feed kiosk: ___   10 Meeting point: ___
8 Toilets: ___

➤ **HELP**

6 This question refers to the feeding area being between the large pond and enclosure number two. Can you locate this?

> **TEST STRATEGY**
> In this map-labelling task, there are several areas with similar names, for example there are two ponds and two enclosures and you must make sure you pick the right one.

Task analysis

5 Did you find any questions particularly difficult? If so, listen to the audio again. Why do you think these questions were particularly difficult?

Language development and vocabulary

> **COURSEBOOK** page 32, **EXPERT GRAMMAR** page 177

Relative clauses

1 Read the sentences and answer the questions.

   1 **A** All the passengers, who were wearing seat belts, survived.

      B All the passengers who were wearing seat belts survived.

      Did **some** or **all** of the passengers referred to in the sentence survive?

   2 **A** The islands, which are near to Stockholm, are inhabited.

      B The islands which are near to Stockholm are inhabited.

      Are **some** or **all** of the islands referred to in the sentence inhabited?

2 Add commas to the sentences as necessary.

   1 Archaeology is particularly important for learning about prehistoric societies for whom there are no written records.

   2 There is no single approach to archaeological theory which has been followed by all archaeologists.

   3 The cuckoo whose calls used to be regarded as the first sign of spring is now absent from many of its former breeding grounds.

   4 There are no other languages related to the Basque language which is spoken in parts of Spain and France.

   5 Aerial photographs can detect many features which are not visible at ground level.

   6 Olympic athletes who receive financial support from their governments are able to train full time for their events.

3 Complete the text with the words below. You can use the words more than once.

where	which	who	whose	why

Wikipedia

When Jimmy Wales launched the website in 2001, he imagined a world 1 _____ every single person on the planet has free access to human knowledge. Now there are more than half a million people 2 _____ visit Wikipedia every month. It is the most linked-to website in the world.

Wikipedia isn't a profitable internet giant like Google, Facebook or Apple, 3 _____ have won the loyalty of global consumers through sleek, refined products and services. Instead, Wikipedia has always been a sparse, no-frills text-based site 4 _____ design has been almost untouched since its launch.

The purely volunteer-driven site operates as a non-profit organisation, 5 _____ is primarily supported through small donations from its vast global community. The reason 6 _____ Wikipedia intends to keep the donor model, rather than allowing advertising on its site, is that this is part of its identity.

4 Combine the sentences below, using a relative pronoun.

   1 Wikipedia has upset several commercial businesses, such as encyclopaedia and school textbook publishing companies. Wikipedia itself does not make a profit.

      Wikipedia, which does not make a profit, has upset several commercial businesses, such as encylopaedia and school textbook publishing companies.

   2 The print business of encyclopaedia was seriously affected. Computers did this.

   3 Teachers and students from around the world have contributed more than 88,000 new articles to Wikipedia. They were not paid for writing them.

   4 Wikipedia has to focus on being accurate and relevant in this modern age. It is constantly being updated.

   5 Our method of getting information has switched from PCs to other devices. These devices are smaller and more mobile.

6 Billions of new internet users will come online for the first time. They will use a mobile device first.

_____

7 Many new internet users will come from the developing world. They will speak languages other than English.

_____

8 Wikipedia needs to reach out to people in the developing world. They will benefit greatly from its educational materials.

_____

5 Write about yourself. Complete the sentences below using a relative clause.

1 I come from a city/an area which _____ .
2 The person in my family who _____ is _____ .
3 One of my earliest memories is of a time when _____ .
4 One of the most exciting things that has happened to me took place on a day when _____ .
5 My best friend is someone who _____ .
6 One of my friends has a brother/sister who _____ .
7 One of my favourite films is about a man/woman who _____ .
8 I'm really looking forward to a time when _____ .

> **TEST STRATEGY**
>
> You will get a higher score in the IELTs Writing papers if you are able to use complex sentences. Sentences which contain relative clauses are complex.

Sequencing with prepositions and adverbs

6a Complete the sentences with the words below.

after	as	before	during	when	while

1 Merchants first brought tea to Europe _____ the 16th century.
2 _____ silk was widely worn in China, it was reserved for use by the Emperor.
3 The Italian cities of Herculaneum and Pompeii were destroyed _____ a volcano erupted in 79 AD.
4 _____ the introduction of the motor car, horse-drawn carriages generally went out of use.
5 In 1492, Christopher Columbus landed in America _____ searching for a route to Southeast Asia.
6 _____ wheat and other cereals were being cultivated in the Middle East, people in other parts of the world were largely hunter-gatherers.

b Choose the correction option in _italics_ to complete the text.

Tim Berners-Lee and the World Wide Web

There were many great scientific and technological advances **1** _during / while_ the 20th century, but few would deny that the world wide web was amongst the most important. Communication became almost instantaneous **2** _before / when_ the internet became widely available. The person responsible for this revolutionary development was Tim Berners-Lee. Tim Berners-Lee was born in London in 1955. **3** _As / When_ he was a child, he occupied himself by building computers out of cardboard. He then went on to study Physics at Oxford University. In 1982, **4** _during / while_ he was working as a scientist at the European Organisation for Nuclear Research, in Switzerland, Tim Berners-Lee published a proposal for allowing physicists to share electronic documents. Then, **5** _during / while_ the same decade, he proposed a way of adapting the system for general use. This system was to revolutionise the way we live. Fourteen years **6** _after / as_ he received a grant to develop this big idea, Berners-Lee was honoured by Queen Elizabeth II, and became Sir Tim Berners-Lee.

c Write about yourself, using the words in Exercise 6a.

1 <u>My grandfather died</u> before <u>I was born</u>.
2 My most memorable experience was when _____ .
3 While I was still at school my parents _____ .
4 After leaving school I _____ .
5 _____
6 _____

Speaking (Part 2)

➤ **COURSEBOOK** page 33

Vocabulary development

1 Put the words/phrases about buildings in the correct place in the table below.

irregular   plain   at the end of the last century
ornate   five years ago   symmetrical   in 2005   recent
stone   in the city centre   by the river   rectangular
futuristic   bold   on a hilltop   wood   circular
unusual   in the 21st century   steel   glass   concrete
tall   traditional   overlooking a park

Period	Materials
Location	Style

2 Make notes to help you with the following speaking task. Use the words/phrases in Exercise 1 to help you.

> **TEST STRATEGY**
> Try to spend no longer than one minute writing your notes.

Describe a modern building that you like or dislike.
You should say:
  where it is
  what it looks like
  what it is used for
and explain why you like or dislike it.

3 🔊 2.3 Listen to a student doing this task and answer the questions.

1 Does he answer all the questions?
2 If not, which one(s) does he omit?

4 Underline the word on the left which best describes the noun on the right.

1 surprising   startling   stunning   **scenery**
2 remote   reserved   difficult   **island**
3 fussy   active   bustling   **town**
4 pure   unharmed   unspoilt   **landscape**
5 rare   matchless   unique   **environment**

5 Add a relative clause to the sentences below.

1 I know a lovely place that you _can only get to on foot_ .
2 A place I often go to attracts tourists, who _____ .
3 It's a remote area that's only accessible at certain times of the year, when _____ .
4 There's a stunning view from the top of the mountain, that _____ .
5 The town is bustling, especially during the summer when _____ .

Test practice

6 Make notes to help you with the test task below. Then record yourself as you do the task.

Describe a change which has improved the area where you live. You should say:
  what the change was
  when it happened
  why it happened
and explain how the change has improved the area where you live.

Assess and improve

7 Listen to your recording from Exercise 6 and answer the questions.

1 Did you use the full minute for making notes?
2 Did you have enough to say?
3 Did you worry about making grammatical mistakes?
4 How could you improve your fluency?

Writing (Task 1)

> COURSEBOOK pages 36–37, EXPERT WRITING page 192

Understand the task

1   Look at the process diagram task below and answer the questions.

   1   What is the process shown in the diagram? Where is the starting point? What is the result?

   2   How many main phases are there in the process?

   3   What information should you include in an overview of the process?

You should spend about 20 minutes on this task.

The diagram below shows how water is processed to make it drinkable.

Summarise the information by selecting and reporting the main features, and make comparisons where relevant.

You should write at least 150 words.

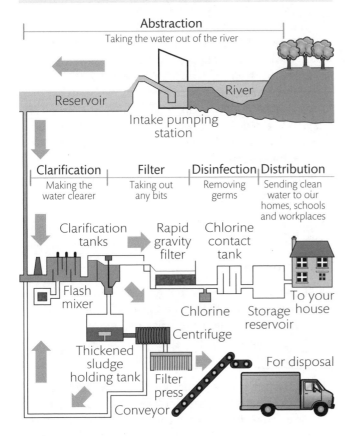

Plan the task

2a   Look at the topic sentences taken from two different sample answers to the task in Exercise 1. Which do you think is the most effective? Why?

   1   At the beginning of the process, water is in the river and after passing through different stages it is safe enough to drink.

   2   There are essentially five main stages involved in the processing of natural rainwater to make it of good enough quality to drink safely.

b   Complete the next part of a sample answer with the words/phrases below.

is taken   being cleaned   is called   via   passed through

The first stage 1 _____ abstraction, where the water 2 _____ out of a river 3 _____ a pumping station and is 4 _____ to a reservoir. The next major stage is clarification, with the water 5 _____ by passing it through a flash mixer.

c   Think about the following linking words/phrases. In which part of your answer could you use them?

the first stage   the next stage   the final stage
from here it is   so it must be pumped
the water is then   before being returned to

Language and content

3a   Choose the correct option in *italics* to complete the phrases about the diagram in Exercise 1.

   1   water is *pumped / passed* forward

   2   waste material is *pressed / pulled* into

   3   water is *returned / cycled*

   4   chlorine is *treated / added*

   5   water is *stored / stocked*

b   Can you think of any other verbs you could use to describe stages in this process?

Write your summary

> **EXPERT LANGUAGE**
>
> For process diagram tasks, try to vary the grammatical structures. Aim to use a mix of simple present passive (e.g. *is taken*) and other forms such as the present continuous passive (e.g. *with the water being cleaned*).

4a   Make brief notes as a plan for the task in Exercise 1.

b   Write your answer. Spend no more than 20 minutes and make sure it is at least 150 words.

Assess and improve

5a   Check your answer. Have you included the following?

   • An introductory sentence or sentences about the process

   • Sequential linking

   • A clear description of all the different stages

   • Mainly the passive voice (a few verbs in the active voice, when it is useful to know the agent)

   • Relative clauses to add information

b   Leave your answer for several hours, then re-read it. What would you change?

The feel-good factor

Reading (Matching headings; Multiple choice: select two answers)

➤ COURSEBOOK pages 40–41

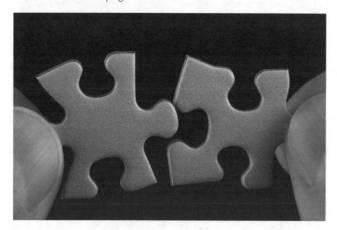

Before you read

1 Look at the title of the reading passage. Which idea in each of the following pairs (A or B) will be the main focus of the passage?

1 A vitamins in general
  B one particular vitamin
2 A mistaken beliefs
  B scientific findings
3 A a positive development
  B a negative development

> **TEST STRATEGY**
>
> The exam sometimes has a question about the main idea of a reading passage, so it is important to be able to recognise the difference between details and main ideas.

Identify the main idea

2a The ideas below are mentioned in section A of the reading passage. Read this section quickly. What is the main topic of section A?

1 a change in lifestyles
2 a scientific finding
3 an increase in bone disease

b Look at the list of headings in the test task in Exercise 3. Which of these headings is closest to the topic you chose in Exercise 2a?

c Read the rest of the passage and try to express the main topic of sections B–E in a few words, as in 1–3 in Exercise 2a.

Test practice

3 Complete the test task.

> *Questions 1–5*
>
> *The reading passage has five sections, A–E.*
>
> *Choose the correct heading for each section from the list of headings below.*
>
> *Write the correct number, i–vii.*
>
> > **List of Headings**
> > i The significance of seasonal variations in the incidence of disease
> > ii A limited response to recent medical findings
> > iii The rejection of previous theories about vitamin D
> > iv A growing understanding of the cause of a medical problem
> > v A revolutionary treatment for sufferers of MS
> > vi A rise in disease levels in new regions of Europe
> > vii The biological connection between a range of different diseases
> >
> > 1 Section A _____   4 Section D _____
> > 2 Section B _____   5 Section E _____
> > 3 Section C _____

Test practice

4a Look at the question below. Underline the key words and use them to find the section in the passage that relates to this question.

Which two statements does the writer make about birthdays?

b Underline the key words in the statement below. Scan the passage and look for either paraphrases or words/phrases with the opposite meaning to those you underlined. Underline the relevant part of the reading passage.

Scientists have long recognised the significance of birthdays in relation to MS.

c Now decide whether the statement is correct or not, according to the information in the passage.

Increasing evidence for the health benefits of Vitamin D

A Scientists often liken the process of discovery to doing a jigsaw. At first, few pieces fit and the picture is a mystery. Then suddenly two or three pieces lock together and an image starts to take shape. This is what is now happening in the study of several, apparently unrelated, chronic diseases which are increasingly common both in the UK and elsewhere. The causes of these diseases have baffled doctors and scientists for decades.

Now pieces of the jigsaw are starting to fit together, and they focus on vitamin D, which is produced naturally in the skin when it is exposed to sunlight. Thanks to our increasingly indoor lifestyles, a deficiency in this crucial vitamin is already blamed for the reappearance in the UK of rickets, a painful and deforming bone disease in children. But gradually, evidence is emerging that links low vitamin D levels to a rise in a whole host of 'modern' diseases, some of which were virtually unheard of in the pre-industrial era.

B One of these diseases is multiple sclerosis (MS). It is well recognised that multiple sclerosis has become increasingly common in the UK over the last century. Today, in cloudy Orkney, off the north of Scotland, one in 150 women suffer from MS, believed to be the highest prevalence in the world. Less well known is that a generation ago, the disease was much less common in southern than in northern Europe. But MS has increased rapidly in the Mediterranean in the last few years, reflecting the increased movement of people away from rural subsistence farming to towns and a life in urban apartments. On the Greek island of Crete MS has increased almost four fold over the last generation.

C One crucial piece in the jigsaw has come from the study of birthdays. Links between birthdays and future life events have long been the territory of people who claim to have psychic powers; so when evidence first emerged, almost two decades ago, that people born at the end of winter were more likely to get MS, and those born in autumn less so, many scientists found it hardly credible. But now we know that MS is associated with end-of-winter births, when shortage of sunshine is demonstrable and vitamin D levels are lowest. This suggests, in line with other observations, that vitamin D protects against the disease.

In the northern hemisphere summer sun is at its maximum strength in June and July, but vitamin D which is generated in the skin by sunlight takes two or three months to get into the body's general circulation. So we reach our maximum level of vitamin D in about September. Babies born in October or November have the best chance of a relatively high level of vitamin D during their final months in the womb. And this, the birthday evidence suggests, can protect them from MS, while the risk is higher for babies born at the end of winter. This pattern in the risk of MS has now been found in eight different countries, including Australia, and has convinced previously sceptical scientists.

D Less well known is the link between end-of-winter birthdays and an increased risk of several other diseases. Studies of thousands of birthdays in Europe, Canada and Australia over some 30 years have found that people born at this time are also at greater risk of type 1 diabetes, coeliac disease (gluten intolerance), schizophrenia and autism.

For a long time experts did not know what to make of this data, since these diseases had no obvious links. But now more conditions are being added to the list by a team of researchers from Oxford University in the UK. And what links these is the fact that they are all, like MS, autoimmune diseases, which occur when the body is attacked by its own immune system. Diabetes type 1 is also an autoimmune disease. To date, at least 18 autoimmune diseases have been linked to low vitamin D levels – more than enough to demonstrate a pattern. According to one of the team of researchers, Dr Ramagopalan, 'These auto-immune diseases are one of the most common disease groups in modern economies today, affecting some 10% of the world population. Vitamin D deficiency is the most obvious risk factor.'

E Highlighting the benefits of vitamin D has led to at least some degree of change in official attitudes. UK citizens are now advised to spend some time in the sun at midday, while vitamin D supplements are advised for everyone during the winter months. However, the UK government could go much further. Vitamin D, given freely to all women in pregnancy, could be used to curb or prevent some major diseases including multiple sclerosis, diabetes, schizophrenia, asthma and several cancers. It might also be used to treat established disease, at least in the early stages.

5   Follow the procedure in Exercises 4a–4c and complete the test task.

Questions 6–7

Choose **TWO** letters, **A–E**.

The list below contains some possible statements about birthdays.

Which **TWO** of these statements are made by the writer of the passage?

A Scientists have long recognised the significance of birthdays in relation to MS.

B People with psychic powers were the first to predict MS based on an individual's birthday.

C There is a link between a person's birthday and their likelihood of developing MS.

D In the northern hemisphere, vitamin D in the bloodstream is at its highest level in June and July.

E Findings relating to birthdays and the risk of developing MS are the same in a number of countries.

➤ HELP

C The passage says at first the scientists found the idea *hardly credible*. This means they found it *almost unbelievable*.

Task analysis

6   Look again at any answers you got wrong. Can you see why they were wrong? Use your dictionary if necessary.

Vocabulary

> **COURSEBOOK** page 42

Problems and solutions

1 Choose the correct option in *italics* to complete the sentences.

1 The *danger / threat* of consuming too much fat and sugar is that it can lead to medical problems.
2 One *outcome / issue* concerning medical research is whether the funding for it comes from a company with commercial interests.
3 A reduction in government funding presents a *threat / priority* to ongoing and future medical research.
4 The main *test / danger* of the government's anti-smoking campaign will be whether sales of cigarettes decrease.
5 *Results / Methods* of diagnosing major health problems are much more effective than they used to be.
6 A key *outcome / challenge* for all governments is how to meet the rising costs of health and social care.
7 One *outcome / approach* of recent research findings is that people are spending less money on skin-protection products.
8 Many health *problems / outcomes* can be avoided by taking regular exercise.

Academic collocations

2 Underline the verb on the left which collocates best with the noun in bold.

1	locate	find	uncover	**a solution**
2	face	meet	view	**a challenge**
3	grab	seize	tackle	**an issue**
4	make	create	produce	**a priority**
5	cause	pose	set	**a threat**

3 Complete the sentences with the correct form of the collocations in Exercise 2.

1 Many parents are reluctant to *tackle* the *issue* of trying to get their children to eat well.
2 According to medical experts, the government should _____ mental health as much a _____ as physical health.
3 Resistance to antibiotics _____ a major _____ in the fight against infectious diseases.
4 It is not a simple affair to _____ a _____ to the growing problem of childhood obesity.
5 Health professionals have found that the biggest _____ they _____ when dealing with the problem of infectious diseases is good hygiene.

Idiomatic phrases for problems and solutions

4 Match the sentence beginnings (1–7) with the correct endings (A–G).

1 One new case of the Ebola virus in Europe
2 Whether or not people should be required to stop smoking before undergoing surgery
3 Although underlying problems may remain, taking pills to relieve pain
4 Depression can lead to overeating, which leads to further unhappiness due to weight gain, and thus
5 In the case of many widespread health problems, a willingness to accept a change of lifestyle
6 When an individual has success in one sphere of life, it
7 Extracting teeth to relieve toothache

A can have a positive impact on other areas.
B is a useful quick fix.
C should be a solution of last resort.
D might be just the tip of the iceberg.
E a vicious cycle is created.
F is a bone of contention.
G remains the crux of the matter.

5 Complete the sentences below, using your own ideas.

1 Next year I intend to make _____ a priority as a way of remaining healthy.
2 Some of my friends _____ because they enjoy facing a challenge.
3 For me, _____ as a method of keeping fit would be a last resort.
4 Doing yoga is probably one of the best methods of _____ .
5 In my opinion, the biggest issue for people who work long hours is _____ .
6 One of the consequences of _____ is that I feel more relaxed.

TEST STRATEGY

The topic of health and fitness often comes up in the Speaking test as well as in the second part of the Writing test, so it is useful to extend your vocabulary in these areas.

Language development

> COURSEBOOK page 45, EXPERT GRAMMAR page 177

Real and unreal conditionals review

1 Do the following sentences describe real or unreal situations?

1 If people spend too much time indoors, they probably don't get enough vitamin D.
2 If pregnant women took vitamin D tablets, their babies would possibly have some protection against multiple sclerosis.
3 People get too little exercise if they go everywhere by car.
4 Manufacturers will continue adding too much sugar to drinks if the government doesn't regulate them.
5 A lot of people would cycle to work if the government created special cycle lanes.

2a Read the following sentences. Does the writer think the situation is *possible* or *unlikely* to occur?

1 If cars were banned from the city centre, there would be far fewer road accidents.
2 If cars are banned from the city centre, there will be far fewer road accidents

b The following sentences all describe situations which the writer thinks are unlikely to occur. Complete the sentences with the correct form of the verbs in brackets.

1 If more parks were created, people living in cities _____ (get) more opportunity to take exercise.
2 People would suffer less stress if they _____ (work) fewer hours.
3 If the government _____ (raise) fuel prices, fewer people would use cars.
4 There _____ (be) fewer dental health problems if everyone visited the dentist regularly.
5 If people regularly _____ (use) stairs instead of lifts, they would generally be healthier.

3 Write sentences like those in Exercise 2b, using the notes to help you.

1 develop a vaccine for malaria → save a lot of lives
If a vaccine were developed for malaria, it would save a lot of lives.
2 more organic farms → fruit and vegetables safer to eat

_____

3 children get more sleep → make better progress at school

_____

4 people wash hands more often → infections spread less quickly

_____

5 people have better health education → cost of healthcare reduced

_____

Other ways to express conditionality

4a Choose the correct option in *italics* to complete the sentences.

1 There will soon be no effective treatment for common infections *provided that / unless* new antibiotics are developed.
2 People shouldn't need to take food supplements *unless / as long as* they have a balanced diet.
3 *Supposing that / Provided that* children are vaccinated against TB at an early age, they are unlikely to develop the disease in later life.
4 *Supposing that / As long as* a vaccine could be developed for malaria, millions of lives would be saved.
5 Parents should stop driving their children to school, *unless / otherwise* children will become unfit from an early age.
6 *Otherwise / As long as* you don't get sunburnt, daily exposure to the sun is good for you.

b Complete the sentences with the words/phrases below.

_____

as long as/provided that   otherwise   supposing   unless

EXPERT LANGUAGE

As long as and *Provided that* have the same meaning.

---

1 _____ you get regular exercise, you don't need to go to a gym.
2 New babies don't need to drink water, _____ they are bottle fed.
3 _____ you had more free time, how would you spend it?
4 It's better not to study every day, _____ you'll have no chance to relax.

5 Complete the sentences according to your own ideas and experience.

1 Supposing that I had more free time, I would

_____ .

2 As long as I don't feel too tired, I'm going to

_____ .

3 I won't be able to do more exercise unless _____ .
4 I'm not going to call my friend today, otherwise

_____ .

5 I think I'll get a good grade in the IELTS test, provided that _____ .

Writing (Task 2)

> **COURSEBOOK** page 46, **EXPERT WRITING** page 193

Understand the task

1a Read the test task. What kind of essay is it asking you to write?

> *Write about the following topic.*
>
> *Despite evidence that certain types of food are harmful, many people make the choice to eat unhealthy food.*
>
> *What do you think are the causes of this problem and what measures can be taken to solve it?*

b What is the core problem you need to write about? What two major elements must there be in your answer?

Write about problems and solutions

2 Match the sections of an answer to the essay task in Exercise 1a (1–5) with their functions (A–E).

Section	Function
1 It has long been known that eating certain kinds of food – processed meat, greasy hamburgers, sugar-laden cakes – causes a wide range of problems, from obesity to heart disease.	A A suggested solution
2 However, many people choose to ignore warnings and eat large amounts of unhealthy food. Why do they do this and what can be done to prevent it?	B A description of one cause of the problem
3 Firstly, processed food is generally cheaper than fresh food because it tends to be mass produced and often also contains chemicals to preserve it for longer.	C Further explanation of the solution
4 The solution to this is therefore to make the food more expensive and consequently less attractive.	D A more detailed explanation of the core issue
5 It is common to impose massive taxes on cigarettes and the same levy should be put on things like sugar or trans-fats.	E A summary of what the essay will cover

Develop a paragraph

3a Put the sentences (A–E) in the correct order to make the second paragraph of the essay in Exercise 2.

  A In addition, advertising and texts like menus should also be required to show clearly how much sugar and fat is in each meal.

  B For example, many fast food outlets are owned by large corporations and they promote their products through expensive promotional campaigns and slick adverts, many of them specifically designed to 'hook' children to the products early on.

  C A second reason why many people choose unhealthy foods is because there are numerous temptations to buy and consume them.

  D Many people feel that this issue can best be handled by banning advertising of unhealthy food to children, for example to prohibit commercials on children's TV or other media and on mainstream channels before the 9p.m. watershed.

  E These adverts make no mention of the high number of calories the food contains or of the amount of fat used in its preparation.

b Match the sentences in Exercise 3a with their functions (1–5).

  1 A summary of one solution to this problem

  2 An outline of a second cause of the problem

  3 A further detailed analysis of why the problem is so serious

  4 More detail of how the solution can be made effective

  5 An example to give more detail about how the issue causes problems

Write your essay

4 Think of another cause of the problem in the essay task in Exercise 1a. Write a paragraph following the structure in Exercise 3b, outlining a possible solution to this problem. Then write a concluding sentence for the whole essay.

> **TEST STRATEGY**
>
> For problem-solution essays, aim to include several different causes of the problem as this will allow you to generate a number of different solutions. This will make it easier to develop your paragraphs and fulfil the 250-word requirement.

Listening (Section 4)

> COURSEBOOK pages 44 and 47

Before you listen

1   Read the notes in the test task below and answer the questions.

1   What do you think is the main focus of this section of the lecture?
2   How many gaps do you need to fill?
3   What is the maximum number of words you can write for each answer?

Questions 1–3

Complete the notes below.

Write **NO MORE THAN ONE WORD AND/OR A NUMBER** *for each answer.*

Allergies
Background
– Allergies are becoming more widespread: 4–8% of population in developed world, 25% in UK
– Allergies cause different symptoms:
– Milder reactions, e.g. temporary itching, problems with 1 _____
– More severe reactions, e.g. 2 _____
– Some types of food allergies tend to improve in adulthood, e.g. 3 _____ , eggs and soy

Identify specific information required

2   Match the words/phrases below with the underlined words in the test task in Exercise 1. There may be more than one answer.

serious common minor short-term quickly disappear result in later life difficulties reactions

Test practice

3a   Read the headings and subheadings in the test tasks in Exercise 4. Predict what type of information will be given under each sub-section.

b   Underline the key words in questions 4–10 which act as guide to the correct answer. Think of alternative ways of expressing these words.

4   ◀)) 3.1 Complete the test task.

Questions 4–7
Answer the questions below.
Write **NO MORE THAN THREE WORDS** *for each answer.*

Managing allergies
What are the two main risk factors for allergies?
• 4 _____
• 5 _____
What are the names of the two main techniques for identifying allergens?
• 6 _____
• 7 _____

TEST STRATEGY

The instructions for note completion give the maximum number of words for each answer. Note that this number is the maximum – many items will only require one-word answers.

Questions 8–10
Complete the notes below.
Write **NO MORE THAN ONE WORD** *for each answer.*

Research: neutralising allergens in sesame seeds
Scientists:
• established that protein in foods causes the allergic reaction
• turned the seeds into 8 _____
• used pulses of electricity, which changed the structure of the protein in the seeds
Outcomes
• 95% of the allergic qualities disappear
• the treatment doesn't change the seeds' 9 _____ or taste
• unsure of reason for success – believed to be affected by changes to the 10 _____ inside the molecules

TEST STRATEGY

Sub-headings and sub-sub headings on the question paper are a valuable guide when listening. Note that the heading 'Scientists:' is followed by bullet points which follow on from this stem.

Language development

> COURSEBOOK page 48, EXPERT GRAMMAR page 177

Modal forms; Degrees of certainty

1a Underline the errors in the sentences.

1 You can't not take your phone into the X-ray room.
2 In some countries people don't must pay for their medication, but in other countries they do.
3 I need spend more time training if I want to enter the marathon race.
4 If you have antibiotics, you must to finish the whole course.
5 Doctors should prescribe a treatment unless it has been approved by the government.
6 You needn't pick up heavy objects without bending your knees.

b Correct the errors you underlined.

> **EXPERT LANGUAGE**
>
> *Must* and *have to* mean the same thing, but *mustn't* and *don't have to* have a different meaning. *Mustn't* means 'it is prohibited', *don't have to* means 'it is not necessary'.

2 Choose the correct option in *italics* to complete the text.

The problem with antibiotics

In 1945, when Alexander Fleming accepted a prize for discovering the antibiotic penicillin, he warned that bacteria **1** *must / could* become resistant through inappropriate use of the drug. 'The time **2** *should / may* come in future when penicillin **3** *can / must* be bought by anyone in the shops,' he said. That time is getting closer, and antibiotics are no longer as effective as they used to be. As a result of their over-use, an invisible army of super-resistant bacteria has evolved.
A further problem is that new antibiotics are not being developed fast enough. In order to make a profit, pharmaceutical companies **4** *have to / ought to* sell large volumes of drugs. Many have pulled out of development altogether, focusing attention instead on drugs for conditions such as diabetes or blood pressure, which patients **5** *should / have to* take for years, rather than courses lasting just days or weeks. According to Professor Anthony Kessel, we **6** *must / might* urgently engage in a discussion about the lack of new drugs. He says that we may soon arrive at a situation where we **7** *can / have to* think about rationing antibiotics. However, this **8** *would / can* be politically unacceptable. Meanwhile, doctors **9** *shouldn't / wouldn't* prescribe antibiotics unless it is absolutely necessary.

3 Complete the sentences with the words below. Use the word with the degree of strength indicated.

could/might   will   won't   would

1 I _____ take part in the next London marathon race. (moderate strength)
2 Some doctors _____ go abroad to work unless they get a pay rise. (maximum strength)
3 Certain food products _____ be withdrawn from sale if the government tightens safety regulations. (moderate strength)
4 Some people _____ change their lifestyle until they become ill. (maximum strength)
5 If children didn't have computer games, they _____ play outside more. (maximum strength)
6 The government _____ decide to put a tax on sugar if obesity continues to rise. (moderate strength)

4 Complete the second sentence so that it has a similar meaning to the first. Use the modal verb in brackets.

1 Louis Pasteur was probably motivated to cure infectious diseases because three of his children had died of typhoid. (might)
If three of Louis Pasteur's children hadn't _____ .
2 After Louis Pasteur suggested that infections were caused by micro-organisms, other scientists developed antiseptic methods for surgery. (wouldn't)
If Louis Pasteur hadn't _____ .
3 To develop new treatments, greater investment in the pharmaceutical industry is required. (could)
With greater investment, the pharmaceutical industry _____ .
4 The smallpox vaccine, which Edward Jenner pioneered in the 19th century, saved thousands of people from dying of the disease. (would)
If Edward Jenner hadn't pioneered _____ .
5 It isn't a good idea to keep unused medicines when they have passed their expiry date. (shouldn't)
People _____ .
6 It is essential for people using mosquito nets to make sure that there aren't any holes in them. (need)
People using mosquito nets _____ .
7 It isn't necessary for people to take vitamin supplements, as a balanced diet contains all the nutrients the body needs. (have to)
As a balanced diet contains all the nutrients a body needs, _____ .
8 It is a legal requirement for doctors in the UK to be registered with the General Medical Council before they can practise medicine. (must)
UK doctors _____ .

5 Finish the sentences below about yourself and your plans. Use a suitable modal verb.

1 If I get a good grade in the IELTS test, I _____ .
2 Unless I get the grade that I want in the IELTS test, _____ .
3 Before the end of the year I _____ .
4 To get the kind of job that I want, I _____ .

Vocabulary

➤ COURSEBOOK page 48

Adverbs of attitude

1a Which of the adverbs (1–6) usually appear at the beginning of a sentence, followed by a comma?

1 apparently	4 undeniably
2 evidently	5 undoubtedly
3 naturally	6 unfortunately

b Which of the adverbs in Exercise 1a have a very similar meaning?

c Which of the adverbs in Exercise 1a almost always appear in the middle of a sentence?

d Match each of the words in Exercise 1a with one of the meanings (A–D). Some of the meanings have more than one answer.

A I have heard or read this, and I believe it is probably true.
B This is obvious, it hardly needs to be said.
C This is a pity.
D No-one could claim that it's untrue.

2 Choose the correct option in *italics* to complete the sentences, so that they match the writer's attitude in brackets.

1 *Naturally / Evidently*, too many doctors are prescribing antibiotics unnecessarily. (I've read or heard this.)
2 *Unfortunately / Apparently*, my sister isn't coming because she has a doctor's appointment this evening. (I wish she was coming.)
3 *Naturally / Evidently*, experts are very worried about the threat of a global infection which doesn't respond to drugs. (It's obvious that they would be worried.)
4 *Apparently / Unfortunately*, the race is only open to runners who have passed a time trial. (I've heard this.)
5 *Naturally / Apparently*, it's possible to do too much exercise as well as too little. (It's obvious to most people.)
6 Antibiotics were *evidently / undoubtedly* the biggest medical development of the 20th century. (I feel certain about that.)
7 *Unfortunately / Undeniably*, pharmaceutical companies often have to charge high prices for medicines to compensate for the high costs of research. (It's a pity.)

3 Express your opinion about the following topics. Use adverbs from Exercise 1a to show your attitude about what you're saying.

1 swimming and health	5 vitamin supplements and health
2 chocolate and weight gain	6 walking and bones
3 money and happiness	7 age and memory
4 music and relaxation	8 yoga and stress

TEST STRATEGY

The use of adverbs of attitude can give your writing greater cohesion, and you will gain extra marks for this in the Writing test.

Speaking (Part 3)

> **COURSEBOOK** pages 43 and 49,
> **EXPERT SPEAKING** page 186

Vocabulary development

1a Read the Part 3 questions in Exercise 1c below. What is the general topic of the questions?

1 personal characteristics
2 social attitudes
3 child development

b Put the words below into the correct category.

anxious   attitude   cheerful   contented   optimistic
outlook   pessimistic   therapy   treatment   worried

Positive	Negative	Neutral
_____	_____	_____
_____	_____	_____
_____	_____	_____
		_____

EXPERT LANGUAGE

The adjectives *optimistic* and *pessimistic* are opposite in meaning.

---

c Read the questions below and think about how you might answer them.

1 What effect do you think a person's early life has on their personality?
2 Some people say that people with a positive attitude are generally more successful. What's your opinion about that?
3 People who have a good position in society or a lot of possessions are not necessarily contented. How would you explain this?
4 Who do you think worries more, young people or adults?
5 Which do you think is better for treating people who suffer from anxiety, medication or therapy?

d 🔊 3.2 Listen to five different people answering one of the questions in Exercise 1c. Match each speaker (A–E) with one of the questions.

A _____
B _____
C _____
D _____
E _____

e 🔊 3.3 Close your book. Listen to the questions and answer them yourself. Try to give examples and explanations for your opinions.

Test practice

2a Read the questions below about social relationships and think about how you might answer them. Make notes.

1 Why do you think some individuals are more sociable than others?
2 How important is it to teach children social skills?
3 Do you think individuals with different personalities can be close friends?
4 Some people say that a cheerful person makes others feel cheerful. Do you agree?
5 In your opinion, what kind of individuals make good group leaders?
6 Do groups work better together when the members are similar to each other, or when they are different?
7 When people apply for a job, which is more important, general attitude or qualifications?

TEST STRATEGY

In the Speaking test, if the examiner asks you a question that you don't understand, ask for repetition or clarification before you answer.

---

b 🔊 3.4 Listen to two people answering question 1 in Exercise 2a. Which one uses more adjectives like the ones in Exercise 1b?

c Answer the questions yourself. If possible, record your answers.

Assess and improve

3a Did you have any problem understanding the questions? Listen to them again to check. If you did, try to get more practice by listening to interviews on the radio or television.

b Were you able to use the new adjectives that you have learnt in this section?

Writing (Task 2)

> COURSEBOOK pages 52–53, EXPERT WRITING page 193

Understand the task

1 Read the writing task question below. What is the core problem?

Despite advances in medicine, mental ill health is becoming more common amongst young people. What do you think are the causes of this problem and what measures can be taken to solve it?

Plan the task

2a Look at the table below. The first column lists possible causes of mental health problems in young people. The second column suggests measures which might be taken to address each of these. Add further points to the two columns.

Possible cause	Suggested solution(s)
Alienation from wider society	Encourage older and younger generations to mix more
Stigma related to talking about mental health problems	Raise awareness through open discussion – reduce fear/normalise mental health problems
Reduced physical activity	More emphasis on getting young people into sports

b Highlight the issues in the table in Exercise 2a which you think are most relevant and which you feel you have enough to write about.

3 Think about how you'll organise your essay. Choose one of the essay types below and draft your plan.

Essay Type 1	Essay Type 2
Cause 1 → solution(s) Cause 2 → solution (s)	Causes 1, 2, 3 Solutions for 1, 2, 3

Language and content

4a Look at the extract below from a sample answer for the task in Exercise 1. Underline phrases which indicate tentative views.

> **LANGUAGE EXPERT**
>
> Problem-solution essays often include speculations about possible causes and effective solutions. Use tentative language to introduce speculations in your writing.

Because of improvements in care and in living conditions, many people in different parts of the world are living longer and healthier lives. However, there are certain problems which appear to be resisting this trend. In particular, it is believed that mental ill health is on the rise, especially amongst younger people. The reasons for this are many and varied. Perhaps the most powerful cause could be that some young people feel alienated from wider society. Nowadays, communities tend to be less multi-generational than they used to be and young people have fewer role models to look up to or respected older figures they can ask for advice and guidance.

b Complete the sentences with the phrases you underlined in Exercise 4a. There may be more than one possible answer.

1 Sports and other physical activities _____ less popular with young people nowadays.
2 One solution _____ to have more sports and games at school.
3 _____ that there is a link between mental and physical well-being.
4 Research shows that young people _____ to be more interested in sedentary activities.

Write your problem and solution essay

5 Write your answer to the essay task in Exercise 1. Try to include tentative language for both causes and solutions. Write at least 250 words.

Assess and improve

6a When you have finished writing, leave your essay for a while. Re-read it after a few hours and answer the questions.

1 Is the core problem explained clearly?
2 Have you included at least two reasons and relevant solutions for the core problem?
3 Did you use paragraphs effectively?
4 Is there a satisfying conclusion which gives a sense of overall cohesion?
5 Have you used a variety of forms to convey the fact that your views are tentative?
6 Can you see any grammar, spelling or puntuation mistakes?

b Work on improving your answer. Focus on TWO areas you want to improve, using the questions in Exercise 6a to help you.

4a The cost of buying

Reading (Matching information; Summary completion)

> **COURSEBOOK** pages 56–57

Before you read

1 Read the title of the reading passage. What do you think the 'threat' might refer to?

Identify functions

2a Read the title and skim the first and last paragraphs of the reading passage. What kind of passage is it?

    1 an argument (a reasoned opinion)
    2 a narrative (an account of a series of events)
    3 a description

  b Read the passage. Has your answer to Exercise 2a changed?

3 Read the first two paragraphs of the passage and follow these steps.

    1 Underline words/phrases relating to how widespread advertising is. What examples are given of products or services which display advertisements?
    2 Underline words/phrases relating to official policies on advertising. Which words signal a contrast?

Test practice

4 Complete the test task.

Questions 1–5

The reading passage has SEVEN paragraphs, A–G.

Which paragraph contains the following information?
Write the correct letter, A–G.

You may use any letter more than once.

    1 a list of groups who have expressed concern about levels of public consumption
    2 mention of one useful but uncommon function of advertisements
    3 reference to measures taken by one country to defend people of a certain age against advertisements
    4 a contrast between past and present attitudes to advertising among one group of people
    5 examples of activities which are known to be more beneficial for individuals than shopping

Test practice

5a Read the title of the summary below. Scan the reading passage to find a reference to the environment. Which paragraph is it in?

  b Look at the gaps in the summary below. Which kind of word would fit in each gap?

> **Advertisements and the environment**
>
> The global economy is increasing very quickly, and this has an impact on global warming. According to experts, developments in **1** _____ by themselves will not avert a crisis: we must also reduce our levels of **2** _____ . Advertising is a threat to such an aim.

  c Complete the summary in Exercise 5b with one word from the passage in each gap.

6 Complete the test task.

> **TEST STRATEGY**
>
> In a summary task the information may not be in the same order as in the reading passage.

Questions 6–8

Complete the summary below.

*Choose **ONE WORD ONLY** from the passage for each answer.*

> **How society must change**
>
> Unless we make fundamental changes, our future prosperity is at risk. We should no longer aim for continuous **6** _____ in our economy. In terms of the goods that we buy and sell, we should recognise the importance of **7** _____ : we must recycle goods instead of simply buying new ones. And if we cut manufacturing output by reducing working hours, **8** _____ will not automatically result.

> **Expert language**
>
> The prefix *re-* can either mean *back* or *again*. *Recycled* goods are used items which are adapted for further use, for example empty bottles which are processed to produce new glass goods.

The threat posed by advertisements

A Advertising is everywhere. Media that were once largely free of commercials, such as movies and the internet, now come full of commercial messages. Not so long ago, most musicians were reluctant to see their work used to endorse shampoo or footwear. Today, the music and advertising industries are united in a profitable relationship. We now have advertisements in our schools and on our clothes. Our main TV genre – in terms of volume – is not comedy, drama or sport, but advertising. The average British viewer is now exposed to 48 TV commercials a day. Recent studies showed that around a third of Australian TV time is now taken up by advertisements. In the USA the figure is closer to 40 percent.

B Advertising has become such a routine part of everyday life that we rarely stop to think about its significance. Governments, regulators and media companies tend to regard advertising purely as a source of income, and have allowed it to increase. There are a few exceptions to this: governments are prepared to limit the promotion of harmful substances such as tobacco, and they monitor advertisements for modesty and respectfulness. Some governments – like Sweden – have acted to protect young children from the worst influence of TV advertisements, but most treat each advertisement on its individual merits. The larger question – what is the overall effect of so many advertisements – is rarely asked. However, in an age where economists, social scientists and climate scientists, among others, are seriously questioning the value of consumerism, this approach is no longer acceptable.

C For all their differences, advertisements share one basic value system. The message of the thousands of different stories they tell is that the only way to secure pleasure, popularity, security, happiness or fulfilment is through buying more; more consumption – regardless of how much we already have. However, there are two major problems with this set of values.

D First, the promise of advertising is entirely empty. Studies have shown that, beyond a certain point, there is no connection between the volume of consumer goods a society accumulates and the well-being of its people. The research shows that a walk in the park, social interaction or volunteering – which cost nothing – will do more for our well-being than any amount of shopping. Reviewing the evidence on consumerism and quality of life, Richard Layard argues that legislation banning advertising is far more likely to increase quality of life than extending consumer choice is.

E The second problem with advertising's value system is environmental. In a finite world, our current growth in consumption is unsustainable. The global economy has expanded five-fold in the last 50 years. By the end of the century, if we continue consuming at the current rate, it will be 80 times larger. Climate scientists insist that if we are to meet the targets required to avoid catastrophic levels of global warming, we cannot do it by new technology alone: we must begin to consume less. In this way, advertising and the culture it promotes threatens the sustainability of life on earth.

F It follows from this that we must change the way we live at the moment. If we are to prosper and develop as a species, we must begin to imagine economic models which recognise that resources are limited, and that do not rely on endless economic growth. We must pursue a way of working that values durability over short-term use, on repairing and reusing goods, rather than dumping and replacing them. We can avoid high unemployment in manufacturing industries by giving workers more free time rather than more money.

G Advertising runs counter to all these ideas and so it stifles our imagination. It keeps us hooked on a cycle of borrowing and spending, and it supports the idea that human progress is measured purely by our ability to acquire as many consumer goods as possible. Occasionally, advertising can provide us with useful information. But in the world of branding, imparting useful information has become increasingly old-fashioned. What we have instead is a vast global industry that promotes one activity above all others: shopping.

Vocabulary

➤ **COURSEBOOK** page 58

Academic verbs for thoughts and beliefs

1 Choose the correct option in *italics* to complete the sentences.

1 When referring to things that they buy, different people *define / contradict* 'need' in different ways.
2 Most economists *speculate / assume* that economic growth is a desirable objective.
3 Nowadays, many people cannot *consider / conceive* of life without a phone.
4 Even some business leaders *acknowledge / convince* that producing too many consumer goods is bad for the environment.
5 It is proving difficult for environmentalists to *contradict / convince* people to buy fewer goods.
6 It is interesting to *speculate / assume* on the kind of new products that will be invented over the next few decades.

EXPERT LANGUAGE

Conceive is followed by *of* + noun phrase; *speculate* is followed by *on* or *about* + noun phrase.

2 Match the sentence beginnings (1–6) with the endings (A–F).

1 When defining 'consumerism', dictionaries usually mention that this word is often used in
2 Our experience of certain products sometimes contradicts
3 A lot of people regard shopping as
4 Advertisements are very good at convincing people of
5 Supermarkets now acknowledge that 'Best Before' dates on food result in
6 The growth of online shopping has led planners to speculate on

A an enjoyable hobby.
B considerable waste.
C a negative sense.
D the value of a particular product.
E the future of conventional stores.
F claims made by advertisements.

Use an impersonal style in writing and speaking

3a Complete the sentences with the phrases below, so that they match the meaning of the words in brackets.

there is a widespread belief
there is a common misconception
it is formally acknowledged
there is an underlying assumption

1 _____ that there is a minimum wage below which employees cannot meet the basic costs of living. (The government has defined minimum wage levels.)
2 _____ that the economy is more important than the environment. (It is widely believed, but untrue.)
3 _____ that cheap goods are produced at the expense of the workers who make them. (It's the opinion of many people.)
4 _____ that higher prices are an indication of better quality. (It is a view which is not stated, but is taken for granted.)

TEST STRATEGY

If you write in an impersonal style in the Writing paper, you will get credit for appropriacy, as academic writing is usually impersonal.

b Write sentences about the following information, using the phrase from Exercise 3a which you think is most appropriate. You can use the phrases more than once.

1 Supermarket prices are higher than necessary.
2 Discarded packaging from consumer goods is polluting the oceans.
3 It is always better to buy locally produced goods than imported goods.
4 Glass bottles are more environmentally friendly than plastic ones.
5 Some companies pass on information about our shopping preferences without our knowledge.

Collocations for thoughts and beliefs

4a Underline the word on the left which best collocates with the phrase in bold.

1 bring take get **something into consideration**
2 resign leave accept **oneself to something**
3 own keep have **a lot of/little faith in something**
4 allow give pass **judgement on something**
5 be stay become **open to ideas**

b Complete the text with the correct form of the collocations in Exercise 4a.

Improving working conditions

When employees are dissatisfied with their working conditions, they often 1 _____ the situation, and do nothing about it. They 2 _____ in the employer's willingness to change things, and assume that management is unconcerned with their welfare. However, before 3 _____ their employer, the employee should consider being open about the problems. Not all employers are unsympathetic: some 4 _____ and can be persuaded to 5 _____ their employees' suggestions for change. It's certainly worth a try.

Language development

> COURSEBOOK page 61, EXPERT GRAMMAR page 178

Form clauses

1 Complete the text with the clauses A–F.

Car boot sales in the UK

At car boot sales, people get together to sell their unwanted items from the back of their car. Recently, the number of both visitors and sellers has increased, **1** $\boxed{D}$ or sell things to raise money.

This increased interest is partly due to the fact that people **2** ___ have left the site due to an increase in charges. Another reason for the car boot sale's rise in popularity may be environmental, as **3** ___ and now think more about recycling.

One outdoor market manager explained that **4** ___ , and car boot sales are basically a massive recycling exercise. Also, as supermarket food has become more expensive, **5** ___ .

Thousands of people flock to car boot sales every weekend, with pitches costing around £10 for the day. Sellers will often queue overnight, **6** ___ .

A who previously sold their things on an online auction site

B people are now much more conscious of the environment

C people want to save money

D as people either go on the hunt for a bargain

E so that they can be sure of securing the best pitches

F people have become less inclined to throw things away

2 Match the sentence beginnings (1–8) with the endings (A–H).

1 A charity shop is a retail outlet
2 Charities such as Oxfam sell goods to
3 The goods sold by charity shops
4 Compared to the goods in conventional shops
5 Most charity shops are staffed
6 The popularity of charity shops has increased since
7 Environmentalists prefer buying second-hand goods, as
8 Re-using second-hand items reduces

A they use fewer natural resources.
B the first one opened in 1947.
C which is owned and run by a charity.
D raise money.
E those in charity shops are more affordable.
F the amount of waste that goes to landfill.
G are donated by members of the public.
H by volunteers.

Subordinate clauses

3 Complete the sentences with the words below.

although as if unless whenever whereas whether
while

1 I never buy shoes _____ I can try them on.
2 I only buy clothes online _____ I'm short of time.
3 My mother hates shopping, _____ my father loves it.
4 _____ I buy things online that aren't suitable, I return them and get a refund.
5 It's better to buy electrical goods online than from a store _____ they're usually cheaper.
6 _____ shops sometimes use bags, there is far more packaging around posted goods.
7 _____ my sister takes ages choosing what to buy, I do my shopping very quickly.
8 _____ it's more expensive or not, I prefer getting my shopping in the old-fashioned way.

EXPERT LANGUAGE

Whereas and *while* can both be used to signal a contrast. They are usually used in formal writing.

4 Write five more sentences like the ones in Exercise 3, using subordinate clauses. Make any necessary changes so that they are correct for you.

Express opinions with *that*

5a Which of the following is a full sentence?
1 I disagree that packaging is unnecessary.
2 I think that buying unnecessary things.
3 I doubt that wrapping vegetables.

b Insert *that* in the correct place in the following sentences.
1 It is widely believed shopping is good for the national economy.
2 It is my belief people shop when they are bored.
3 A lot of people think supermarket prices are too high.
4 There is a common misconception food should not be eaten after its 'Best Before' date.
5 It seems to me having a wide choice of products is unnecessary.
6 Children should be taught to recognise adverts are designed to persuade them.

EXPERT LANGUAGE

In spoken English, *that* is often omitted, but it is usually used in written English.

6 Answer the questions, using *that*.
1 What is your opinion about online shopping?
2 What do you think about the use of packaging for food?
3 What do most of your friends think about buying imported goods?
4 What is your attitude towards throwing things away?

Writing (Task 2)

➤ **COURSEBOOK** page 62

Understand the task

1a Look at the test task below. What type of statement is in the first line?

1 a statement giving both sides of a question
2 a controversial statement designed to catalyse argumentation
3 a nuanced statement suggesting a particular view

'Advertising is a positive feature of life and brings many benefits to society as a whole.'
To what extent do you agree or disagree with this statement?

b What is the core meaning of the statement in the task in Exercise 1a?

1 advertising is very beneficial for society in general but damaging for individuals
2 advertising is has both positive and negative outcomes
3 advertising adds value to people's existence and has tangible benefits

Give your opinion

2a Carefully consider the statement in the task in Exercise 1a. To what extent do you agree with it? Choose a number on a scale of 1–5, where 1 means 'strongly disagree' and 5 means 'strongly agree'.

b Look at the points 1–9 and decide whether they would be a suitable in an argument for (✓) or against (✗) the statement in the test task in Exercise 1a.

1 It promotes choice in business.
2 You have to be able to advertise to get your message across to your customers.
3 It is easy to be misled by adverts – they give a false picture.
4 It reduces prices because it enhances competition.
5 It tempts people to spend money they do not have.
6 It leads young people astray, e.g. to smoke or drink heavily.
7 I often find myself laughing at adverts: many are genuinely funny.
8 It can be controlled if it is carefully monitored.
9 I dislike having adverts all around me.

c Decide which points in Exercise 2b are made from an academic perspective (Ac) and which from a more personal (P) perspective.

d Reword the points you labelled P to make them more suitable for an academic piece of writing.

Develop your arguments

3a There are four main ways to organise an opinion essay. Which way you do think is most effective?

1 Agree with the statement and answer only from that point of view.
2 Disagree with the statement and answer only from that point of view
3 Start with the arguments made by people who hold a different view from yours. Then give your arguments in support of your opinion.
4 Discuss both for and against arguments and then finish by making clear your own position.

b Complete the sample answer with the words/phrases below. There is one extra word/phrase you do not need.

although   firstly   however   in addition   lead to   most of which   particularly

There are a number of convincing arguments against advertising, **1** _____ portray adverts as a blight on society. **2** _____ , our constant exposure to commercial images is said to **3** _____ poor mental health. **4** _____ , adverts are considered to misrepresent the truth. **5** _____ they are often glossy and humorous, they sometimes deliberately give false information and fool people into believing that they must have a particular product, forcing them to spend money they can ill afford to part with. Adverts, it is said, deliberately 'hook' people, **6** _____ youngsters, ensuring they will be addicted to certain products for the rest of their lives.

c Which organisational structure in Exercise 3a do you think the writer of the sample in Exercise 3b was following?

Write your opinion essay

4a Consider your opinion and plan your answer to the writing task in Exercise 1a. Think about:

1 How much you agree (1–5 on the scale) and how you will make your position clear.
2 What main reasons you have for this opinion, from an academic perspective.
3 Explanations and examples you can use to support your main reasons.
4 How the different sections are signposted.
5 How you can link your explanations and examples together.

b Write your essay.

TEST STRATEGY

IELTS Writing tasks require you to take an academic rather than a personal perspective. So for this task, you must argue about potential effects of advertising on society as a whole rather than just on you personally (as a consumer) or on certain individuals such as business owners.

Listening (Section 2)

> COURSEBOOK pages 60 and 63

Before you listen

1a Look at the instructions for the test task in Exercise 3. What is the maximum number of words you can use in each answer?

b Look at the table in the test task. What type of gadgets do you think the speaker will talk about? How many gadgets will be described?

c For each question, predict what kind of word (noun, adjective, verb) you need to write.

Identify links between ideas

2a Look again at the table. In what order will the information be given in the talk?

b The second and third columns of the table are Good points/Special features and Disadvantages. Which of the words/phrases below relate to a) positive and b) negative points?

1 There are lots of positives
2 On the downside
3 The main shortcoming
4 It's got a lot of great features
5 It has several snazzy functions
6 The negatives are
7 What makes it special is

c Match the phrases (1–3) with the functions (A–C).

1 The first, the second, the last
2 basically, the idea is
3 I have to say, research shows

A reinforcing a point
B moving from one gadget to the next
C introducing the core features

Test practice

TEST STRATEGY

For IELTS Listening tasks you only listen to the recording once so it's important to pick up on cues which tell you what type of information is about to be given. When filling in tables, listen for words and phrases which relate to the titles of the rows and columns.

3 🔊 4.1 Complete the test task.

Questions 1–10
Complete the table below.
*Write **NO MORE THAN TWO WORDS** for each answer.*

Gadget trial

Gadget and purpose	Good points/ Special features	Disadvantages
UV Bracelet Gauges UV radiation while sunbathing Warns of high levels Also gives a detailed 1 _____	Free to download Available in several 2 _____ Comfortable to wear while doing 3 _____	Shorter 4 _____ than expected No indication when it stops working so it can be dangerous Rating: 7/10
Vibrapower Disc Vibrations help tone your body	5 _____ to use Strong evidence that it improves speed of fat loss Helps maintain 6 _____	Very large Difficult to find a good position because of problems with 7 _____ Rating: 7/10
Smart BP Monitor Monitors blood pressure	Can work with a smartphone or on a 8 _____ Lots of functions, e.g. to check your pulse and count steps Can send stats directly to a 9 _____	Gave inconsistent readings Difficult to 10 _____ Rating: 5/10

EXPERT LANGUAGE

For productive tasks in the Listening paper, you must listen for words actually used by the speaker and in exactly the same form, e.g. question 2 requires a plural answer – the answer is wrong if your write the singular form.

Task analysis

4 Did your answers contain any of the following?

1 misspelling
2 too many words/too few words
3 incorrect answer
4 unnecessary information

Language development

> **COURSEBOOK** page 64, **EXPERT GRAMMAR** page 178

Pronoun referencing

1 Match the pronouns in bold (1–6) with the word(s) they refer to (A–F).

Banana leaves have long been used across India as a natural alternative to food packaging. **1 They** are cheap to buy, waterproof, hygienic and degrade quickly when binned.

Inspired by the simplicity of this low-cost alternative to plastic and polystyrene, entrepreneur Jaydeep Korde decided to launch a packaging company **2 which** makes disposable packaging out of waste rice and wheat straw.

It took **3 him** seven years to develop a process that can turn any kind of cereal waste into packaging. 'Straw is annually renewable, which makes **4 it** a more sustainable raw material than paper,' he explains.

Producers of other natural alternatives, such as corn starch packaging, have to compete for raw materials with food producers and biofuel manufacturers.

The downturn in newspaper sales has also created a shortage of recycled paper products. **5 This** has created a growing niche for alternatives to environmental paper, says Korde. 'Recycled paper has become an expensive commodity. Trendwise, **6 that** is only going one way.'

A Jaydeep Korde
B a shortage of recycled paper products
C banana leaves
D a packaging company
E Recycled paper has become an expensive commodity.
F straw

TEST STRATEGY

Pronouns are extremely important for creating cohesion in an essay. If you are able to use them correctly in the IELTS Writing papers, you will get a higher score.

2 Choose the correct pronoun in *italics* to complete the sentences.

1 There are various alternatives to packaging material made from non-renewable material. One of *this / these* is made out of a fungus called mycelium.
2 An American company developed the new packaging product, *this / which* it calls Mushroom Packaging.
3 Mycelium is the part of a fungus that attaches to the soil, or whatever else *it / this* is growing on.
4 The mycelium fibres are allowed to grow around clean agricultural waste, such as corn stalks or husks. Over the space of a few days *this / they* bind the waste together.
5 The waste binds together, forming a solid shape, *this / which* is then dried to stop the fungus growing any further.
6 Polystyrene takes thousands of years to decompose, but mycelium packaging can be simply thrown into the garden, *where / which* it decomposes naturally within a few weeks.
7 Another advantage of mycelium is that *it / they* can be grown in a mould of any shape or size.
8 Buyers of the packaging include the computer giant Dell, which uses *this / it* to cushion large computer servers.

3 Complete the text with suitable pronouns.

A ban on polystyrene

In 2016 San Francisco decided to ban polystyrene products, such as the cheap insulating foam **1** _____ cushions goods and keeps drinks hot or cold. They say the lightweight plastic, **2** _____ is extremely slow to decompose, pollutes waterways, harming marine life and birds.

Polystyrene is the latest plastic to be targeted by U.S. cities, much like the single-use plastic bag, which disappeared in San Francisco **3** _____ the city outlawed it in 2007. The latest measure builds on a 2006 regulation **4** _____ requires food vendors and restaurants to use recyclable or compostable containers for **5** _____ carry-outs. Other cities in the USA followed suit. New York City tried, but a state judge recently overturned a ban on plastic foam containers and packing there, saying **6** _____ could be recycled.

4 Answer the questions about yourself, using full sentences.

1 Do you usually buy fruit and vegetables which are pre-packed?
2 Apart from food, what kinds of things that you buy are usually pre-packed?
3 How do you carry things that you buy from a shop?
4 What do you do with packaging after unwrapping things?
5 How do you feel about buying things which have a lot of packaging material?

Vocabulary

> **COURSEBOOK** page 64

Signposting words

1 Choose the correct option in *italics* to complete the sentences.

1 As people become wealthier, they buy more luxury goods. *However / For instance*, when incomes fall, the demand for luxury goods falls too.

2 Between 1996 and 2000, sales of watches and jewellery grew in value by 23.3 percent, *therefore / whereas* sales of clothing and accessories grew by only 11.6 percent.

3 Prior to 2012, Japan was the world's biggest market for luxury goods. *In addition / However*, in that year China became the biggest market.

4 Virtually every category of goods includes a subset of products which are regarded as luxurious on account of certain features. *Consequently / For instance*, they may be better designed, or more durable.

5 Some so-called luxury goods, which are bought to demonstrate the wealth of the owner, may not be better made than similar, cheaper goods. *On the contrary / Nevertheless*, they may be inferior in quality.

6 *Initially / Furthermore*, a certain product may not be regarded as a luxury item. However, if a celebrity buys the product, it can then become one.

7 Some individuals regard accessories as a status symbol. *In addition / In particular*, they like to wear a showy watch.

8 In general, the market for luxury goods in China has declined recently. *Although / Nevertheless* certain well-known brands have retained their popularity.

2 Replaced the words/phrases in bold with the words/phrases below.

as a result   at first   furthermore   in particular
nevertheless   on the contrary   while

1 **Whereas** the price of clothes has remained steady recently, the price of food has risen.

2 Women tend to be more cautious shoppers than men. **For instance**, they spend more time comparing prices.

3 **Initially** people bought Fairtrade goods as a way of helping those on a low income. Later they bought them on account of their quality.

4 Most people claim to be concerned about the environment. **However**, the same people are happy to use plastic bags whenever they go shopping.

5 For some people, shopping is an enjoyable experience. **Consequently**, they feel more relaxed after a shopping trip.

6 Supermarkets try to compete with each other on price. **In addition**, they try to do better than their competitors on customer service.

7 It is often assumed that shoppers are attracted by low prices, but this is not always the case. **In fact**, given the choice between two similar products, some individuals choose the more expensive one.

TEST STRATEGY

In the IELTS Writing paper, cohesion is one of the marking criteria. Using signposting words is one of the main ways of achieving cohesion in an essay.

---

3 Put the sentences (A–H) in the correct order to form a coherent text.

The value of works of art

A The expert has also claimed that the content of paintings affects their value.

B For one thing, some aspects of an artist's life make them more interesting to collectors, and therefore more valuable.

C Consequently, they can afford to buy expensive paintings, and they choose subjects which appeal to younger buyers.

D In addition, paintings are more valuable if the artist dies young.

E For example, sunny weather, beautiful scenery or lovely young women generally make them more valuable.

F One of the reasons for this may be that in today's world, individuals are becoming wealthy at an early age.

G For instance, a history of rebellion, or even madness, often makes paintings more desirable.

H A leading art expert, who has spent 35 years working in the art market, has said that there are several factors which affect the price of a painting.

4 Complete the sentences using your own experience and opinions.

1 Although _____ , I enjoy looking at paintings in an art gallery.

2 I like the work of some artists more than others. In particular, _____ .

3 I usually like paintings of _____ . For instance, _____ .

4 I rarely buy luxury goods. However, _____ .

5 Whereas my friend prefers shopping online, I _____ .

6 I try to care for the environment. Therefore, I don't _____ .

Speaking (Part 3)

➤ **COURSEBOOK** pages 59 and 65

Vocabulary development

1 Choose the correct option in *italics* to complete the sentences.

1 A *brand / symbol* is the name of a product, its appearance and its characteristics.
2 Another name for 'products' is *imports / goods*.
3 Things which are not essential, but which are desirable, are called *basic / luxury* items.
4 Items such as food and warm clothing are regarded as *necessities / goods*.
5 Things which are produced in the area near our home are known as *local / luxury* products.
6 *Exported / Imported* products are things which one country buys from another country.
7 Something which is bought to demonstrate the wealth of the buyer is a status *product / symbol*.

2a Complete the spidergram with the words in Exercise 1. Use a dictionary if necessary.

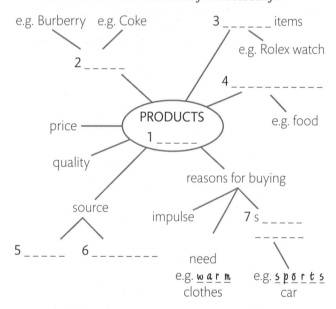

b Answer the questions about yourself.

1 Are you an impulse buyer, or do you spend a lot of time choosing what to buy?
2 When you buy clothes, is the price more important, or the quality?
3 What are your favourite brands, if any?
4 What is the most luxurious thing you have ever bought?
5 Are you interested in buying things as a status symbol?
6 How important to you is the quality of the things you buy?

Expand your ideas using conjunctions and phrases

3 Match the sentence beginnings (1–6) with the endings (A–F).

1 Some people like to buy food at the market, but others
2 Since they spend more time on a computer, younger people are more likely to
3 Some people don't buy second-hand clothes, because they only
4 Busy workers buy meals at market stalls, as they don't
5 If people don't want things anymore, they usually
6 Buying things online is very easy, so it encourages people to

A like new things.
B throw them away.
C get it from a supermarket.
D spend more money.
E have time for shopping and cooking.
F buy things online.

Test practice

4a Read the questions about imports and exports and think about how you would answer them.

1 Some people prefer buying imported goods to locally produced goods. Why do you think this is?
2 What are the benefits for the environment if people buy goods which are produced locally?
3 A few countries rely on imports for some of their basic needs. Why might this be the case?
4 What sort of facilities do countries need to develop if they want to export goods to other countries?

b 🔊 4.2 Close your book and listen to the questions. Practise answering them.

Assess and improve

5 Answer the questions.

1 Were you able to produce the vocabulary that you needed to answer the questions fully?
2 If not, what will you do to expand your vocabulary on this topic?

Writing (Task 2)

> **COURSEBOOK** pages 68–69, **EXPERT WRITING** page 194

Understand the task

1a Read the writing task and answer the questions.

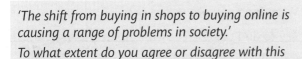

1 What is the general topic of the essay?
2 Do you need to write about both sides of the argument?
3 What does the 'shift' refer to?

> *'The shift from buying in shops to buying online is causing a range of problems in society.'*
>
> *To what extent do you agree or disagree with this statement?*

b What is your opinion on this issue? Decide on your position on a scale of 1 (do not agree at all) to 5 (completely agree).

Plan the task

2a Plan your essay by adding more ideas and supporting points/illustrations to the table. Some examples have been done for you.

Ideas	Support/Illustration
1 Rise in internet shopping means many shops have been forced to close	• Many city centres no longer thriving, empty • Deprives vulnerable people of social encounters in face-to-face shopping
2 Online shopping tends to be run by bigger companies – smaller ones struggle to compete	• Small companies can't match efficiency in advertising or delivery • Craftsmanship declines

b Decide which method of organising your essay (1–4) you are going to use.

1 Agree with the statement and answer only from that point of view.
2 Disagree with the statement and answer only from that point of view
3 Start with the arguments made by people who hold a different view from yours. Then give arguments in support of your opinion.
4 Discuss both for and against arguments and then finish by making clear your own position.

Language and content

3a Complete the sentences with the words/phrases below. Use a dictionary/thesaurus to help you if necessary.

thriving far-reaching high street squeeze out outsource no-go areas

1 In many small towns, the _____ is becoming less important than out-of-town shopping centres.
2 The disappearance of large shops means many city centres are now _____ with high crime levels.
3 Some established businesses are _____ but others are being forced to cut prices or close down.
4 Large online retailers are beginning to _____ many smaller shops and businesses.
5 Retailers are choosing to _____ the making of their clothes to overseas suppliers.
6 The effects of this change in shopping habits are likely to be _____ .

b Read the extract from a sample answer to the task in Exercise 1a. The writer has made five errors. Underline and correct them.

> It is true that online shopping seems to benefit individual shopper by offering wider choice and lower prices. However, it is important to look more deeper at the range of consequences for society as a whole. Firstly, because of the raise of internet shopping, many high-street stores have been force to close down. A large proportion of town centres have numerous empty spaces where shops once were, and the absent of a thriving commercial centre makes these places dangerous, no-go areas.

c What type of mistake has been made in each case? Match the words you underlined with the types of error (A–E).

A adverb   D verb form
B noun   E wrong word
C plural

Write your opinion essay

4 Write your answer to the task in Exercise 1a, using ideas from Exercises 1 and 2 and any relevant language from Exercise 3. Write at least 250 words.

Assess and improve

5 When you have finished, evaluate your essay by answering the following questions.

1 Is the core issue – the shift from shops to online – explained clearly?
2 Have you made the organisation of the essay clear (using one type 1–4), with effective paragraphing?
3 Have you given relevant support and illustration for your points?
4 Have you used topic-specific vocabulary to give authority to your assertions?
5 Can you see any grammar, spelling or punctuation mistakes?

5a Making life easier

Reading (Matching features; Note completion; *True/False/Not given*)

➤ **COURSEBOOK** pages 72–73 and 82–83

Before you read

1 You are going to read about a house which is environmentally friendly. Tick any words below which you might expect to find in the passage.

energy light heat luxury rent efficient spacious

Recognise reference words

2a Look at the underlined words in the first five paragraphs of the reading passage. What does each one refer to?

b In the sixth paragraph, which word refers back to the idea that 'the only way to store excess electricity was in batteries'?

3a Look at the test task in Exercise 4. Scan the reading passage to find a reference to the first feature of the house (question 1), and underline it. What is said in the passage about the function of this feature?

b Now look at the list of functions (A–F). Which one is the most similar in meaning to the function you identified in Exercise 3a?

Test practice

4 Follow the same procedure as in Exercises 3a and 3b and complete the test task.

Questions 1–4

Look at the following features of the house and the list of functions below.

Match each feature (1–4) with the correct function (A–F).

1 wall paints
2 glass panes
3 movement and daylight sensors
4 smart plugs

List of functions
A control the electric lighting
B control the water supply
C convert heat to electricity
D contain a section of the power network
E check energy consumption at individual power points
F prevent heat from escaping

Test practice

5a Look at the title and the first line of the notes below. Scan the reading passage to find the part which gives information about this.

b Look at the first gap (question 5) in the notes. What kind of word would fit?

c Try to find the correct word in the passage

6 Complete the test task.

Questions 5–8

Complete the notes below.

*Choose **ONE WORD ONLY** from the passage for each answer.*

The water supply
1998: The Smart Home was built.
Rainwater was collected from beneath the ground.
Problems: The 5 _____ stopped working.
       The system was blocked by 6 _____ .
Present day: Rainwater is collected under the house's 7 _____ .
It supplies the toilets, etc. using 8 _____ .

➤ **HELP**

5 *Stopped working* means *failed*.

Test practice

7a Look at the statement in question 9 of the test task on page 47. Underline the key words.

b Scan the reading passage to find words which are the same or similar in meaning.

c Read the part of the passage which contains the information, and decide whether the statement in question 9 is True or False, or whether there isn't enough information to decide.

An eco-house for the future
A journalist reports on his visit to a model home

Imagine a house that switches the lights off for you when the sun comes out; a house that will tell you, while you are at work, that your son has left his Xbox on, a house built with such smart materials that even the paints used on its walls have insulating properties.

This house actually exists – at least as an experimental model – on parkland just north of London in the UK. Currently being tested by scientists at the Building Research Establishment (BRE), it holds out a fascinating glimpse of the kind of energy-saving gadgets and materials which we can expect to see inside our homes in just a few years' time.

I am visiting the prototype house on a chilly November day. From the outside, the large, angled conservatory roof looks like conventional glass. From inside, however, each pane of glass now reveals that it has tiny wires embedded inside it, because it is part of a 5-kilowatt solar electricity circuit. These panes of glass, although transparent, are shaded orange, which is the best colour for tracking ultraviolet light. The colour is slightly confusing, as if a sodium street light were shining directly overhead.

According to John O'Brien, a scientists at the BRE, 'The development of eco materials is moving at such a rapid rate that we have moved from the conventional opaque, blue-coloured solar collectors that you normally see on roofs, to these transparent orange-coloured panes of glass. Very soon, manufacturers will be able to make colourless glass collectors, and then every office, and ultimately every home in the country would, in theory, be able to generate its own electricity unobtrusively.'

Not only is the conservatory roof a giant solar electricity generator, but, acting as a buffer between the main living quarters of the house and the outside, it operates as a 'solar space'. In winter, its design captures warmth from the low-hanging sun and warms the air inside, protecting the rest of the house from the cold. However, as with all solar panel systems it is affected by seasonal variations, generating more than it needs in the summer, and less than it needs in the winter, an obvious weakness in the technology.

'People used to think that the only way to store excess electricity was in batteries,' says O'Brien. 'This is both inefficient and cumbersome: you would need a battery the size of a submarine buried under the house to provide electricity to last the winter.' However, the BRE is currently working with partners on storing solar electricity as heat, which is converted back to electricity when needed. 'This development is still a fair way off, but one day it will be achievable. It will avoid the main disadvantage of solar electricity, which is that, in northern latitudes like our own, it doesn't provide electricity when it is most needed.'

Inside the house, motion and light sensors ensure the most efficient use of the low-energy lighting system. In addition, 'smart plugs', which are enabled by a smart-phone app, allow socket-by-socket monitoring of electricity use. O'Brien tells me that not only would I be able to find out, remotely, whether my son has left his computer on, but I could also remotely shut it down.

The BRE Smart Home is a renovated house which was originally built in 1998. While the existing walls still perform well, before the refurbishment this year the so-called 'House of the Future' only scored an E on current Energy Performance ratings. Now it has

an A/B rating (the highest), so the Smart Home demonstrates just how much energy-efficiency technologies have improved in a short space of time.

'When it was first built, this house was at the cutting edge of technology, but a lot of the original materials and designs have become outdated,' says O'Brien. He points to the original rainwater-harvesting system, which has become obsolete. 'The water was collected underground, but the pumps failed and leaves clogged up the system,' he says. The refurbished house uses a rainwater tank which is located under the edge of the roof instead. It is a wide, shallow collector that distributes the weight of the water evenly inside the roof. This means it will feed the toilets and other appliances by gravity rather than needing a pump, which can go wrong. Futuristic materials are also being tested in the house. They include the hi-tech wall paints, as well as insulating panels which are embedded in paraffin-wax. These store heat in the day and release it at night.

I have caught a glimpse of the future, and it's full of energy-saving opportunities.

---

8 Complete the test task.

Questions 9–14

Do the following statements agree with the information in the reading passage?

Write

TRUE *if the statement agrees with the information*

FALSE *if the statement contradicts the information*

NOT GIVEN *if there is no information on this*

9 In future, all homes and offices will have glass panes which are orange.

10 The solar panels on the experimental house produce as much heat in the winter as in the summer.

11 The BRE and others are trying to find an alternative to batteries for storing electricity.

12 At present, no one lives in the BRE Smart Home.

13 The Smart Home is more energy-efficient now than when it was first built.

14 There are plans for the Smart Home to collect wind energy soon.

Vocabulary

> **COURSEBOOK** page 74

The language of invention and innovation

1a Choose the correct option in *italics to* complete the sentences.

1 New building materials undergo lengthy *automation / experimentation* in laboratory conditions before they are used in construction.

2 As more routine housework is done by *automation / innovation*, people have more leisure time.

3 In the UK, any proposal to build new houses in the countryside is *accessible / controversial*.

4 To encourage *intelligence / innovation*, some companies offer prizes for ideas on how to reduce energy use in the home.

5 Artificial *experimentation / intelligence* has produced phones that can assess the contents of a refrigerator and create a shopping list.

6 Eco-houses must be inexpensive to construct, to make them *accessible / controversial* to people on low incomes.

b Complete the sentences, according to your own experience and opinions.

1 In my country, the suggestion that _____ is very controversial.

2 Although automation has reduced the number of jobs available, it has _____ .

3 In the early part of the 20th century, artificial intelligence was regarded as _____ .

4 The best way to encourage innovation is to _____ .

5 Despite lengthy experimentation, some new products never _____ .

6 _____ should be accessible to everyone, regardless of their social background.

Express quantity

2a Look at the diagrams. Which word(s) below best describe(s) the number of shaded figures in each one? One has been done for you as an example.

a third   both   few   three quarters   ~~most/the majority~~

1 ♦♦♦♦♦♦♦♦♦♦ _most/the majority_
2 ♦♦ _____
3 ♦♦♦♦♦♦♦ _____
4 ♦♦ _____
5 ♦♦♦ _____

b Complete the sentences with the correct form of the words/phrases in Exercise 2a.

1 According to surveys, _____ of the general public in the UK support solar technology; the remaining 25 percent regard it as too expensive to install.

2 _____ wind and solar energy are suitable for generating domestic electricity.

3 At present, _____ people can afford the luxury of domestic robots, but the price of these will eventually decrease.

4 In the UK, two thirds of household paper is recycled; the remaining _____ goes to landfill.

5 The overwhelming _____ of households in Wales recycle their waste.

6 In Denmark, _____ domestic waste is burnt rather than buried.

EXPERT LANGUAGE

A *household* is the people who live together in one house.

---

c Look at the list of things below. Using words like those in Exercise 2a, say how many of your friends and/or family own each one.

smartphone   laptop computer   car   Xbox   pet   electronic activity tracker

Both my parents own a smartphone.

Agreement and disagreement

3a Read the opinions (1–6) and circle the response which is stronger, A or B.

1 Some people are too lazy or too selfish to recycle their unwanted things.
   A I'm slightly in agreement with you.
   B I wholeheartedly agree with you.

2 The government should raise taxes on domestic oil and gas to reduce use.
   A I thoroughly disagree.
   B I partly disagree.

3 We should destroy old buildings and replace them all with eco-buildings.
   A I utterly agree.
   B I'm somewhat in agreement with you.

4 People are getting less fit because more and more domestic work is being done by machines.
   A I'm marginally in agreement.
   B I totally agree.

5 It's very expensive to adapt older houses so that they are more energy efficient.
   A I'm slightly in agreement with you.
   B I'm entirely in agreement with you.

6 Modern houses look out of place in areas with a lot of traditional buildings.
   A I'm firmly of that opinion.
   B I'm partly of that opinion.

b Imagine that someone expresses the opinions (1–6) above. How would you respond? Try to use some of the words from Exercise 3a. Give reasons for your opinions.

Language development

> COURSEBOOK page 77, EXPERT GRAMMAR page 178

Reported speech patterns

1 Choose the correct reporting verb for each sentence. Then complete the sentences with the correct form of the verb you chose.

1 The builders _____ (tell/argue) that the air-conditioning system would be too expensive.
2 The architect _____ (explain/promise) how the new houses were made to withstand earthquakes.
3 The designer _____ (argue/mention) several ways in which labour-saving devices could be used in new houses in the future.
4 The government _____ (tell/explain) that residents would be consulted about future development plans.
5 The planners _____ (argue/promise) to take account of residents' concerns before proceeding with building work.
6 The developers _____ (tell/mention) the builders to improve the insulation of the new houses.
7 The builders _____ (suggest/say) increasing the amount of storage space in the new houses.
8 The house buyers _____ (tell/say) that they were very pleased with their new home.

EXPERT LANGUAGE

Tell is followed by an indirect object. All the other verbs in Exercise 1 can be followed directly by *that* and a clause.

2 Rewrite the sentences in reported speech. Use the verb in brackets as the main verb.

1 The scientists said, 'Buildings technology is developing very quickly.' (explain)
2 He said to the reporter, 'Why don't you come and see our eco-house?' (suggest)
3 When they entered the house, he said to the reporter, 'Look closely at the conservatory roof.' (tell)
4 The reporter said 'The light coming through the orange glass is like street lighting.' (argue)
5 The scientists said to the reporter 'Before long, we'll all be able to produce electricity in our houses using colourless glass panes.' (promise)
6 The reporter said, 'The temperature inside the house is very comfortable.' (mention)
7 The scientist pointed out, 'Technology is developing so fast that houses soon become outdated.' (say)
8 The official said, 'The government's target is for all new houses to generate their own energy by 2025.' (promise)

Other reporting structures

3a Write sentences using the prompts.

1 I asked / electrician / replace / old wires / in house
   I asked the electrician to replace the old wires in the house.
2 I asked / shopkeeper / have / tinned fish / or not
   _____
3 I asked / one / friends / if / pick me up / from my house
   _____
4 I asked / cousin / meet / at the cinema / or / at the car park
   _____
5 I asked / teacher / if / borrow / the book
   _____
6 I asked / taxi driver / go / station
   _____
7 I asked / police officer / where / central market
   _____
8 I asked ask / friend / wanted / eat / noodles / or / rice
   _____

EXPERT LANGUAGE

We use *whether ... or* if there are two possible answers to a question.

b Decide whether each of the sentences you wrote in Exercise 3a is an instruction, a question or a request.

c Rewrite the following sentences as if you were reporting what you said.

1 'Take me to the hotel please.' (taxi driver)
   I asked the taxi driver to please take me to the hotel.
2 'Would you like tea or coffee?' (Lisa)
   _____
3 'Please can I borrow a pen?' (the clerk)
   _____
4 'Where is the bus station?' (police officer)
   _____
5 'Do you use gas or electricity for cooking?' (the customer)
   _____
6 'What time will you be ready?' (my girlfriend)
   _____

Writing (Task 1)

> COURSEBOOK page 78, EXPERT WRITING page 195

Understand the task

1   Look at the task below and answer the questions.

   1   In general terms, what does the chart show?
   2   How many household items are included?
   5   What do the figures on the *y* (vertical) axis indicate?

You should spend about 20 minutes on this task.

The chart shows the average percentage of household income spent on different items, in one country in 2012.

Write at least 150 words.

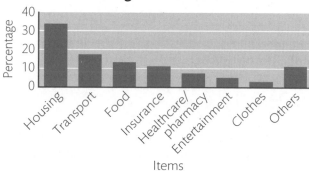

**Spending on different items
– average household 2012**

Interpret statistical data

2a   Look at the sentences below, which give specific details relating to the chart. Which are true (T) and which are false (F)? Correct the false sentences, retaining the underlined sections.

   1   Approximately one third of people spent money on housing costs in 2012.
   2   Eleven percent of total expenditure was spent on insurance.
   3   The smallest percentage of total spending was given over to healthcare costs.
   4   Only 5 percent of households spent money on some form of entertainment.
   5   About 60 percent of total expenditure was on just three areas.
   6   Other items (not specified) accounted for 11 percent of household expenditure.

b   Complete the sentences using information from the bar chart.

   1   Approximately _____ of household spending was on food.
   2   _____ of outgoings was spent on healthcare.
   3   Transport and Insurance accounted for _____ and _____ of spending respectively.
   4   _____ of average outgoings was spent on clothes.
   5   After housing, the next two most important areas of expenditure were _____ .

Support trends with details

3a   Look at the exam task in Exercise 4 and answer the questions.

   1   What does the chart show?
   2   What do the different colours represent?
   3   How many areas of expenditure are covered?

b   Look at the summary sentence below. Which option best completes the sentence?

The chart shows that having a more advanced educational level made _____ difference in the way people spent their income

   1   no major difference
   2   a striking difference
   3   a small but significant difference

c   Look at the percentages for the different areas of expenditure. Identify which areas of expenditure are larger (+) or smaller (-) with higher levels of education.

   1   Food eaten in the home   5   Pension
   2   Food eaten in restaurants, etc.   6   Travel abroad
   3   Rent/mortgage   7   Other
   4   Transport

d   Look at the extent of the effect of higher education levels on expenditure. Which areas show the most marked difference?

Test practice

4   Write your answer to the question below, using ideas from Exercises 1–3.

The chart below shows the proportion of expenditure on different items in an average household in one European country in 2015, according to educational level.

Summarise the information by selecting and reporting the main features, and make comparisons where relevant.

You should write at least 150 words.

Percentage of income spent on different items

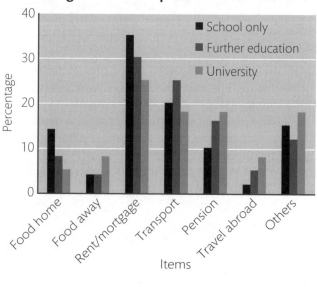

Listening (Section 3)

> COURSEBOOK pages 76 and 79

Before you listen

1   Read the instruction from the question paper. What do you have to listen for?

What action do Leo and Kerry agree they will need to take for each stage of their presentation?

Listen for agreement and disagreement

2a Look at the two extracts from the first part of the discussion. Underline the key phrases that show:

   A what action is being suggested.
   B how agreement is signalled.
   C how disagreement is signalled.

Extract 1

Kerry: I've got the notes we made about what the various stages of the talk will be, but we ought to agree on what we include in each part.

Leo: Sure. Well, we'll obviously need something really striking for the introduction.

Kerry: I always think it's helpful to start with something simple like the meaning of the word 'television' ...

Leo: Meaning 'far sight' ... of course, we could start with that on the first slide.

Kerry: Simple but clear – great.

Extract 2

Kerry: Could we say something about how he set up a telephone exchange in his bedroom ... act out how it worked?

Leo: That'd be great ... but only if we had another 30 minutes!

Kerry: OK ... fair enough. What about focusing on him studying at Glasgow University, which had a world-renowned engineering faculty? I think it'd be good if we could give the audience some idea of what the laboratories were like.

Leo: Hmm ... I'm not sure how easy it would be to get video footage.

Kerry: I saw some stills photos on the university website – they're just rooms, not his colleagues, but I still think they'd work well.

Leo: Then let's go for that.

b   Look at the test task in Exercise 3. How many stages are there in the presentation? How many actions are listed? Underline the key words in the different actions.

Test practice

3   🔊 5.1 Complete the test task.

Questions 1–7

What action do Leo and Kerry agree they will need to take for each stage of their presentation?

Choose SEVEN answers from the box and write the correct letter A–I, next to questions 1–7.

Agreed actions
A show pictures of Baird's colleague
B compare TV with other gadgets
C read out a quotation
D show a short video
E act out a scene
F show a picture of a lab
G explain using a diagram
H discuss the meaning of a word
I ask the audience to give their opinion

Stages of the presentation
1 Introduction   _____
2 Baird's early life   _____
3 1st experiment, 1924   _____
4 Famous demonstration, 1926 _____
5 Developments after 1927   _____
6 Baird's other work   _____
7 Preserving Baird's legacy   _____

TEST STRATEGY

Section 3 Listening matching tasks frequently involve listening for agreement between two or three speakers. This agreement is signalled in a variety of ways – it can be through individual words indicating acceptance, for example *OK* or *fine*, or it can be through longer utterances, for example *That's a better idea* or *Let's go with that*. Make a note of expressions used to signal agreement and add them to a list as you continue to practise doing Section 3 Listening tasks.

Task analysis

4   Analyse your answers using these questions.

   1 How easy did you find it to identify the speakers?
   2 Did you generally hear the phrases for agreement and disagreement? How many can you recall?
   3 What paraphrases of the 'actions' did you hear in the recording?

Language development

> COURSEBOOK page 80, EXPERT GRAMMAR page 179

Noun phrases 1

1   When are we *most* likely to use noun phrases? Choose one.

   1   in direct speech
   2   in informal writing (e.g. text messages)
   3   in formal writing (e.g. essays)
   4   in indirect speech

2   Underline the noun phrases in the following text. One has been done for you as an example.

> Nearly half of <u>Britons who have not managed to buy a house by their mid-thirties</u> doubt they will ever be able to do so, a report has found.
>
> The research from Yorkshire Building Society found 49 percent of people aged 35 to 40 who are not homeowners but would like to be, think it is now 'unlikely' or 'very unlikely' they will ever own a property.
>
> The survey, carried out by NatCen Social Research, found that more than two thirds (69 percent) of young adults aged 18 to 40 felt owning their own home was a source of social and financial security.
>
> Nearly a third (31 percent) of non-homeowners aged 35 to 40 have completely given up even trying to buy a home due to affordability issues, the research found.
>
> The situation is unlikely to change unless there is a dramatic downward shift in house prices.

3   Complete the sentences with the noun phrases below.

> the recommended minimum size   switches on the wall
> buildings designed in the 1960s   central heating systems
> children under the age of six months   smart homes
> people who have a disability   almost two thirds of people

   1   Electric lighting is usually controlled by _____ .
   2   _____ often need special adaptations inside their homes.
   3   _____ can be operated remotely in some new houses.
   4   _____ are designed to reduce their impact on the environment.
   5   In the Netherlands, _____ live in semi-detached houses.
   6   Most new homes in England are only 92 percent of _____ .
   7   _____ usually sleep in their parents' room.
   8   _____ were often energy-inefficient.

EXPERT LANGUAGE

Sometimes a noun phrase consists of two nouns, the first of which has the function of an adjective, for example *window blinds*.

4   Complete the second sentence so that it has a similar meaning to the first. Use noun phrases.

   1   More recycled materials are used nowadays.
      The use _____ .
   2   The price of raw materials is going down, so they will soon be more affordable.
      The falling _____ .
   3   The design of the house is relatively simple, so it is cost-effective.
      The relative _____ .
   4   A major part of the government's policy with all new homes is to improve their efficiency.
      An improvement _____ .
   5   Over 20 years ago, people in a Swedish town made a hotel out of ice. It was the first ice hotel in the world.
      The world's _____ .
   6   They first exhibited manufactured goods from all over the world in 1851. It was known as the Great Exhibition.
      The Great Exhibition of 1851 was _____ .

5a   Decide whether you agree or disagree with the following statements.

   1   The place where I'd most like to live in future is the one where I live now.
   2   Having an eco-house equipped with all the latest technology doesn't really interest me.
   3   Reducing household bills is the most important thing for me.
   4   Cutting down on waste and energy consumption is a priority.
   5   I'd like to build my own energy-efficient house from recycled building materials.

b   Rewrite any of the statements (1–5) that you disagree with.

The place where I'd most like to live in future is Maine in the USA.

TEST STRATEGY

If you can use noun phrases in the IELTS test tasks, you will gain marks for stylistic appropriacy and for the range of grammatical structures you are able to use.

Vocabulary

> COURSEBOOK page 80

Reporting verbs

1a Complete the table with reporting verbs.

The original speaker/writer	Reporting verbs
made a positive statement	c _ _ _ m, h _ _ _ _ _ _ _ _ t, i _ _ _ _ _ _ _ _ e, p _ _ _ _ o _ t, p _ _ _ e
made a negative statement	d _ _ y
made a hesitant statement	i _ _ _ _ _ e, s _ _ _ _ _ t
made a statement about danger	w _ _ n

b Complete the table with the reporting verbs in Exercise 1a.

The person reporting a statement	Reporting verbs
is unsure whether the statement is correct or not	
accepts the truth of the statement	

EXPERT LANGUAGE

There are many verbs which can be used to report what other people said or wrote. The exact verb that you choose gives information both about the original speaker/writer and about your attitude to what was said/written.

2 Choose the correct option in *italics* to complete the sentences.

1 The Committee on Climate Change *warned / suggested* that each year in the UK 1,500 new homes were being built in areas of high flood risk.

2 The environment minister *denied / pointed out* that last year there had been an increase in investment in flood defence schemes.

3 Villagers often *claim / deny* that new eco-towns are spoiling rural areas and threatening wildlife, but those in charge of planning *warn / deny* that this is the case.

4 A recent survey *suggested / proved* that homelessness is a growing problem in UK cities, although it is quite difficult to obtain exact figures due to the changing nature of the problem.

5 A spokesperson for homeless people has *prove / warned* that the situation could get much worse unless more houses are built as a matter of urgency.

6 A nationwide survey has *claimed / highlighted* concerns about the rising costs of housing in the UK.

7 Community leaders consistently *point out / prove* the need for planners to consult communities before a housing development is authorised.

8 New guidelines *deny / indicate* that house builders should increase levels of insulation in future.

EXPERT LANGUAGE

Highlight and *illustrate* are followed directly by a noun phrase, not by *that*.

3 Match the sentence beginnings (1–6) with the endings (A–F).

1 Scientists have warned
2 A report by building surveyors has highlighted
3 A survey of people in their twenties indicates
4 Insurance companies have denied
5 Many house owners claim
6 Surveys of families with young children illustrate

A being slow to deal with claims for flood damage.
B the need for safe play areas in residential areas.
C that sea levels are continuing to rise.
D that many are still living with their parents.
E that their homes are poorly constructed.
F the need to avoid coastal areas when building new homes.

4 Rewrite the following statements as reported speech. Use the person/group and verb in brackets.

1 'The domestic water supply is completely safe.' (engineers/claim)
_____

2 'We didn't say that the house is suitable for a family.' (estate agents/deny)
_____

3 'There are insufficient houses to meet current demand.' (a government spokesperson/point out)
_____

4 'Families with young children should have priority over single adults.' (a housing officer/suggest)
_____

5 'The housing shortage is going to get worse over the next five years.' (an urban planner/warn)
_____

6 'Bus services in this area are inadequate.' (a local resident/claim)
_____

5 Write about a housing problem in your city or town, and how the public and officials have reacted to it. Use reported speech.

TEST STRATEGY

Try to vary the reporting verbs that you use, don't always choose *say*. In the Writing test you will get credit for using a range of words.

Speaking (Part 2)

> **COURSEBOOK** pages 75 and 81

Vocabulary development

1 Match the words/phrases (1–6) with the meanings (A–F).

1	labour-saving	A	modern
2	outdated	B	adaptable
3	revolutionary	C	reduces time and effort
4	state-of-the-art	D	old-fashioned
5	user friendly	E	easy to operate
6	versatile	F	results in huge changes

2a Use the prompts to write questions.

1 Which / more / labour-saving / brush / vacuum cleaner?
2 Which / more / outdated / candle / torch?
3 Which / more / revolutionary / when / first produced / paper / silk?
4 Which / more / state-of-the-art / robotic surgery / gene therapy?
5 Which / more / user-friendly / driverless car / conventional car?
6 Which / more / versatile / piece of cloth / pair of scissors?

b Answer the questions in Exercise 2a.

3a Read the Part 2 task card below. How many points do you need to talk about?

> *Describe a piece of equipment in your home that you only use occasionally.*
>
> *You should say:*
> *what the equipment is*
> *how long you have had it for*
> *what you use it for*
> *and explain why you only use it occasionally.*

b 🔊 5.2 Listen to a speaker talking about the topic in Exercise 3a and answer the questions.

1 Does the speaker mention all of the points on the card?
2 If not, which point(s) does she omit?

c Listen again and answer the questions.

1 Does the speaker provide many details in her answer?
2 Can you think of any other detail that this speaker could have provided?

Focus on grammatical range and accuracy

4a Look at what another speaker said about the same topic. Did the speaker cover all the points on the task card?

> 'A piece of equipment that I only use occasionally is an electric blender – it's a motor with two small blades that rotate very quickly. There's also a glass container that you put food in, and the blender chops it up. I've had it for at least 12 years, maybe longer, and most of the time it sits in a cupboard. There are two things that I use it for. One is making smoothies – I don't know if you know what a smoothie is, but it's a mixture of fruit or vegetables and cream or yogurt. Smoothies were supposed to be healthy, but then the advice about them changed and dieticians said there was too much sugar in some of them – natural sugar from the fruit that is. So that's one reason I stopped making them so often.
>
> Another thing that I use the blender for is chopping nuts for the birds that visit my garden. I make a paste with nuts and fat that they really like.
>
> The reason why I only use it occasionally is probably because you have to get it out and assemble it, and it's quite hard to clean it afterwards without getting the motor wet. I'm a bit lazy I suppose!'

b Which of the following structures did the speaker use?

1 present simple tense	5 relative clause
2 present perfect tense	6 reported speech
3 past simple tense	7 complex noun phrase
4 future tense	8 comparative

c Underline an example of the structures you ticked in the list and write 1, 2, etc. next to each one.

Test practice

5 Read the task card below and make notes. Speak for about 2 minutes and record yourself if possible.

> *Describe a gadget in your home that you use every day and find very useful.*
>
> *You should say:*
> *what the gadget is*
> *how long you have had it for*
> *what you use it for*
> *and explain why you find this gadget very useful.*

Assess and improve

6 Answer the questions.

1 Were your notes useful? How might you improve the notes that you make?
2 Were there any important words that you didn't know? Will you look them up?
3 Did you speak for around two minutes?
4 Did you use a range of grammatical structures?

Writing (Task 1)

> **COURSEBOOK** pages 64–65, **EXPERT WRITING** page 195

Understand the task

1   Look at the Part 1 writing task below and the charts. Answer the questions.

1   What period of time do the charts cover?
2   Which items declined in importance as part of the household budget? By how many percent?
3   Which items increased in importance? By how many percent?
4   Which stayed the same?
5   What was the biggest change?

The charts below show the percentage of spending on different areas in the average household in one country in 1910 and 1960.

Summarise the information by selecting and reporting the main features, and make comparisons where relevant.

You should write at least 150 words.

Average household expenditure

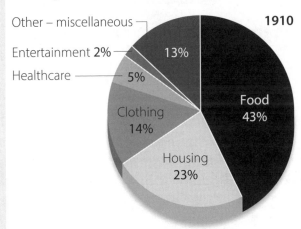

1910

Other – miscellaneous 13%
Entertainment 2%
Healthcare 5%
Clothing 14%
Housing 23%
Food 43%

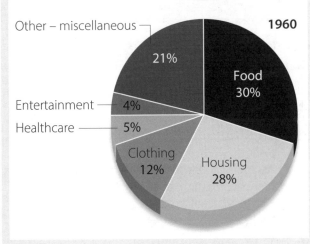

1960

Other – miscellaneous 21%
Entertainment 4%
Healthcare 5%
Clothing 12%
Housing 28%
Food 30%

Plan the task

2   Look at the sample answer below. Match the sections (A–E) with the questions (1–5) in Exercise 1. You can use the questions more than once.

> **A** The two charts show that there was a significant difference in the proportion spent on different items over the 50 years between the beginning and the middle of the 20th century in an average household in one country. It should be noted that although the relative importance of the different items remained constant, some areas declined whilst others increased in percentage. **B** The most notable change was in the proportion of the budget spent on food. This fell from 43 percent in 1910 to 30 percent in 1960. **C** By contrast, there was a slight increase, of 5 percent, in spending on housing – from 23 percent to 28 percent. **D** The next item in order of importance – clothing – held fairly steady, dropping just 2 percent to 12 percent in 1960. **E** The proportion spent on healthcare remained exactly the same: 5 percent.

Language and content

3a   Identify the words/phrases used in the sample to express the following:

1   rising   4   large
2   falling   5   small
3   staying the same 6   percentage

b   Underline any other expressions in the sample answer which you think will be useful for writing similar reports.

Test practice

4   Using ideas from Exercises 1 and 2, write a report comparing the the chart for 1960 with the chart for 2010, below.

Average household expenditure 2010

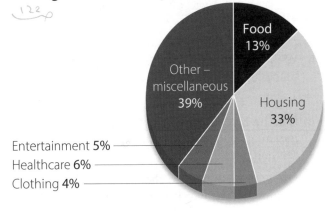

Food 13%
Other – miscellaneous 39%
Housing 33%
Entertainment 5%
Healthcare 6%
Clothing 4%

Assess and improve

5   Check your writing. Does it contain

1   an introductory sentence or sentences summarising the key points in the chart?
2   a clear description of key differences and similarities?
3   a variety of different vocabulary to express change, avoiding repetition of lexis?
4   relative clauses to add information?

6a Preventing crime

Reading (Flow chart completion; Sentence completion)

> **COURSEBOOK** pages 88–89

Before you read

1a Look at the title of the reading passage. Which of the following do you think will be the main topic of the passage?

  1 crime detection   3 psychology
  2 the legal system

b Read the passage quickly. Do not stop to use a dictionary. Was your answer to Exercise 1 correct?

Work out the meaning of unknown words

2a Try to guess the meaning of the underlined word in the first paragraph of the reading passage. Which of the following is it most likely to mean?

  1 the police who came to investigate the robbery or accident
  2 the people who were responsible for the robbery or accident
  3 the people who were robbed or hurt in the accident

> **TEST STRATEGY**
>
> When you come across a word that you don't know, use the context as well as the form of the word to try to guess the meaning.

b What are the approximate meanings of the following prefixes?

  1 con-   2 re-   3 mis-

c Use the context and the prefixes to guess the meanings of the other underlined words in the reading passage.

d Use your dictionary to check if you guessed the meaning of the words in Exercise 2c correctly.

Test practice

3a Look at the test tasks in Exercise 3c and answer the questions.

  1 How many words/numbers are permitted in each gap?
  2 What kind of words are missing (e.g. verb, noun, etc.)?

b Underline the words around each gap to help you find the information you need in the passage.

c Complete the test tasks.

> *Questions 1–5*
>
> *Complete the flow chart below.*
>
> *Choose **ONE WORD AND/OR A NUMBER** from the passage for each answer.*
>
> > **Yuille and Cutshall's study**
> > Police interviewed witnesses about an actual 1 _____ incident
> >
> > ⬇
> >
> > Five months later, police interviewed 2 _____ witnesses again. The researchers had added two confusing 3 _____ .
> >
> > ⬇
> >
> > A check showed that witness accounts were 4 _____ .
> >
> > ⬇
> >
> > The researchers concluded that 5 _____ had not affected witness reliability.

> **Help**
>
> 5 Look back to the first sentence of the third paragraph.

> **TEST STRATEGY**
>
> The order of the questions in flow charts may not be exactly the same as the order of information in the reading passage.

> *Questions 6–11*
>
> *Complete the sentences below.*
>
> *Choose **ONE WORD ONLY** from the passage for each answer.*
>
> 6 In criminal trials, _____ often find eyewitness testimony convincing.
> 7 According to Bartlett, people often mistakenly compare memory to a _____ .
> 8 People store information according to categories which are known as _____ .
> 9 In a well-known study, Bartlett used a procedure similar to that of a particular _____ .
> 10 Each time the folk tale was repeated, it was shorter, more rational and more _____ .
> 11 The storytellers in Bartlett's study left out details of the _____ .

The reliability of witness statements following a crime

Eyewitness testimony (EWT) is a legal term. It refers to an account given by people of an event they have witnessed. For example, they may be required to give a description at a trial of a robbery or a road accident they have seen. This includes identification of perpetrators, details of the crime scene, etc. Juries tend to pay close attention to eyewitness testimony, and generally find it a reliable source of information. However, research into this area has found that eyewitness testimony can be affected by many psychological factors, such as stress or memory issues.

Eyewitness testimony is an important area of research in cognitive psychology and human memory. A number of studies have shown that, for tasks of moderate complexity (such as EWT), performance increases with stress up to a certain point, and then starts to decline. For example, one study found that people who watched a film of a violent attack remembered fewer details about the event than a control group who watched a less stressful version. And as witnessing a real crime is probably more stressful than taking part in an experiment, memory accuracy may well be even more affected in real life.

However, a study by Yuille and Cutshall (1986) contradicts the importance of stress in influencing eyewitness memory. They showed that witnesses of a real-life incident (a shooting outside a gun shop in Canada) had remarkably accurate memories of the event. The police interviewed witnesses, and 13 of them were re-interviewed five months later. In spite of the fact that two misleading questions had been inserted by the research team, when these witness accounts were compared to the earlier ones, recall was found to be accurate, even after such a long time. On the other hand, one weakness of this study was that the witnesses who experienced the highest levels of stress had been closer to the event, and this may have helped with the accuracy of their memory recall.

Another important factor regarding the reliability of EWT is the nature of memory. Bartlett's theory of reconstructive memory is crucial, as he suggested that recall is subject to personal interpretation, and is dependent on our norms and values, and the way we make sense of our world.

Many people believe that memory works something like a video: storing information is like recording, and remembering is like playing back what was recorded, with information being retrieved in much the same form as it was captured. However, memory does not work in this way. It is a feature of human memory that we do not store information exactly as it is presented to us. Rather, people extract from information the gist, or underlying meaning.

People store information in the way that makes the most sense to them, and we make sense of information by organizing it into schemas. These are mental patterns that correspond to frequently encountered people, objects or situations. They allow us to make sense of what we encounter in order that we can predict what is going to happen and what we should do in any given situation. These schemas may, in part, be determined by social values, and therefore by prejudice. Schemas are therefore capable of distorting unfamiliar or unconsciously 'unacceptable' information, in order to 'fit in' with our existing knowledge or schemas. This can result in unreliable eyewitness testimony.

In a now famous study, Bartlett tested this theory using a variety of stories to illustrate that memory is an active process and subject to individual interpretation or construction. In the experiment, his participants heard a story and had to tell the story to another person and so on, like a game of 'Chinese Whispers'. The story was a North American folk tale called *The War of the Ghosts*. When asked to recount the detail of the story, each person seemed to recall it in their own individual way. With repeated telling, the passages became shorter, puzzling ideas were rationalized or omitted altogether, and details changed to become more conventional.

For example, the information about the ghosts was omitted as it was difficult to explain. On the other hand, participants frequently recalled the idea of someone 'not going because he hadn't told his parents where he was going' because that situation was more familiar to them.

Bartlett concluded that memory is not exact but is distorted by existing schemas, or what we already know about the world. It seems, therefore, that each of us 'reconstructs' our memories to conform to our personal beliefs about the world. This clearly indicates that our memories are anything but reliable, 'photographic' records of events. They are individual recollections which have been shaped and constructed according to our stereotypes, beliefs, expectations, etc.

Task analysis

4   Check your answers to the test tasks and answer the questions.
    1   Did you write a maximum of one word for each answer?
    2   Did you copy the spelling of each word correctly?
    3   Did you change the form of any words in your answers?

> **TEST STRATEGY**
>
> If you have to change the form of a word from the passage (for example, change a singular noun to a plural noun), your answer is wrong, so you need to go back to the reading passage and choose another answer.

Vocabulary

> **COURSEBOOK** page 90

Verbs for argument and opinion

1a Choose the correct word in brackets to complete the sentences. Change the form of the word if necessary.

1 After hearing all the evidence, the jury _____ (identify/conclude) that the accused person was innocent.

2 The study of microbiology has _____ (facilitate/derive) new methods of crime detection, such as DNA testing.

3 Roadside cameras help traffic police to _____ (involve/identify) drivers who are speeding.

4 It is likely that falling levels of poverty _____ (contribute/conclude) to falling levels of crime.

5 Community service _____ (involve/derive) criminals doing unpaid work to benefit the community, instead of serving a prison sentence.

6 A number of English laws _____ (contribute/derive) from ancient customs.

b Complete the sentences with the correct form of words from Exercise 1a.

1 The witness successfully _____ the woman he had seen stealing goods in the supermarket.

2 Police training _____ learning how to overpower criminals without injuring them.

3 The task of law enforcement is _____ when police officers develop good relations with community leaders.

4 Because one boy ran away from the scene of the robbery, the police _____ that he was responsible for the crime.

5 The provision of leisure activities for young people probably _____ to reduced crime rates.

6 Victims of theft may _____ some comfort from having their property returned to them.

Academic words

2a Match the words (1–10) with the definitions (A–J).

1	appropriate	A	arguably
2	beneficial	B	basically
3	debatably	C	likely to succeed or be effective
4	feasible	D	not matching
5	fundamentally	E	unrealistically
6	idealistically	F	sensibly
7	inconsistent	G	suitable
8	logical	H	making good sense
9	practical	I	having a good effect
10	reasonably	J	possible

b Tick any of the following opinions which you agree with.

1 It is not appropriate to put anyone under the age of 18 in prison.

2 Prison sentences are debatably ineffective in reforming criminals.

3 It is not feasible for the police to investigate every minor crime.

4 It is fundamentally right for people to defend themselves if attacked.

5 People idealistically suppose that children will always obey their parents.

6 When suspects make statements which are inconsistent, the police may not believe anything they say.

7 When a car is stolen, it is logical for the police to suspect anyone who has stolen cars in the past.

8 Reformers reasonably claim that prisoners should have access to books and television.

c Change any of the opinions in Exercise 2b that you disagree with so that they are true for you.

Collocations for argument

3a Complete the sentences with the words below.

convincing   flawed   line of   rejected   sides   supports

1 The judge _____ the defence lawyer's argument that her client was sorry for his behaviour, and gave him a lengthy prison sentence.

2 The case against the accused woman was declared invalid, because the argument for her prosecution was felt to be _____ .

3 A decrease in re-offending rates _____ the government's argument that new rehabilitation projects are working.

4 The government will consider both _____ of the argument concerning raising the age of criminal responsibility before reaching a decision.

5 The prosecuting lawyer's _____ argument was so logical that it persuaded the jury to reach a unanimous 'guilty' verdict.

6 Neither the defence nor the prosecution made a _____ argument, so the jury was unable to reach any decision.

b Choose the correct option in *italics* and complete the sentences with your own words.

1 In my opinion, the argument for longer prison sentences is *convincing / flawed* because _____ .

2 I *accept / reject* the argument for raising the legal driving age because _____ .

3 Some people argue that everyone should be allowed to own a gun in case they need to defend themselves. However, the other *side / line* of the argument is that _____ .

4 It is sometimes argued that social problems are the real cause of crime. I *reject / support* this view, because _____ .

5 Studies showing a link between drug abuse and crime *support / reject* the argument for _____ .

6 Lawyers are trained to present a *side / line* of argument which is logical, and which can _____ .

Language development

> COURSEBOOK page 93, EXPERT GRAMMAR page 179

Link ideas

1a Put the words below into three groups, according to their grammatical functions.

~~although~~   ~~conversely~~   ~~despite~~   likewise   similarly
whereas   while

Conjunctions	Adverbs	Prepositions
although	_conversely_	_despite_
_____	_____	
_____	_____	

b Put the words in Exercise 1a into two groups, according to their approximate meaning.

This is a different idea	This is the same idea
_____	_____
_____	_____
_____	
_____	
_____	

c Which of the words in Exercise 1a connect ideas in different sentences? Which of the words connect ideas within the same sentence?

2 Choose the correct option in *italics* to complete the text.

The legal system in the UK and the USA

1 *Despite / Whereas* some minor differences, there are many similarities between the two countries. The English legal system is based mainly on judgements made in previous court cases. 2 *Conversely / Likewise*, the U.S. system is based on decisions made by judges in the past. 3 *Although / Despite* legal practitioners in the UK are generally referred to as 'lawyers', the term 'attorney' is used in the USA. In addition, 4 *despite / while* in both countries there are two main types of lawyer – those who deal directly with clients and those who represent clients in courts of law – they have different names. In the UK they are referred to as 'solicitors' and 'barristers', 5 *similarly / whereas* in the USA they are known as 'litigators' and 'non-litigators'. Another difference lies in the fact that, 6 *although / likewise* in the USA lawyers choose the members of a jury, in the UK jurors are selected at random by a civil servant.
Finally, there are differences in the penalties for criminal behaviours. Most notably, the UK has outlawed capital punishment. 7 *Conversely / Likewise*, the USA has retained it.

3 Complete the second sentence so that it has a similar meaning to the first.

1 The various legal systems around the world share certain features, but very few are exactly alike.
Despite _sharing certain features, very few of the legal systems around the world are exactly alike_ .

2 The Japanese legal system is based on civil law, but the U.S. legal system is based on common law.
Whereas _____ .

3 There are many differences between the legal systems of the two countries, but a number of U.S. law firms have opened successful offices in Japan.
Although _____ .

4 Law-makers try to write laws that are as clear as possible, but there will always be occasions when this is difficult to do.
While _____ .

5 In some countries it is the responsibility of an accused person to prove their innocence. In others, it is the responsibility of the accusers to offer proof.
Whereas _____ .

6 Lawyers have to spend a long time training, but jurors have no training at all.
_____ . Conversely, _____ .

7 In the USA, the legal powers of the federal government are limited. In Germany too, some legislation is enacted by the country's member states.
_____ . Similarly, _____ .

8 In ancient Rome, justice was symbolised by a picture of a woman holding scales and a sword. The scales are also used in many modern cultures too.
_____ . Similarly, _____ .

Both, neither, either

4a The three words below all refer to two things. Match the words with the meanings (1–3).

both   either   neither

1 X or Y
2 Not X and not Y
3 X and Y

b Rewrite the sentences using the words in Exercise 4a.

1 Some convicted criminals are sent to prison. Others are made to pay a fine.

2 Community police officers can help to prevent crime and so can people living in the area.

3 Keeping people in prison for a long time is not cheap, and it is not effective.

4 Prisoners can choose the kind of training they want. Some study for a qualification, while others learn a new skill.

Writing (Task 2)

➤ **COURSEBOOK** page 94, **EXPERT WRITING** page 196

Understand the task

1 Look at the writing task below. What is the proposal being made?

> 'Teenage offenders should be dealt with completely differently from the way adult criminals are treated.'
>
> To what extent do you agree or disagree with this statement?

Structures to compare and contrast

2a Look at the following ideas which could go into an essay on the treatment of teenage offenders. Which points support the proposal and which oppose it?

1 Young offenders should do work in their victims' community, instead of a prison sentence, so they begin to understand the consequences of their actions.
2 The prospect of strict punishment will deter young criminals as well as old.
3 The effects on the victim are the same irrespective of the age of the perpetrator
4 Teenagers are a slave to their hormones – they behave out of character at this time.
5 Prisons are 'schools of crime' and young offenders should be kept out of them.
6 Young people don't understand the real difference between right and wrong.

b Read the extract from a sample answer. Does this paragraph make points for or against the proposal in the task? Which of the points in Exercise 2a (1–6) are mentioned?

> In some parts of the world, teenagers who commit crimes are dealt with in exactly the same way as adults are. The arguments in favour of this approach are usually as follows. The punishment should fit the crime rather than the criminal. If a shop is robbed by an armed teenager, it is just as brutal and terrifying for the victim as if it had been carried out by someone older. For this reason, the punishment should be equally harsh to act as an equal deterrent. If teenagers believe they will get away with a lighter sentence, they will be more willing to break the law. Many people believe that one of the reasons for the increase in criminal activity is the lenient treatment of young offenders.

c Match the words (1–5) with their synonyms (A–E).

1 delinquency	A chance
2 enlightened	B belief
3 opportunity	C not harsh
4 lenient	D crime
5 view	E open-minded

d Complete at the final paragraph of the sample answer with the words (1–5) from Exercise 2c.

> I am persuaded by the 1 _____ that teenagers should be given the 2 _____ to redeem themselves before they become stuck in a life of 3 _____ .
> For this to happen we need more 4 _____ methods of dealing with young offenders.

Contrast your opinions

3a Choose the correct option in *italics* to complete the sentences.

1 In some countries young offenders are given counselling and let off with a warning *despite / whereas* in others they are treated in the same way as adult criminals.
2 *Although / Despite* the fact that statistics show high levels of crime committed by teenagers, many people deny that there is a youth crime problem.
3 *While / However* it is widely accepted that many young criminals come from disadvantaged homes, this cannot be an excuse for more lenient treatment.
4 *In spite / Although* there is evidence that community service is more effective than imprisonment for teenagers, many people choose to ignore it.

b Identify words in the sentences in Exercise 3a which have the same meaning as the words/phrases below.

1 criminal
2 carried out
3 believed
4 underprivileged

Test practice

4 Write the second paragraph of the essay, following on from the first paragraph in Exercise 2b. Start it as follows: 'However, there are many who take the opposite view ...'

Listening (Section 4)

➤ **COURSEBOOK** pages 92 and 95

Before you listen

1 Read the context rubric for a listening task. Tick the sentence (1–4) you think summarises the content of the talk.

> *'You will hear a talk, given by a first-year Criminology student, on Elizabeth Fry, a prison reformer in the early 19th century.'*

1 the history of prison reform in general
2 what is wrong with our current prisons
3 the life story of one prison reformer
4 a portrait of prison life in the 19th century

2a Look at the summary task below. What type of word would fit in each gap (1–3)?

Complete the summary below using no more than ***ONE WORD*** *for each answer.*

Elizabeth Fry
Elizabeth Fry was born in 1780, with the name Elizabeth Gurney, into a wealthy family in East Anglia. Her home is now part of the local 1 _____ . Following her mother's death she spent her teenage years teaching her younger siblings. As a young adult she took an interest in the poor and organised 2 _____ collections. She also set up lessons in the grounds of her home and taught local people to 3 _____ . In 1800 she married Joseph Fry, a banker, moved to London and went on to have 11 children.

b Read the extract from the first part of the audio script and complete the summary in Exercise 2a.

… [Elizabeth Fry] was born Elizabeth Gurney … in 1780 in Norwich, in East Anglia, a relatively remote area of Southeast England. She was born into a prosperous family of bankers and the family home was a large mansion – Earlham Hall – which now forms a section of the University of East Anglia. It was a large family and when her mother passed away, when Elizabeth was just 12, she spent much of her youth educating her younger brothers and sisters. When she was 18, Elizabeth attended a lecture by a charismatic preacher, whose words inspired her to take an interest in those less advantaged than herself. She began to look beyond the walls of her privileged home and to see the plight of the poor and the sick. She arranged to make collections of clothing for the poor, visited the sick in the villages nearby and invited local people to a small building in the grounds of her home, where she taught them to read. It was during this period that she met Joseph Fry, a banker. In 1800, when she was 20 years old, they married and moved to London. The couple went on to have 11 children.

c Look at the underlined words in the summary in Exercise 2a and identify the sections in the audio script which express the same thing.

Test practice

3 🔊 6.1 Complete the test tasks.

Questions 1–6
Complete the summary below.
Write ***NO MORE THAN ONE WORD*** *for each answer.*

After arriving in London, she visited Newgate Prison and was particularly concerned about 1 _____ , especially in the women and children's section of the prison. Women were required to 2 _____ in their cells – which was very unhealthy. Financial problems delayed action until 1816 when Fry returned and started a 3 _____ in the prison. She also helped women to sell their needlework to make cash.

Fry worked tirelessly for prisoners. She created a nationwide organisation – the ARFP – and also wrote a book on prison conditions. Fry's work eventually led to The Gaol's Act of 1823 (though this was undermined by a lack of 4 _____ who were to put her ideas into practice). Following a harsh winter, in 1820, Fry started to work with 5 _____ people, and in 1840, she opened a college for 6 _____ which improved conditions in war zones.

Question 7
Choose the correct letter, ***A***, ***B*** *or* ***C***.

7 According to the speaker, what is Fry's most famous memorial?
A stained-glass windows
B a copy of a key to a prison cell
C appearing on bank notes

Language development

> **COURSEBOOK** page 96, **EXPERT GRAMMAR** page 179

Cleft sentences

1a Compare the sentence below with the sentences (1–3) in Exercise 1b. What is the difference between them?

The writer Conan Doyle based the character of Sherlock Holmes on a surgeon he knew.

b The sentences below (1–3) contain the same information as the sentence in Exercise 1a, but they are in a different form. What does each sentence imply? Choose the correct letter, A, B or C.

1 It was on a surgeon he knew that the writer Conan Doyle based the character of Sherlock Holmes.
2 It was the writer Conan Doyle who based the character of Sherlock Holmes on a surgeon he knew.
3 It was the character of Sherlock Holmes that the writer Conan Doyle based on a surgeon he knew.

A not the character of Dr Watson
B not the writer H.G. Wells
C not on a detective he knew

c Rewrite the sentences, so that they imply the meaning shown in brackets. Begin your sentences with *It*.

1 In the story called *His Last Bow*, Sherlock Holmes had retired to a small farm in the country and taken up beekeeping. (not in the story called *The Second Stain*)
2 The author of the Sherlock Holmes stories was a clerk at a hospital in Edinburgh. (not at a hospital in London)
3 The American writer Edgar Allan Poe is best known for his tales of mystery. (not for his poetry)
4 The novel *Miss Smilla's Feeling for Snow* probably prompted the current wave of Scandinavian crime stories and films. (not the novel *The White Lioness*)
5 Keigo Higashino wrote the popular crime story called *The Devotion of Suspect X*. (not Natsuo Kirino)
6 The fictional detective in the French novel *The Man in the Eiffel Tower* was Maigret. (not Hercule Poirot)
7 A Spanish author originally wrote *The Depths of the Forest*. (not a French author)
8 A woman called Candice Fox wrote the Australian crime novel *Eden*. (not a man)

2 Match the sentence beginnings (1–8) with the endings (A–H).

1 What the government should do now is
2 What the police said was
3 What the witness saw was
4 What led to the arrest of the gang was
5 What surprised the police was
6 What the victim told reporters was
7 What the judge said was
8 What the prisoners appreciated most was

A that she felt sorry for the boy who took her money.
B someone climbing out of a window.
C the chance to learn a new skill before they were released.
D order a review of prison conditions.
E a telephone call from a member of the public.
F the fact that there were no signs of a break-in at the house.
G that the offender should do community service for six months.
H they were still looking at the evidence.

EXPERT LANGUAGE

The structures in Exercises 1 and 2 are not the most common way of making a statement. They are used when the speaker/writer wants to emphasise something.

---

3 Complete the sentences, using your own ideas.

1 What would help in reducing juvenile crime is
_____ .
2 What would encourage more witnesses to report crimes is _____ .
3 What house owners should do to protect their property is _____ .
4 What would help ex-prisoners to fit into society again is _____ .
5 It is the responsibility of _____ to report suspicious activities.
6 It is the duty of _____ to protect the public.
7 It is the job of the jury to _____ .
8 It is the _____ to pass new laws.

Vocabulary

> **COURSEBOOK** page 96

Using *there* and *it*

1a Complete the sentences with *there* or *it*.

1 _____ is often said that watching crime films encourages real-life crime.
2 _____ is important to have a logical mind if you want to become a lawyer.
3 If you're looking for a police station, _____ is one on Queen Street.
4 _____ is a tendency to exaggerate levels of crime.
5 In relation to the population size, _____ are a lot more lawyers in the USA than in Japan.
6 _____ is almost a hundred years since cameras in courtrooms were banned in the UK.
7 _____ looks as if it's about to rain.

b Match the sentences in Exercise 1a with one of the rules for choosing *it* or *there* (A–G).

Use *there*:
A before saying where something is.
B before quantities and numbers.
C before introducing a new topic.

Use *it*:
D before dates and times.
E before adjectives expressing opinion.
F before describing the weather.
G before passive forms.

2 Choose the correct option in *italics* to complete the text.

Dealing with cyber-crime

1 *It / There* is strong legal protection in place for consumers against unauthorised transactions on their bank card or account. **2** *It / There* is now much more difficult for criminals to steal money in this way, because banks use highly sophisticated security systems to protect their customers. Instead, criminals are now targeting consumers directly. **3** *It / There* are various tricks aimed at getting people to give away their personal or financial details.

4 *It / There* is vital that everyone is extremely wary of any unsolicited calls, texts or emails asking for such information.

Police have warned that faceless crime is being conducted over the internet on an 'industrial scale': **5** *it / there* is thought to cost £1 billion a year in the UK alone. However, **6** *it / there* is a range of measures which can prevent cybercrime, such as the use of more effective passwords and regularly updating security software.

3 Match the sentence beginnings (1–6) with the endings (A–F).

1 There was a big fall last year in
2 It is very encouraging that
3 It is usually helpful for the police to have
4 There have been many cases in which
5 It was only recently that a decision was made to allow
6 There are many similarities between

A photographic evidence of a crime.
B children to give evidence in court via a video link.
C the number of crimes which are solved is increasing.
D the US and UK legal systems.
E the number of cars that were stolen.
F fingerprint evidence has been used to convict thieves.

4 Complete the second sentence so that it has a similar meaning to the first.

1 The use of drones to catch criminals is very controversial.
There is considerable <u>controversy about the use of drones to catch criminals</u> .
2 You can't legally download music and films without consent.
It _____ .
3 The police can use various hi-tech devices to catch criminals.
There _____ .
4 If you send spam in the USA you can receive a maximum sentence of five years in prison.
In the USA _____ .
5 Using the internet for betting on a sports match is a federal crime.
It _____ .
6 The number of email accounts which are hacked has increased sharply recently.
There _____ .

5 Write 5 sentences about law and order in your country. Start the sentences with *It* or *There*, and follow the rules in Exercise 1b.

EXPERT LANGUAGE

If you read extensively in English, you will probably learn when to use *it* or *there* correctly without thinking about it.

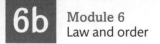

Speaking (Part 3)

> **COURSEBOOK** pages 91 and 97

Vocabulary development

1a Match the words/phrases (1–7) with the definitions (A–G).

1 data sources
2 drones
3 facial recognition
4 crime hotspots
5 prediction
6 social media
7 suspects

A places where there's a lot of illegal activity
B aircraft without a pilot
C people who the police believe may have committed a crime
D identifying a person by the features of their face
E an attempt to say what will happen in the future
F places where information is stored
G electronic ways of communicating with people informally

b Complete the sentences using the words in Exercise 1a.

1 By recording the places where crimes have taken place, the police can identify _____ .
2 Police forces can now use _____ to secretly follow and film criminals from the air.
3 The police have identified a number of _____ who they intend to question about the robbery.
4 Criminal records are one of the most useful _____ for police investigations.
5 There are now computer programmes that use _____ techniques to identify people by their appearance.
6 Criminals often provide the police with valuable information when they write about their activities on _____ .
7 By using information from their records, the police are sometimes able to make a _____ about when a robbery is going to take place.

Focus on fluency and coherence

2a In the months or weeks before you take the IELTS test, how can you best improve your speaking fluency? Number the four activities below according to what you think about their importance for fluency practice.

• Learn and practise new words
• Learn and practise new grammatical forms
• Practise listening to oral questions
• Practise speaking, by yourself and with others

b When you do a test practice, or when you take the test, which of the following will help increase your fluency? Write 'yes' or 'no' for each one.

1 Concentrate on accuracy
2 Try to give expanded answers to questions
3 Don't try to correct mistakes

3a Look at the questions about law and order. Underline the key words in each question.

1 Some people think that if more people are sent to prison, crime will be reduced. What do you think about that?
2 Which is more common where you live, people stealing on the street, or people stealing from houses?
3 What kinds of things do you think people can do to protect themselves from crime?
4 Do you think having more police would help to reduce crime?

b Check the meaning of any unknown words in the sentences in Exercise 3a.

c Make notes on how you might answer the questions.

4a Match the two answers below with two of the questions in Exercise 3a.

A Well, they can avoid going to areas which are known to be crime hotspots, for one thing. I mean, if that's possible of course – if they live in one of those areas, it's not. Also they can avoid going out late at night, especially if they're alone. And thirdly, people can carry alarms. They're easy to put in your pocket or bag and they're not very expensive. And the last thing is, I've read somewhere that people who look frightened are more likely to become victims of crime. So if possible, people should try and appear confident even if they're scared.

B I don't really agree with that, because it's a well-known fact that spending time in prison can create so-called 'career criminals'. For example, when they go in for the first time, often after committing some minor crime, petty criminals meet and spend time with criminals who've committed more serious crimes, or who've committed a lot of crimes, and it's like being in a school – they're influenced by those people. So when they finally leave prison, they've got a lot of criminal contacts and they're less likely to give up crime. On the other hand, if petty criminals received some other kind of punishment, they'd be more likely to change their behaviour.

b Underline the words in A and B above which link the speaker's ideas.

Test practice

5a 🔊 6.2 Listen to the questions about the causes of crime and practise answering them. If possible, record yourself.

b Listen to your answers and make notes of anything which you could improve. Then try answering the questions again.

Writing (Task 2)

> **COURSEBOOK** pages 100–101, **EXPERT WRITING** page 196

Understand the task

1 Look at the 'for and against' essay task. What is being proposed? What would be the opposite view?

'It is sometimes justifiable to break the law for a good cause.'

To what extent do you agree or disagree?

Plan the task

2a Match the sentence beginnings (1–3) with the endings (A–C) to create the first paragraph of the answer to this essay.

1 There have been several instances in the news recently

2 For example, activists who believe that nuclear power is damaging for the environment and have climbed perimeter fences to disable equipment

3 The question is: although activists are breaking the law,

A so that energy production is disrupted.

B should their transgressions be regarded in a completely different light from other crimes?

C where people have been put in prison for fighting for a cause which many people would regard as worthwhile.

b Put the sentences in the correct order to make the second paragraph of the essay, which sets out the case against the statement in the task.

A Taking the example of breaking into the power station, many people would say that we need to find sources of energy which do not emit greenhouses gases and that nuclear energy, whilst far from perfect, is an acceptable solution.

B A second argument is that such actions cause immediate danger, not just to the workers in the plant but to the protesters themselves and that the law is in place to protect people and should be respected.

C Firstly, there is not always agreement about what constitutes a righteous cause.

D There are a number of arguments against giving such people special treatment in law. People who disrupt the supply of power to places like hospitals are actually causing criminal damage and should therefore be punished as criminals.

c Complete the third paragraph with the words/ phrases below. There is one extra word/phrase.

flawed	legislation	reversed	badly	moral	allow
awareness					

On the other hand, there is a clearly a 1 _____ difference between breaking the law for your own gain – to steal money, for example – and in order to raise 2 _____ of wrong practice. Many people would argue that if a law is 3 _____ , then it should be broken. In the past, bad laws were only 4 _____ after people broke them and drew attention to them. Without the 'illegal' activities of suffragettes, for instance, the 5 _____ relating to elections would never have changed to 6 _____ women to vote.

d Which of the following do you think would make the best conclusion to this sample essay? Why?

1 On balance, I feel that the intentions of the perpetrator should be taken into account when sentencing and that it is indeed sometimes justifiable to break the law for the common good.

2 Taking into account the arguments on both sides, I believe that it is justifiable to break the law for a good cause.

e Looking back at the sample answer in Exercises 2a–2d, decide which structure the writer has used. Choose from the following list.

1 statement of own position → arguments in support of this

2 arguments supporting proposal → statement of own position

3 arguments supporting proposal → arguments against → statement of own position

Write your opinion essay

3 Write your answer to the task below. Use ideas from Exercises 1–2 to help you.

It is a good idea to have fixed penalties for crimes, e.g. murder should always result in life imprisonment.

To what extent do you agree or disagree?

Assess and improve

4 When you have completed your essay, leave it for some hours. Then re-read and check your writing, using the following questions.

1 Is there an introduction, clear paragraphs and a conclusion?

2 Do you make clear your level of agreement with the statement?

3 Is each main point introduced clearly?

4 Is each point well developed and supported?

5 Is there a well-structured conclusion?

Reading (Matching sentence endings; Summary completion)

Before you read

1 Look at the title of the reading passage. Which of the words below might you find in the passage?

architecture   construction   modern   population
roof   salary   site   structure   traffic

Link ideas; Paraphrase

2 Read the passage once quickly and answer the questions.

1 Which four different parts does the market hall contain?

2 What is the most impressive feature inside the market hall?

3 What has the public reaction been to the market hall?

3a Look at question 1 and the sentence endings (A–H) in the test task in Exercise 4. Which of the sentence endings must be wrong?

b Look at the first paragraph of the reading passage and find words that correspond to the key words underlined in Exercise 4 question 1.

c Identify a reason why there was a positive change in Bilbao's economy.

d Choose a sentence ending that corresponds to that reason.

Test practice

4 Follow the same procedure as in Exercise 3 for questions 2–6 and complete the test task.

Questions 1–6
Complete each sentence with the correct ending, A–H.

1 A positive change in Bilbao's economy is thought to be due to

2 The characteristic building style in Amsterdam is quite unlike

3 Archaeological remains found at the construction site can be viewed while descending

4 Residents who live above the market hall have linked its appearance to

5 The aspect of the market hall which gets most attention is

6 The metal panels inside the market hall have been treated to achieve

A a huge picture of plants and wildlife.
B its shape and colour.
C a reduction in general noise levels.
D a new museum.
E that of another building in the vicinity.
F increased visitor numbers to Rotterdam.
G to lower levels of the building.
H that of Rotterdam.

Test practice

5a Using your memory of the passage, decide which words/phrases are missing in questions 7–10 below.

b Use the title of the summary below to find the area of text which the summary is based on. Then use the strategies in Exercise 3 to check your answers to questions 7–10.

Questions 7–10
Complete the summary using the list of words/phrases, A–I, below.

The Eiffel Tower

In the nineteenth century, the 7 _____ of buildings in Paris led to a comprehensive reconstruction of the city. As a result, it was 8 _____ in appearance. So when the Eiffel Tower was built it received a 9 _____ . Nevertheless, for countries outside France it served as a 10 _____ , and gave the city a reputation for being modern.

A crowded layout   B mixed reaction   C model
D more exciting   E poor condition   F symbol
G unanimous welcome   H unfashionable style
I uniform

TEST STRATEGY

In the IELTS test, a summary may be based on the whole passage, or on just one particular part of it.

Markthal:
how the design of a new building has transformed a city in the Netherlands

The power of new architecture to regenerate a city is well documented. Notably, Bilbao's transformation from a declining industrial city to a booming cultural destination is often attributed to the opening of the Guggenheim Museum Bilbao, designed by Frank Gehry, in 1997. More than one million people visited in the first year, three times more than forecast. Since then many other cities, such as Doha, Hull and Valencia, have commissioned architects – often big names – to design buildings that will pull in the crowds.

Usually these buildings are museums or art galleries, sometimes hotels – but rarely are they as prosaic as a covered market with apartments and underground parking. Yet Rotterdam is experiencing a surge in visitors since its new Markthal, the first covered hall in the Netherlands, opened in October 2014. According to Rotterdam Partners, the organisation that promotes the city's economy, the building had received six million visitors before the end of 2016. At weekends there are queues to get in.

The city's mayor, Ahmed Aboutaleb, argues that the influence of the new architecture extends beyond visitor numbers. 'The Markthal contributes immensely to the image and attractiveness of Rotterdam as a city ... where national and international businesses want to invest,' he says.

Rotterdam already has a reputation for bold architecture. While Amsterdam is all quaint old canal houses, the port city of Rotterdam, heavily bombarded during the Second World War, is best known for thrusting skyscrapers. But it is the fairly low-rise market hall that everyone wants to see. A photograph of the structure, designed by Rotterdam-based architects MVRDV, graces the cover of the city's official tourist information material. The building contains 228 apartments, which arch over 96 market stalls and eight restaurants. Below ground there is parking for 1,200 cars.

The market is located on the original site of Rotterdam dating back to the 13th century. Historic artefacts such as pottery and the remains of a horse's jawbone used as skates, were found during construction. These are now displayed in cases adjacent to escalators serving the car parks four floors below ground. However, for many residents the new market hall trumps the location's history. They have given their new architectural attraction a nickname. The horseshoe-shaped tubular structure, clad in the same grey Chinese granite as the city's new pavements, is the 'sharpener' for a neighbouring 'pencil' – a columnar apartment block with a conical lead roof.

Nevertheless, it is the colourful mural inside the hall, on the 11,000-square-metre ceiling, that is the main attraction. A visit will make you feel as if you're in Wonderland: stacks of barley, six storeys tall, sprout towards the sun, while an enormous strawberry tumbles from the sky. A giant butterfly flits through the scene, its turquoise wing containing a window from which someone waves. Within the mural, the windows of the apartments overlook the hubbub of commerce and the dreamlike scene. Visible from outside through two enormous glazed arched facades, the decorated ceiling brightens up dark evenings. 'In winter, from outside it looks so festive – the colour and the lights – it's like Christmas', says the market manager.

The mural, entitled *Cornucopia*, is by Dutch artists Arno Coenen and Iris Roskam, who used software from a film studio to create the 1,470-gigabyte image that is printed on 4,500 aluminium panels. These are perforated with tiny holes to deaden sound, so that despite the hustle and bustle, conversation at normal volume is easy. 'We wanted a calm environment,' says the principal architect Winy Maas. It is an architectural quality that might only be otherwise noticed if seriously deficient. Neither does noise from the market disturb the apartments that arch over the top. The windows that face the market are sealed and triple glazed.

Not everything went smoothly, however: some teething problems soon became apparent. Some apartments get too warm on hot days, because there's no through-breeze, and the market hall also overheats. The two huge glass facades, held together by a grid of steel cables, are a feat of engineering, but the expanse of unshaded glass means the building acts like a greenhouse. While this design provides welcome warmth most of the year, on hot summer days it is a problem which will take time to address.

Although not everyone agrees that a single building can transform a whole city, there are instances where a structure has been able to shift perceptions, so that it can appear to herald a new urban era. It is difficult to think of a better example than the Eiffel Tower in Paris. In the mid-nineteenth century, the city's decaying, medieval fabric was radically rebuilt by Baron Hausmann as a city of boulevards and squares. It was then aesthetically harmonious and, in a way, monotonous. The building of the Eiffel Tower in 1889 was hugely controversial, but it gave Paris a modern image and came to represent the city on the international stage.

Vocabulary

> COURSEBOOK page 106

Academic nouns

1a Choose the correct option in *italics* to complete the sentences.

1 During long-distance cycle races, water and snacks are delivered to feeding stations on the route for *distribution / investment* to cyclists.
2 Regular *implementation / maintenance* of road surfaces is essential for cyclists' safety.
3 Japanese *initiative / investment* in new roads has meant that in many places the quiet, old roads are perfect for cyclists.
4 The Netherlands, Denmark and Germany aim for the full *integration / implementation* of cycle lanes with public transport systems.
5 Racing bikes are designed according to strict *parameters / infrastructure*.
6 Due to the growing popularity of cycling, Amsterdam is to bring forward plans for the *initiative / expansion* of its bicycle parking spaces.
7 The *distribution / construction* of new cycle paths and improved road junctions are two of the projects currently being undertaken in Barcelona.
8 When several local groups are campaigning for improvements to cycling facilities, *compensation / co-ordination* makes the campaigns more effective.

b Complete the sentences with the correct form of the words below.

compensation	construction	implementation
infrastructure	initiative	investment
maintenance	parameter	

1 _____ began on a railway line between Tokyo and Osaka in 1883.
2 In Texas, the _____ defining a child's eligibility to travel by school bus are set by the state education authority.
3 A major complaint in surveys of passenger satisfaction is that airlines rarely offer _____ for the late departure of flights.
4 After the successful _____ of various high-speed-train projects, Spain is now focusing on establishing a good tram network.
5 New transport _____ are usually government led, due to the high costs involved.
6 In the UK, different companies are responsible for the railway _____ and the train services.
7 The frequent breakdowns experienced on long-distance coaches are evidence of poor _____ .
8 Most economists agree that _____ in transport systems has long-term economic benefits.

c Describe one aspect of the transport system in your country. Use the words in Exercise 1b.

Word families

2 Choose the correct option in *italics* to complete the text.

Transport in Brazil

Approximately 20 percent of Brazilians spend more than one hour to go from home to work, and recently demand for public transport has fallen considerably. This is because buses are poorly **1** *maintained / maintenance*, and there are insufficient subway lines.

One of the main problems is that until recently, new **2** *invest / investment* has been in private transport infrastructure, mainly for cars. And while in some countries road lanes have been **3** *construction / constructed* which are available only for cars with more than two people, the scheme hasn't yet reached Brazil. However, there are some websites which specialise in **4** *coordinating / coordination* car drivers and potential passengers.

Another welcome initiative is the **5** *expansion / expand* of the cycle network. In São Paulo, for example, the government has **6** *investment / invested* in the construction of a further 86.5km of paths.

In Rio de Janeiro, the flagship transport **7** *initiate / initiative* for the 2016 Olympic Games was a new metro line to the western neighbourhood of Barra da Tijuca, where the main Olympic park was located. This new line will benefit the citizens of Barra de Tijuca by taking a great deal of traffic off congested roads.

Collocations with *plan*

3a Tick the verbs/verbs phrases that collocate with *plan*.

1 combat	5 go ahead	9 oppose
2 conduct	6 guide	10 put forward
3 draw up	7 keep	11 shelve
4 expose	8 offer	12 unveil

b Complete the flow chart using the correct form of the verbs in Exercise 3a.

The government wants to construct a new airport. They ask their advisers to **1** _____ a plan.

⬇

The advisers gather information of various kinds and then **2** _____ their plan to the government.

⬇

The government considers the plan which the advisers have suggested. They decide on a date when they will **3** _____ the plan to the general public.

⬇

Some people are enthusiastic about the government's plan for the airport, but many **4** _____ it.

⬇

For the time being, the government decides to **5** _____ the plan, so no action is taken.

⬇

The government makes some changes to satisfy those against the plan. Then five years later they announce that they will **6** _____ with it.

Language development

> COURSEBOOK page 109, EXPERT GRAMMAR page 179

Sentence fragments and run-on sentences

1a Underline the sentences in the advertisement below which are incomplete.

> ## Emirates Aviation Experience
>
> The **Emirates Aviation Experience**, one of London's newest attractions, is the first of its kind globally. Is located next to the Greenwich Peninsula terminal. The exhibition gives visitors information about the operations and modern achievements of commercial air travel. Using state-of-the-art technology, interactive displays, and life-size aircraft models, something for people of all ages.
>
> So we've included a new on-board 'tour' as part of the Discovery experience. The audio-guide commentary complements the visual 'journey' with a series of fascinating stories about East London. The tour presents a selection of our most famous London landmarks including the Thames Barrier and Royal Docks. Also gives information about East London's exciting plans for the future.

b Choose one of the phrases below to complete the sentences in Exercise 1a. Write the letter in the place in the advertisement where it fits.

A it offers
B the commentary
C we wanted to tell you about the local area too
D the building

2a Tick the sentences that can be split into sentences.

1 The London Cable Car, officially known as 'The Emirates Air Line', is a cable car which crosses the River Thames in East London.
2 It is sponsored by Emirates Airline that is why it is called the Emirates Air Line.
3 The terminal on the north side of the river is close to the Excel Centre while that on the south side is close to the O2 Arena.
4 The cable cars leave each terminal every few seconds the normal journey time is 5 minutes.
5 From 10a.m. to 3p.m. the journey time is longer, visitors can have more time to enjoy the view.
6 Each cable car can seat up to ten people and two bicycles, and boarding is supervised by staff.
7 The cable car opens at 7a.m. from Monday to Friday, 8a.m. on Saturday and 9a.m. on Sunday.
8 Passengers can buy a '360' trip which allows them to stay on and go back to the original terminus this costs the same price as a return trip.

b In the sentences you ticked in Exercise 2a, write // to mark the place where the first sentence ends.

Punctuation

3a Underline the punctuation mistakes in the sentences.

1 There are three major airports in the Washington DC region, Ronald Reagan Airport, Washington Dulles Airport and Washington Thurgood Marshall Airport.
2 Sydneys airport is the oldest commercial international airport in the world.
3 Flights from Tokyo to Sydney depart at 19.25; 22.00 and 22.10.
4 travelling by cargo ship can be a good alternative to travelling by cruise ship, as cargo ships travel to more destinations.
5 There are several reasons why people prefer travelling by public transport, including lower costs compared to car or taxi. the reduced impact on the environment. and the convenience of not needing to find a parking space.
6 As Singapore is a small city, it uses sophisticated computer programmes to maximise the capacity of it's roads.

b Match the list of punctuation rules (A–F) with the type of mistake in the sentences in Exercise 3a.

A There should be a capital letter at the beginning of sentences.
B When a statement is followed by a complete list of the items it refers to, use a colon before the first item.
C When a list contains complex noun phrases, use semi colons to separate the items.
D Don't put an apostrophe in a possessive pronoun.
E When a list contains simple, short items, separate these using commas.
F When two nouns appear together, and the first is the owner of the second, use an apostrophe followed by 's' (where the first noun is singular).

> **EXPERT LANGUAGE**
>
> *It's* and *its* are often confused. *It's* is a contracted form of *It is*, while *its* is a possessive pronoun.

c Correct the punctuation mistakes in Exercise 3a.

4 Write a short paragraph about the different kinds of transport you use. Pay particular attention to the punctuation.

Writing (Task 1)

> COURSEBOOK page 110, EXPERT WRITING page 197

Understand the task

1 Look at the writing task in Exercise 2a. Read the rubric and answer these questions.

   1 In general terms, what is the focus of the graph?
   2 Do we know which country supplied the data?
   3 What time period is covered?
   4 Which data are predicted?

Represent data clearly and accurately

2a Look at the bar chart below. What does the x (vertical) axis show? What does the y (horizontal) axis show?

The graph below shows the percentage of car ownership in one country between 1995 and 2015 (with predicted figures for 2025).

Summarise the information by selecting and reporting the main features, and make comparisons where relevant.

Write at least 150 words.

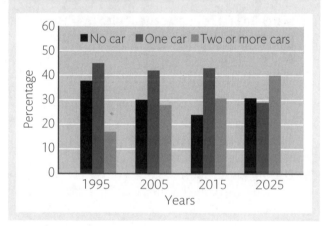

b Look carefully at the data shown in the chart and answer the questions.

   1 How many different categories of car ownership are shown? What are they?
   2 Which category of ownership declined significantly between 1995 and 2015?
   3 Which category increased between 1995 and 2015?
   4 Which category stayed roughly similar between 1995 and 2015?
   5 Which trends are predicted to change by 2025?

c Look at the opening paragraph of a sample answer to the task in Exercise 2a. Choose the correct option in *italics* to complete the paragraph.

The bar chart indicates a number of clear 1 indications / trends / lines in ownership of cars in one European country 2 in / to / between 1995 and 2015, but a 3 decline / reversal / rise of one of these patterns is predicted in the near future.

Identify inaccuracies in writing

3a Look at the rubric for the writing task below. Make notes on what you could include in both the introduction and summary overview.

The table below shows reasons migrants gave for moving from rural to urban areas, in one country, in the period 1980–2010.

Summarise the information by selecting and reporting the main features, and make comparisons where relevant.

	1980	1990	2000	2010
For a definite job	28	23	19	12
To look for work	22	20	25	35
For formal study	13	7	10	12
To accompany spouse/family member	33	32	31	32
No single reason	4	18	15	9

b Read the paragraph taken from the middle part of an answer to this task. The writer has made six mistakes. Underline the mistakes.

By compare, the figures for those moving because they were seeking work arose steadily about the same period – from 22 percent to 35 percent. The percent of migrants moving in order to accompany a spouse or family member was the highest in 1980 and remains steady during the 30 years, only varying at 2 percent in the whole period.

c Match the mistakes you underlined with the type of mistake 1–4.

   1 vocabulary choice   3 preposition
   2 word form   4 tense/aspect

d Write corrections for the mistakes you underlined.

Test practice

4a Write your answer for the test task in Exercise 3a. Write at least 150 words.

b When you finish, proofread your work for accuracy of data, grammar and vocabulary.

TEST STRATEGY

Bar charts and tables enable people to make comparisons very easily. Take time before you start writing to identify differences between different elements, for example number of cars, and dates, for example between 1995 and subsequent years. Make sure you convey clearly what is the same and what is different.

Listening (Section 1)

> COURSEBOOK pages 108 and 111

Understand the task

1   Look at the listening task in Exercise 3a. Underline the key words in questions 1–3. What do you think the recording will be about?

Identify distractors

2a   Read the question and options. Match the options A–C with the paraphrases 1–3 below.

> 1   What surprises Alex about the beginner's gliding lesson?
>
> A   the instructor sits behind the learner
> B   the learner takes control for part of the flight
> C   there is no time to practise before flying

    1   actually flies on her own
    2   trying it out in a controlled environment
    3   with a teacher behind you

b   Read the extract from the audio script and <u>underline</u> where you find the correct answer to the question. Circle the parts of the text which act as distractors.

Beth: It's two hours long and essentially what we do is start by giving a short talk to explain the basics, then you go up. It's a two-seater plane, with an instructor behind you and dual controls … so the learner actually flies on her own for part of the time, though of course the instructor takes off and lands.

Alex: Yes, but I'm amazed that you go straight up in the plane without trying it out beforehand, on a machine, even though it's with an instructor.

Beth: We have very experienced teachers and it's very safe.

Test practice

3a   Look at questions 1–3 of the test task. For each question, decide: 1 what the topic is, 2 what the specific focus is.

b   🔊 7.1   Complete the test task.

> *Questions 1–3*
>
> *Choose the correct letter A, B or C.*
>
> > 1   What is Alex most worried about for the lesson?
> > A   which type of flight will be most comfortable
> > B   having to land far from the launch site
> > C   what happens if there is bad weather
> > 2   Which group of members is increasing fastest in the club?
> > A   retired people
> > B   25–60-year-olds
> > C   under 25-year-olds
> > 3   What does the receptionist enjoy most about gliding?
> > A   the sense of peacefulness
> > B   the excitement of flying
> > C   the new perspective on the world

Test practice

4a   Read the questions below and think about how the speakers might include the different forms of distractors.

b   🔊 7.2   Complete the test task.

> *Questions 4–10*
>
> *Complete the form below.*
>
> *Write **NO MORE THAN TWO WORDS AND/OR A NUMBER** for each answer.*
>
> **Zest Gliding Club**
> Customer information form
>
> Name of learner: Rosie 4 _____
> Date of birth: 5 _____
> Height: 6 _____
> Medical conditions: problem with her 7 _____
> Contact number: 07753 42136
> Package type: 8 _____
> Address: Northbrook House, 9 _____ , Sandbrook, BL2 4PD
> Date of lesson: 25 August
> Time: 3p.m.
> Where client heard about our gliding club: 10 _____

Task analysis

5   What do you still need to focus on for Section 1 of the IELTS Listening paper? Make a list of ways you could improve.

Language development

> COURSEBOOK page 112, EXPERT LANGUAGE page 180

Improve grammatical accuracy

1   Choose the correct option in *italics* to complete the sentences.

   1   *A / The* school I go to is about 2km from my home.
   2   There is *a / the* special bus service to take children to school.
   3   A lot of children *walk / walks* to school with their friends.
   4   Nobody *come / comes* to school by bike.
   5   Both the head teacher and her assistant *travel / travels* to school by car.
   6   There are always one or two children who *arrive / arrives* late.

2a   Read the text below. Tick (✓) the underlined words which are correct, and cross (✗) those which are incorrect.

Travel to school

To assist in shaping its transport policy, **1** a̲ Department of Transport in the UK **2** conducts annual surveys to find out how people usually travel. One of these surveys, which **3** were̲ carried out in 2014, looked at how children travel to school. It found that for very short trips, walking is **4** a̲ main mode of travel for children of all ages. However, for trips of over 2 miles, most primary schoolchildren **5** goes̲ by car, whereas secondary schoolchildren generally **6** take̲ the bus.

b   For each incorrect word in Exercise 2a, say why is it incorrect.

c   Correct the incorrect words in Exercise 2a.

3   Complete the text with the correct form of the words below.

be (x2)	find	give	go	it	one

Going to school with an adult

A 2014 survey **1** _____ that 88 percent of children aged seven to ten **2** _____ usually accompanied to school by an adult. About **3** _____ third of children aged eleven to thirteen also **4** _____ to school with an adult. The children **5** _____ two reasons for this. Firstly, **6** _____ is convenient for the adult to accompany them and carry their bags. Secondly, the distance to school **7** _____ too great for them to travel alone.

4   Put the words in the correct order to make sentences.

   1   solution / ban / One / to / is / cars / near / area / from / traffic / to / the / congestion / schools
   _____

   2   convenience / important / is / adults' / Children's / more / safety / than
   _____

   3   to / for / to / The / is / best / school / get / children / way / walk / to
   _____

   4   inexpensive / safety / increasing / Pedestrian / are / of / an / way / crossings
   _____

   5   benefit / exercise / Both / from / parents /getting / and / children
   _____

   6   problems / by / of / congestion / Air / is / traffic / pollution / the / is / one / caused
   _____

5   Answer the questions.

   1   What kind of grammar mistakes do you usually make?
   2   How could you reduce the number of mistakes you make?

Vocabulary

> **COURSEBOOK** page 112

Prepositions

1 Underline the prepositions in the text.

Rules for Cyclists (enforceable by law)

The speed limit is 15km per hour on footpaths, and 25km per hour on cycle paths.

Bicycles must be equipped with lights which are visible from the front and rear. They must be used during hours of darkness (between 7p.m. and 7a.m.).

A maximum of two people cycling side by side is allowed on roads where there are two or more lanes going in the same direction, except on roads with bus lanes.

2 Complete the text with the prepositions below. You can use the prepositions more than once.

at   between   for   in   of   on   through   to   with

Recommendations 1 _____ cyclists and users 2 _____ disability scooters

The guiding principles for these are safety 3 _____ all road users; simplicity and clarity; and achieving a balance 4 _____ the needs of different road users.

- Always give way 5 _____ pedestrians, especially the most vulnerable.

- Slow down, and be prepared to stop 6 _____ areas 7 _____ a high number 8 _____ pedestrians, e.g. 9 _____ bus stops.

- Push your bicycle when passing 10 _____ crowded pedestrian areas.

- Never ride 11 _____ pavements.

- Always stop and help or exchange contact details when you are involved 12 _____ an accident.

3a Underline the mistakes in the sentences.

1 Among 1990 and 2015, global airline passenger numbers rose from 1 billion to 3.5 billion.

2 In 2016, the two largest markets of domestic airline passengers were the USA and China.

3 Every tonne in aviation fuel burned produces between 3.15 and 3.18 tonnes of CO_2.

4 The efficiency of aircraft and engines has significantly improved after the early 1960s.

5 Jet aircraft today are above 80 percent more fuel efficient than the jets of the 1960s.

b Correct the errors in the sentences in Exercise 3a.

4 Complete the text with suitable propositions.

Buses in Singapore

1 _____ the last 11 years, wheelchair-accessible buses have been serving more routes right 2 _____ the island. 3 _____ 2015, 85 percent 4 _____ the bus fleet has been fitted 5 _____ ramps. We aim to have all buses fully wheelchair accessible 6 _____ the next few years. All bus stops 7 _____ Singapore provide bus route information guides to help you plan your journey 8 _____ your destination. Several bus stops are equipped 9 _____ real-time bus arrival information, to keep commuters better informed. You can use a mobile app to get more information 10 _____ bus arrival times.

5 Underline the preposition in *italics* in the first sentence which matches the meaning given in the second sentence.

1 The highways project will be completed *by / before* 2020.
The highways project will definitely be completed in 2019.

2 The airport was closed *to / between* August and September.
The airport was closed once.

3 The journey time was reduced *by / to* 10 minutes after the road was widened.
The journey took 10 minutes after the road was widened.

4 Ferry fares decreased *by / from* 12 euros in 2016.
Ferry fares were 12 euros cheaper in 2016.

5 The tourists looked out *from / at* the cruise ship.
The tourists were on the cruise ship.

6 There are three classes of airline seating *amongst / besides* the more expensive ones.
There are three expensive types of seating.

6a Choose the correct option in *italics* to complete the quiz questions.

1 Which U.S. airport has the highest number of planes flying *in / through* it?

2 *After / By* which person is New York's international airport named?

3 *At / In* which country are the express trains referred to as 'bullet trains'?

4 Can you name three countries *through / across* which the Silk Road passed?

5 *Between / Through* which oceans does the Panama Canal run?

6 *During / Between* which century did steam train services begin operating?

b Answer the quiz questions in Exercise 6a.

Speaking (Part 1)

> COURSEBOOK pages 107 and 113,
> EXPERT SPEAKING page 187

Vocabulary development

1 Match the words about travel (1–8) with the meanings (A–H).

1	breakdown	5	delay
2	change	6	fare
3	commuter	7	peak time
4	connection	8	season ticket

A a scheduled transport link
B the busiest period in the day
C when a vehicle stops working
D a pre-paid travel pass for a certain length of time
E getting off one bus or train and getting on another bus or train
F the price of a journey
G a person who regularly travels from home to work
H when a bus or other vehicle doesn't start or travel on time

2 Read questions 1–6 about bus travel. Make notes about how you might answer them.

1 How often do you travel by bus?
2 Are bus journeys expensive where you live?
3 Do you have to wait for a long time to get on a bus?
4 How comfortable are bus journeys?
5 What do you do on a bus journey to pass the time?
6 How easy is it for disabled passengers to get on a bus?

Speak more accurately

3 Read some answers to the questions in Exercise 2. Underline any mistakes and suggest a correction.

1 I'm usually only travelling by bus when my car breaks down. Maybe once or twice in a year.
2 It depends when you want to go in a bus with air conditioning or not. The fare on those buses is three times as much as the fare on ordinary buses.
3 Not really. The buses where I live are quite frequent, especially over peak times. Maybe every five minutes.
4 They are very comfortable. Before five years the city council ordered many new buses, so they are clean and they have more space than the old ones.
5 I wear my earphones and I hear music on my phone, so the journey passes very quickly.
6 Some of buses have a special low step that the driver can operate. It makes it easy if you can't walk well.

TEST STRATEGY

The time to improve your accuracy is in the months and weeks before you take the exam. During the Speaking test, don't focus on accuracy as this will have a negative effect on your fluency. Even if you realise you've made a mistake, carry on talking.

Test practice

4a 🔊 7.3 Listen to the questions about getting to work or college. Make notes about how you might answer them.

b 🔊 7.4 Listen to a student answering the questions. Note down any useful vocabulary you hear.

c Listen to the questions in Exercise 4a again and answer them. If possible, record your answers.

Assess and improve

5 Listen to the recordings you made and answer the questions.

1 Which types of mistakes did you make?
 • the wrong verb tense
 • a mismatch between the subject and the verb
 • the wrong word
 • the wrong pronunciation
 • other
2 Can you correct your mistakes?

Writing (Task 1)

> COURSEBOOK page 116, EXPERT WRITING page 197

Understand the task

1a Look at the table in the writing task below. What is the main focus of the data?

> *The table below shows the number of hours' delay experienced by commuters in different-sized cities between 1995 and 2015 (with predicted figures for 2025).*
>
> *Summarise the information by selecting and reporting the main features, and make comparisons where relevant.*
>
> *Write at least 150 words.*
>
> **Hours of delay experienced per commuter per year (average)**
>
> | City (by size of population)/Year | 1985 | 1995 | 2005 | 2015 | 2025 (predicted) |
> |---|---|---|---|---|---|
> | Small (<500,000) | 7 | 21 | 27 | 21 | 20 |
> | Medium (500,000– 1 million) | 9 | 22 | 31 | 21 | 15 |
> | Large (1–3 million) | 11 | 38 | 42 | 36 | 30 |
> | Metropolis (>3 million) | 19 | 50 | 60 | 50 | 40 |

b Answer the questions about the features of the table in Exercise 1a.

1 What do the figures in columns 2–6 show?
2 How are the cities categorised?
3 What is the timeframe for the table?
4 Which column shows predicted figures?

c Answer the questions about the content of the table.

1 Which period shows the biggest increase in figures?
2 Which period shows a decrease?
3 Which categories of city show significant change? When?

d Tick the features (1–5) which you would include in a summary overview for this table.

1 Repeat words used in the task rubric.
2 Use linkers, e.g. *However* or *Also*.
3 Start with some detailed figures for different years.
4 Start with a word like *Overall* to show that you're looking at the bigger picture.
5 Use adjectives/intensifiers for emphasis.

e Write a one- or two-sentence overview for the table.

Language and content

2a Look at the table again and decide if the statements are true (T) or false (F).

1 The table shows the total hours of delay for the population in each city.
2 The figures for 2015 and 2025 are predicted.
3 The smaller cities have shorter delays per person than the bigger ones.
4 There was a steady increase in congestion over the 30 years 1985–2015.
5 The largest increases in delays occurred between 1985 and 1995.
6 The longest delays happened in 2005.
7 All categories of city will experience shorter delays in future but to varying degrees.

b Correct the false statements in Exercise 2a.

3a Which two tenses (verb forms) will you use to write your answer? Why?

b Complete the table with the adjectives below.

significant   slight   major   small   noticeable
serious   minor   striking   relative

Large change	Small change

c Write four sentences about the data in the table using the words in the table.

There was a slight improvement in figures for delay between 2005 and 2015.

Plan the task

4 Plan your answer to the task in Exercise 1a. Make notes about the following.

1 How you can group any trends or features.
2 How you can support these with data.
3 How you can give an effective summary overview.
4 What language you need to use.

Write your report

5a Write your answer to the task in Exercise 1a. Write at least 150 words. You have 18 minutes to write your answer.

b After you have written your answer, spend 2 minutes checking your work. Check for the following:

1 The information is an accurate reflection of the information shown in the table.
2 Any errors in grammar, vocabulary or spelling. If you see any, correct them.

Assess and improve

6 Have you noticed any mistakes you make repeatedly in doing this task? Make a note of them and try to improve your work, focusing on these areas.

8 Social networks

8a Community

Reading (*Yes/No/Not given*; Multiple choice: select two answers)

> **COURSEBOOK** pages 120–121

Before you read

1 Read the passage quickly and answer the question.

What is the main idea in the reading passage?

A Urban planners should take people into account.
B Building developments should be completed more quickly.
C Communities should be consulted before planners make decisions.

Identify the writer's views/claims

2a Look at the underlined phrases in the statement below. Find phrases in the first paragraph of the reading passage which have a similar meaning.

People who go to live in <u>new inner-city buildings</u> may not <u>mix</u> well <u>socially</u> with the <u>other inhabitants</u> in the area.

b Read the first paragraph of the reading passage carefully, and decide whether it expresses an opinion. If it does, is it the same opinion as the one in the statement in Exercise 2a?

Test practice

3 Underline the key words/phrases in questions 1–6 below. Then follow the same steps as in Exercises 2a and 2b to complete the test task.

Questions 1-6

Do the following statements agree with the views of the writer? Write

YES *if the statement agrees with the views of the writer*

NO *if the statement contradicts the views of the writer*

NOT GIVEN *if it is impossible to say what the writer thinks about this*

1 The development of Kings Cross in London has been very successful.
2 Where big community projects are concerned, a sense of community is created relatively quickly.
3 Residents of retiree communities in the USA appear to be generally happy with their new life.
4 Putting privately run facilities at the heart of community developments can create social harmony.

5 The city of Portland provides a positive model of development for other U.S. cities.
6 It is desirable for planners to take social factors into account when designing urban developments.

> **HELP**

3 This statement may or may not be the same as the writer's opinion, but does the reading passage tell us?

Test practice

4 Read the strategies below and complete the test task.

• Underline the key words in the question.
• Find the place in the reading passage which has words/phrases with similar a meaning.
• Read the text carefully in that part of the reading passage.
• Decide which of the five options are correct.

Questions 7-8

*Choose **TWO** letters, **A-E**.*

What does the writer say about gated communities?

A Residents usually go outside the gates for recreation.
B Gated communities are comparable in some ways to high-rise buildings.
C Criticism of gated communities is largely unjustified.
D Such developments are artificial and misguided.
E Members of gated communities enjoy good relationships with each other.

Question 9-10

*Choose **TWO** letters, **A-E**.*

What does the writer say about Milton Keynes?

A It has been a town for several centuries.
B It is generally criticised by people from outside the area.
C It has taken many years to develop fully.
D It was constructed for people living in London.
E It was originally an expensive place to live.

Building Development for Communities

The character of a community isn't just about buildings, it's about people. New urban developments pose a challenge to social cohesion between existing residents and newcomers, putting pressure on urban planners to understand better how neighbourhoods interact.

Interaction with neighbours is an important part of personal wellbeing, according to research published recently by Sheffield University in the UK. Yet a recent Chinese study found that there were low levels of social interaction in new housing developments built in older, deprived areas. In some other Asian cities, developments are often regarded simply as high-rise building projects, but compartmentalising space in this way can make a building exclusive and intimidating. In London, for example, leaders of the Church of England are worried about the social consequences of the wave of new high-rise buildings spreading along the city's waterfront. The Church is so concerned that in one area it has employed an outreach worker to build links between established communities and the incomers.

Another type of development which presents similar challenges is gated communities. These single-entry, private housing estates represent the archetypal closed society. They have long been criticised for their reluctance to integrate new residents into the surrounding community. In addition to restricted access housing, they often offer private outdoor spaces. One email promoting a collection of gated properties in New York reads, 'Rather than trekking to a public park, residents of these luxury residences can enjoy the sun in their own park-like private space.' Such schemes are not real places, and are precisely the wrong approach to development. Another example of such a development can be found in Chelsea Harbour in London. Closed off, it makes no effort to connect with the bits of the city around it, and it denies non-residents the opportunity to interact with it.

One key to making a newly developed area attractive to both prospective residents and visitors is to harness the history and draw in outsiders. A good example of this is the Kings Cross area of London, where retaining some of the older social spaces alongside the new has added richness and variety.

Another key strategy is to consider new developments over a multi-decade timescale at the planning stage. We should recognise that big community developments are 50-year projects. It takes a couple of generations for people to start feeling that they are part of a place, and for the place to have a maturity about it. By this time people have cultural and community connections; they have grown up with the children in the neighbourhood, gone to school together, and got married to someone within the community.

A good example of this is the city of Milton Keynes in the UK. Originally built as a 'new town' for the less well-off in the 1960s, to relieve housing congestion in London, Milton Keynes only recently acquired a positive profile in the external world. Now it is generally regarded as an exciting, growing city, rather than as a place where people went out of necessity because they could not afford to live anywhere else.

An attempt to foster such social bonds within a shorter space of time can be found in the USA. Over the past few decades there, community developments specifically designed for retirees have evolved from catering simply for people in the last stages of their lives, with facilities dominated by medical care. The trend is now to create a more lifestyle-focused product, aimed at baby-boomers[1] who want to downsize, but are still active. These 'active adult' communities offer a wide range of physical and social activities, from golf courses to exercise classes, in a bid to offer their target customers not just a home, but also a ready-made group of friends.

Yet the design of such developments illustrates a significant change in the way in which new communities function. In the UK in the mid-nineties, a church or a community centre would usually be at the heart of a new housing estate. Today, it is more often a cafe, gym or other paid-entry business. This means that social and economic inequalities are being built in. As a result, any sense of community could be hindered before the development even gets underway. All the more reason for architects, planners and politicians to think about the community they are trying to create before they start work on its physical design.

Cities all over the world are approaching the problem in different ways. In New York, where space is at a high premium, the mayor has argued that building at higher densities would preserve the social mix. At present there are strict limits on how high a residential building can rise, but the mayor has pointed out that relaxing the regulations and adding an extra storey to buildings may allow someone who has lived for 40 or 50 years in a neighbourhood to stay on.

The U.S. city of Portland, in Oregon, has established a benchmark for the country on account of its innovative planning, reuse of old buildings and industrial space, really good public and community spaces, green transport with trams, and a proper cycling network.

Holland is also a trail blazer in urban design. Dutch cities have evolved with a community focus: children play on the street, and people cycle instead of driving cars.

In conclusion, understanding how neighbourhoods develop socially can help planners improve their work. Get it wrong, and a new development can become a concrete wasteland, unloved, branded a failure, and torn down within a few decades. Get it right and it can help a city to grow without pricing out the workers it needs.

1 people who were born during the population explosion which occurred between 1946 and the mid-1960s

Task analysis

5   Answer the questions.

1   Can you tell the difference between a *Yes/No* and a *Not given* statement?

2   Can you recognise paraphrases?

Vocabulary

> **COURSEBOOK** page 122

Vocabulary related to community

1a Choose the correct option in *italics* to complete the definitions.

1 A detailed plan for achieving a particular goal is called *a scheme / an inhabitant*.
2 A group of people or things which are connected with one another, and which form a unit or a system, is called a *division / network*.
3 A *sector / project* is one part, or portion, of a whole system, such as the economy.
4 A group of people who have similar characteristics, or who have common interests, is known as a *community / structure*.
5 A person who lives in a particular place for a long time is known as a *network / resident*.
6 A *policy / structure* is a set of procedures for doing something which has been officially agreed.
7 A local area and the people living in it are sometimes referred to as a *neighbourhood / sector*.
8 The basic parts of an object or organisation, and the way that these are connected, is called a *guideline / structure*.

b Complete the sentences with the correct form of the words in Exercise 1a.

1 In the UK, a _____ known as Neighbourhood Watch aims to increase safety; it involves residents sharing information about security issues.
2 A _____ of cycle lanes connects different parts of Copenhagen, and allows residents to visit friends nearby without using a car.
3 Local councils regularly amend some of their social _____ after carrying out surveys of residents.
4 In western countries, far fewer people are employed in the agricultural _____ today than in the nineteenth century.
5 People from different parts of the world who play online games together often regard themselves as a _____ .
6 Universal education has had a considerable impact on the social _____ of many countries.

Academic collocations

2 Underline the word on the left which collocates best with *community*.

1 cultural	ethnic	racial	community
2 local	area	narrow	community
3 countryside	rural	rustic	community
4 virtual	unreal	computer	community
5 open	fuller	wider	community

3 Complete the sentences with the words below.

current   economic   key   national   social

1 There are some issues which are recognised as too important for individual regions to deal with: there has to be a _____ policy.
2 As soon as a new democratic government is elected, it takes the opportunity to implement its _____ policies, of whatever kind.
3 Interest rates on lending were raised by the central bank, in line with the government's _____ policy.
4 There has recently been a change in the government's approach to public health: their _____ policy is to concentrate on health education.
5 It is widely recognised that a new _____ policy is required to support young adults who are at risk of turning to crime.

Describe emotions

4a Match the prepositions below with the adjectives (1–7). You can use the prepositions more than once. Use your dictionary if necessary.

about   by   of   to   with

1 appreciative	5 overwhelmed
2 delighted	6 sympathetic
3 devoted	7 dreadful
4 outraged	

EXPERT LANGUAGE

Outraged, *dreadful* and *overwhelmed* describe very strong emotions.

b Are the adjectives in Exercise 4a usually positive (+), negative (-) or both (+/-)? Write them in the correct place in the table.

+	-	+/-

c Answer the following questions about people and situations.

1 Describe one kind of situation or behaviour that makes you feel outraged.
2 Describe an occasion when you felt appreciative.
3 Describe a person who was very supportive when you had a problem.
4 Describe a character in a book or a film who you feel sympathetic towards.
5 Describe an everyday situation which makes you feel disgruntled.
6 Describe an occasion when you felt overwhelmed by emotion.

TEST STRATEGY

In the second part of the Speaking test, you often have to talk about your feelings.

Language development

> **COURSEBOOK** page 125, **EXPERT GRAMMAR** page 180

Review of future forms

1 Choose the correct option in *italics* to complete the sentences.

1 The mayor *will be awarded / is awarding* prizes at the carnival next week.
2 The builders *will have finished / will have been finishing* repairs to the village hall by the end of the year.
3 A neighbourhood meeting *will have been held / will be held* on the 8th of September.
4 The local choir *will have sung / will be singing* at a concert in aid of Unicef next week.
5 There *is going to be / was going to be* a cricket match in the local park, but it was cancelled because of heavy rain.
6 The town *will be / will have been* a good place for families to live once the new school opens.
7 Next year the village *will have been holding / will be holding* an annual summer fete for a century.
8 Every year the neighbourhood committee *is organising / organises* a sale of flowers and cakes to raise money for charity.

2 Complete the sentences (1–8) with the verb phrases (A–H).

1 In the future the internet _____ more like electricity is today.
2 Twenty five years from now, the term 'social media' _____ .
3 In 2039, extremely fast mobile wireless broadband _____ into every device, even the most affordable ones.
4 In just a few years, electronic tablets _____ a thing of the past.
5 Soon computer-controlled devices in the home _____ how much food we have and generating shopping lists.
6 One thing about the future is sure: the world _____ smaller and smaller as social media continue to develop.
7 By 2030, IT specialists _____ a way of ensuring that social media networks are secure.
8 Soon mobile devices _____ so that they are more suitable for use by the elderly.

A will have become
B is going to get
C will be supplied to our homes
D will be adapted
E will have been incorporated
F will have disappeared
G will be monitoring
H will have found

3 Complete the text with the correct form of the verbs below.

be (x3)   can   double   evolve   integrate   overwhelm   predict

The future of social media

Experts **1** _____ that, in just a few years, social media usage **2** _____ nearly _____ . By then 2.44 billion of the world's population **3** _____ on social networks. Looking further ahead, most experts agree that, by 2039, use of social media **4** _____ into our daily lives in a multitude of ways. The challenge **5** _____ how to cope with the massive amounts of data that **6** _____ us when that happens.

Mobility is the first step towards the portable future of social media, and wearable devices **7** _____ a big part of that. These **8** _____ probably _____ into an implanted device in our bodies that will connect to everything around us. We **9** _____ to share a taste, a sensation and a smell.

Speculate on the future

4 For each of the predictions (1–4), choose the writer's degree of certainty from those below.

35%   75%   90%   100%

1 As more infrastructure is provided, global sales of mobile phones are likely to rise.
2 As more infrastructure is provided, global sales of mobile phones are bound to rise.
3 As more infrastructure is provided, global sales of mobile phones will rise.
4 As more infrastructure is provided, global sales of mobile phones might rise.

5 Write sentences about yourself or your friends, predicting what will be happening in 2025. Use the structures in Exercise 4 to show your degree of certainty about each prediction.

Writing (Task 2)

> COURSEBOOK page 126, EXPERT WRITING page 198

Understand the task

1 Read the exam task below. Which of the following are you required to do in your essay?

1 Explain what in recent years has caused problems in both extended and nuclear families.
2 Discuss what has caused the change in family structure and what effects have resulted from it.
3 Describe the differences between a nuclear and an extended family and how family structures are going to change in the future.

In recent years there has been a significant change in family structure, from a more extended to a nuclear family structure.

What are the reasons for this and what are the possible effects?

Understand situations, causes and effects

2a Read the first paragraph of the sample answer to the task in Exercise 1. The sentences are in the wrong sequence. Put them in the correct order.

A There are a number of reasons for this change, but perhaps the most influential is that people increasingly value individualism and their right to privacy.

B In recent years in many parts of the world, there has been a noticeable shift from a more extended to a nuclear family structure.

C In the past, it was the norm for several generations and members of the immediate family, e.g. aunts and nephews, to live in the same house but nowadays the trend is for smaller households with just two adults living with their offspring.

D A second reason might be economic – it would be difficult to accommodate more than two adults and two or three children in houses of the size which is common today and on current levels of income.

b When you have reordered the paragraph, think about the functions of the different sentences in Exercise 2a and decide if the following statements are True (T) of False (F). Correct any false statements.

1 The function of the first two sentences is to clarify what change has happened in family structures.
2 The function of the third sentence is to make a transition from the introduction, presenting the first reason for change.
3 The function of the fourth sentence is to make a transition to possible effects.

c Think of one more reason (cause) why family structures might have changed.

Develop a situation, cause and effect paragraph

3a Read the essay tasks below. For each one, do the following:
1 Identify the general situation.
2 Decide whether you must write about a) causes, b) effects or c) both causes and effects.
3 Highlight key elements in the first 'statement' sentence.

A Fewer workers nowadays are choosing to join a trade union. Identify the causes and possible effects.

B People without paid employment tend to suffer in social as well as financial terms. What are the reasons for this?

C On average, women tend to have lower-paid jobs than men. What do you think are the main causes of this? What are the effects?

b Choose the correct option in *italics* to complete the first paragraph of a sample answer to question A in Exercise 3a.

Over the past 20 years or so, in certain parts of the world, there has been a decline in the number of people choosing to join trade unions. **1** *This could be despite* / *This could be due to* changes in workplace culture where there is less of a sense of collegiality and more of individualism. These are cogent reasons for the drop in union membership but **2** *this decline can have negative consequences* / *this drop might make people decide that* both for the individual worker and for the workforce as a whole. **3** *A further possible cause* / *The next problem* is that with little disposable income, union fees are seen as too expensive. **4** *The last issue is* / *Another factor could be* that in a time of high unemployment, people have concerns about losing their job and do not want to be seen as subversive and working against the management to secure improved wages and conditions.

Writing practice

4a Make an essay plan for one of the tasks in Exercise 3a. Note down key vocabulary and link phrases from Exercise 3b which you can use in your answer.

b Write the essay for your chosen task.

c When you have finished your essay, consider the following questions.

1 Have you identified causes and/or effects as required in the essay task?
2 Have you shown transitions clearly, using appropriate link phrases?
3 Have you provided an effective introduction clarifying the initial statement?
4 Have you presented your points in a logical sequence?
5 Have you concluded your essay effectively?

8b Communication

Listening (Section 2)

> COURSEBOOK pages 124 and 127

Before you listen

1   Read the instructions for questions 1–6 in the test task in Exercise 3a and answer these questions.

    1   What do you think is the role of the speaker? Where might you hear him/her speaking?

    2   Underline the key words in options A–G. What synonyms can you give for each word you underlined?

Follow lines of argument

2   Below are sentences taken from the first part of the audio script. Put them in the correct order to create a coherent argument.

    A   This basically follows the progress of humankind from its earliest beginnings to fascinating pieces of modern technology like the credit card.

    B   I've been having a great time listening in to some of this year's most popular podcasts – some taken from mainstream radio and others independently produced.

    C   Starting with one of the most respected and widely praised, called *Object Lessons*.

    D   I really like the way the items and themes have been selected.

Test practice

3a   🔊 8.1 Complete the test task.

Questions 1–6

What does the reviewer say is the best feature of each podcast?

Choose SIX answers from the box and write the correct letter A–H, next to questions 1–6.

Opinions
A   combines humour with informed discussion
B   is extremely honest
C   avoids using a lot of technical terms
D   uses technology in a creative way
E   makes an excellent choice of topics
F   doesn't follow audience expectations
G   features multilingual presenters
H   asks searching questions

Podcasts
1   Object Lessons ___   4   Team Science ___
2   Sky Stories ___   5   The Daily ___
3   Football Focus ___   6   Radio Headways ___

b   Were your predictions about the synonyms in Exercise 1 correct?

c   Listen again and note down words which helped you pick out each answer.

Test practice

4a   Look at questions 7–10. Highlight key words in the stem (the first line/question of each item). Match these words with their synonyms below.

gained/understood   present condition
amazed   liking best   appropriate
very difficult situation   primary/major reason

> **TEST STRATEGY**
>
> Be aware that for some questions you are asked to identify the main reason. You will often hear people giving other reasons but you are required to choose the principle one.

b   🔊 8.2 Complete the test task.

Questions 7–10

Choose the correct letter A, B or C.

7   Jake's main reason for preferring radio to TV is because it
    A   encourages people to be critical of editors' choices.
    B   is able to focus on really important issues.
    C   can speed up interaction with the audience.

8   What does Jake believe radio broadcasters have learnt during times of economic crisis?
    A   when to respond to listeners' worries
    B   how to understand what listeners want
    C   what listeners' think about budget cuts

9   What is Jake most surprised about regarding the current position of radio?
    A   It is rapidly growing in popularity.
    B   It is now considered fashionable.
    C   It is well thought of by people in other media.

10   According to Jake, radio is well suited to a digital format because
    A   being easy to carry makes it flexible.
    B   it tends to be very low cost.
    C   it requires minimum technology.

Task analysis

5   Analyse your answers using these questions.

    1   What features of the talk helped you understand where you were on the test paper?

    2   How does analysing the questions before you listen help you understand the talk better?

Language development

> COURSEBOOK page 128, EXPERT GRAMMAR page 181

Cause and effect linking words

1 Answer the questions about the words/phrases below.

as (conjunction)   as a result   because   consequently   since (conjunction)   therefore

1 Which of these introduce the cause of something?
2 Which of these introduce the effects of something?
3 Which of these are normally followed by a comma?
4 Which of these introduce a clause?
5 Which of these introduce the main clause in a sentence?

> **EXPERT LANGUAGE**
>
> *Since* has more than one meaning. As well as introducing a reason for something, it can introduce a phrase or clause about time, e.g. *Since I was six years old.*
> *Because* and *because of* have the same meaning, but they are grammatically different. The former is a conjunction which introduces a clause of reason, and the latter is a preposition which introduces a noun phrase.
> *Due to* is a preposition and is followed by a noun phrase.

2 Choose the correct option in *italics* to complete the sentences.

1 The internet allows people to communicate with large numbers of people over great distances. *As a result, / As a result of* public campaigns are often well organised and effective.
2 In many parts of the world, rural migration is an ongoing trend *because / because of* there are many more job opportunities in cities.
3 Increasing numbers of women now benefit from higher education. *As a result of / Consequently,* there are more women in senior positions in the workplace.
4 *As a result / Due to* the fact that it has the youngest population in the world, one of Africa's key goals is to widen access to education.
5 In the 21st century there are far fewer isolated communities, *since / therefore* long-distance travel is much more affordable.
6 In many societies, the ratio of younger to older people has changed partly *as / because of* improvements in health care.
7 In some countries, many young graduates are unable to find work. *Therefore / Since* fewer people are choosing to go into higher education.
8 *Because / Due to* a shortage of doctors, some countries are recruiting health professionals from overseas.

3 Match the sentence beginnings (1–8) with the endings (A–H).

1 Due to the installation of underground cables
2 As a result of video conferencing systems
3 Some groups of people have been forced to migrate
4 More rural inhabitants can now do business
5 Employment in the electronics manufacturing industry has risen
6 Because of a new mobile phone app
7 It has become easier to obtain investment for business projects
8 Family cohesion may have suffered

A because of successive crop failures.
B fishermen in Uganda can receive storm alerts.
C as a result of time spent on social media.
D mobile phone connectivity in Africa has increased sharply.
E since the internet allows access to crowd funding.
F employees of international companies have to travel less often.
G due to ongoing demand for new hardware.
H as they can order goods and make payments by phone.

4 Complete the sentences using your own opinions and experience.

1 These days, an increasing number of adults live alone. Consequently, _____ .
2 Due to _____ some elderly people feel lonely.
3 Fights sometimes break out at football matches because _____ .
4 Some children experience bullying at school as a result of _____ .
5 In the UK, fewer girls choose to study engineering than boys, since _____ .
6 Because of _____ families are spending less time together.
7 I've been spending a lot of time studying lately, and as a result _____ .
8 As my English has improved a lot, _____ .

Vocabulary

> **COURSEBOOK** page 128

Noun phrases 2

1 Complete the sentences with the phrases below.

---

acute housing shortages   caring for an elderly population
free nursery education   increasing meat consumption
lowering the voting age   national health campaigns
physical punishment   the nuclear family

---

1 The result of _____ is a global shortage of agricultural land.
2 The issue of _____ is more serious in countries without state welfare systems.
3 The problem of _____ has given rise to long-term construction projects.
4 The success of _____ can be measured by examining medical statistics.
5 The average size of _____ has been going down in Europe for several decades.
6 The use of _____ to control children is illegal in many countries.
7 The benefits of _____ have been greatest for children from poor families.
8 The idea of _____ is popular amongst teenagers themselves.

2 Match the sentence beginnings (1–6) with the endings (A–F).

1 The question of how to attract more teachers into the profession
2 One common cause of marriage breakdowns
3 The problem of youth unemployment
4 The costs of providing more counselling services for stress
5 The issue of who should look after elderly people
6 The question of how people from different cultures can get on together

A is known to be financial problems.
B has been highlighted as a result of increasing globalisation.
C would be offset by reduced absenteeism in the workplace.
D could be partially solved by raising salaries.
E needs addressing urgently, as life expectancy is increasing.
F can only be solved by creating more training opportunities.

3 Write sentences from the prompts.
1 subject / family relationships / occur / frequently / young children / conversations
   The subject of family relationships occurs frequently in young children's conversations.
2 problem / youth unemployment / has / not addressed / properly / government

   _____

3 exact cause / autism / currently / not yet / know

   _____

4 topic / animal communication / common choice / psychology research

   _____

5 issue / how control / children's use / social media / not yet / resolve

   _____

6 cause / antisocial behaviour / may be / chemical imbalance / in / brain

   _____

4 Choose the correct option in *italics* to complete the text.

Crime and society

The purpose of the **1** *education system / justice system* is to uphold fairness in society. The welfare of both **2** *the criminal / the judge* and the victim are important.

The exact causes of **3** *criminal behaviour / prison reform* are complex, but the aim of **4** *prison sentences / crime prevention schemes* is to keep people from committing crimes in the first place. The design of the **5** *programmes / crimes* varies: some are run in groups, while others are for the individual.

The question of the **6** *rehabilitation / arrest* of convicted criminals is also important. The willingness of the **7** *police / prisoners* to change their behaviour is one factor in the success of schemes designed to help them.

5 Complete the sentences according to your own opinions and experience.

1 One cause of crime amongst young people is probably _____ .
2 One way of dealing with antisocial behaviour would be to _____ .
3 The problem of _____ is frequently mentioned by people who emigrate overseas.
4 The issue of employers who _____ is often mentioned by people who leave their jobs.
5 The likelihood of young people getting a job which _____ is now decreasing.
6 The failure of parents to _____ has consequences for children in later life.

Speaking (Part 2)

> **COURSEBOOK** pages 123 and 129,
> **EXPERT SPEAKING** page 123

Vocabulary development

1a Answer the questions about the phrases below.

down-to-earth	force of nature	larger-than-life
see eye to eye	tongue-tied	

1 Which of the phrases are adjectives?
2 Which is a verb phrase?
3 Which is a noun phrase?
4 Which phrase describes a temporary kind of behaviour?

b Which of the phrases in Exercise 1a would you use to describe:

1 a person who gets things done in a very determined way?
2 a person who is suddenly unable to think of what to say?
3 a person who is practical and realistic?
4 a person who is very outgoing and stands out in a group?
5 a situation where two people have the same opinion(s)?

2 🔊 **8.3** Listen to five speakers describing someone they know. Match each description to a phrase in Exercise 1a.

Speaker 1 _____

Speaker 2 _____

Speaker 3 _____

Speaker 4 _____

Speaker 5 _____

3a Choose the correct option in *italics* to complete the sentences.

1 My brother is very *warm-hearted / modest*. He's actually very clever as well as being good at sports, but he doesn't think so himself.
2 When you've got a problem and you want to talk about it, you want someone who's *attentive / conscientious* and won't keep interrupting.
3 My friend gave me this watch – it used to be hers but she had two – she's always very *sensitive / generous* like that.
4 I often lose my temper with people and get upset about little things, but my friend is the opposite, she's so *modest / tolerant*.
5 My cousin and I are both planning to run a marathon, but I sometimes skip training – I'm less *conscientious / attentive* than him.
6 My younger sister says she wants to be a nurse, but she hates seeing anyone get hurt, she's very *tolerant / sensitive*, so I don't think it's the right career for her.

b For each of the words below, choose one from Exercise 3a which is opposite in meaning.

1 narrow-minded
2 arrogant
3 distracted
4 lazy
5 mean
6 hard-hearted

Test practice

4a Read the task card below and think about how you will answer. Make notes.

b Talk for as long as you can on this topic. Time yourself, and record yourself if possible.

> *Describe a person you know who you enjoy spending time with.*
>
> *You should say:*
>
> > *how you know this person*
> >
> > *what he/she is like*
> >
> > *what kind of things you do with him/her*
>
> *and say why you enjoy spending time with this person.*

> **EXPERT LANGUAGE**
>
> *To be like* means 'to have a certain appearance or characteristics'. Don't confuse it with *to like*, which means 'to have a positive opinion about something or someone'.

Assess and improve

5 Answer the questions.

1 How long did you speak for?
2 Were your notes helpful? If not, how could you improve your notes?
3 Did you use a range of vocabulary to describe the person you know?

Writing (Task 2)

> **COURSEBOOK** pages 133–134, **EXPERT WRITING** page 198

Understand the task

1   Read the writing task below and answer the questions.

   1   What is the general context or situation being focused on?

   2   What things are being contrasted in the statement?

   3   What do you have to identify reasons for?

> *'These days, people succeed in their chosen profession because they are good communicators and not just experts in a particular field.'*
> *Discuss the reasons why this is the case.*

> **TEST STRATEGY**
>
> The task talks about the situation 'these days' so in your answer it's important to include a mention of what's happening now and how it might be different from the past.

Plan the task

2   Read a student's notes below for her/his plan for the essay in Exercise 1. Match the notes in column A with their functions in column B. Then work out the correct order for the whole essay.

1 Public wants facts about a given situation so they can make up their own minds	A Second reason
2 Research scientists have to persuade funders of importance of their work	B Concluding summary
3 Increasing use of IT means people have access to more facts	C Statement/Clarification of core assertion
4 Communication skills just as important as technical skills	D Example to illustrate main reason
5 Can't succeed in any job without communication skills	E Main reason

> **EXPERT LANGUAGE**
>
> You are strongly encouraged to use examples to give depth and substance to your writing. For this task, think of particular professions or occupations which would provide a good illustration of the importance of communication skills.

Language and content

> **TEST STRATEGY**
>
> It is important at levels 6.5 and above to use a wide range of vocabulary, which expresses ideas in an interesting and accurate way. It is also important to avoid repeating words in your essays.

3a   Complete the sentences with the words below.

> impact   convey   accessible   specialists   technical
> convince

   1   Good communicators are able to _____ key ideas in an engaging and _____ way .

   2   _____ learn their skills over many years of working in their respective fields.

   3   Experienced engineers are able to draw on a wealth of _____ knowledge in their field.

   4   Researchers must _____ funding agencies that their work will have a positive _____ on the public.

b   Read the paragraph below, which is part of a sample answer to this task. Underline and correct four mistakes. Identify which category of error is being made in this paragraph.

> Nowadays it is very difficultly to succeed in any occupation if you do not have the ability to communicate effective with others. This is very large because today there is such a wealth of information technology which is playing an increasing important role in almost all aspects of our lives and people in all walks of life can no longer choose to ignore it: they have to be able to use it well.

c   Correct the errors you found.

Write your essay

4a   Plan your answer using ideas about structure from Exercise 2, but giving your own response to the issue.

b   Write your answer to the task in Exercise 1. You should write at least 250 words and take approximately 30–40 minutes.

Assess and improve

5a   Check your writing and answer the questions.

   1   How well have you answered the question, identifying at least two reasons?

   2   Are your arguments logically ordered?

   3   Is the paragraph structure clear?

   5   Have you provided supporting examples for at least one of your points?

   5   Have you tried to use some of the vocabulary from Exercise 3a?

   6   What improvements can you make?

b   Underline any new/unusual items of vocabulary you have tried to use in your answer. What words and phrases do you now feel you can use in future writing?

9 Being successful

9a A recipe for success

Reading (Multiple choice; *Yes/No/Not given*)

> **COURSEBOOK** pages 136–137

Before you read

1 You are going to read a passage about a science laboratory. Tick any of the words below which you might expect to find in the passage.

measure	test	scientist	mechanic	technician
lecturer	equipment			

Infer meaning and attitude

2 Read the passage quickly and answer the questions.

   1 Which two groups of people is the laboratory designed to investigate?

   2 Is the writer's impression of the laboratory mainly positive or mainly negative?

Test practice

3a Underline the key words in question 1 of the test task below, then follow steps 1 and 2.

   1 Scan the reading passage to locate the section relating to this. Read this section very carefully.

   2 Choose the correct option (A, B, C or D).

b Follow the same procedure and complete the rest of the test task.

Questions 1–5
Choose the correct letter, A, B, C or D.

1 What does the writer say about 'marginal gains'?
  A They can be very difficult to measure accurately.
  B Sportspeople are highly aware of their importance.
  C In some fields the concept has been slow to make an impact.
  D They are most likely to result from changes in the brain.

2 The tests at HPL may take longer if
  A the subject has an extreme goal.
  B brain function is being measured.
  C the subject is relatively unfit.
  D more complex equipment is used.

3 The lab's study of a rugby team assessed
  A physical performance.
  B decision-making skills.
  C scoring frequency.
  D training materials.

4 What is Kelly Holmes' role at HPL?
  A She undergoes tests for research purposes.
  B She advises on the kind of equipment needed.
  C She helps to monitor the performance of other athletes.
  D She gives advice from an athlete's perspective.

5 According to Mark Langley, the main purpose of HPL is to
  A find solutions to health problems in the wider community.
  B help athletes to overcome performance problems.
  C reduce the pain associated with various medical conditions.
  D advise sports trainers on the most effective programmes.

Test practice

4 Follow the same procedure as in Exercise 3a and complete the test task.

Questions 6–10

Do the following statements agree with the views/claims of the writer? Write
YES *if the statement agrees with the views/claims of the writer*
NO *if the statement contradicts the views/claims of the writer*
NOT GIVEN *if it impossible to say what the writer thinks about this*

6 HPL uses the most up-to-date experimental methods and equipment.
7 Studying the performance of athletes is the best way of studying people's performance in general.
8 HPL is the world's leading organisation for training athletes.
9 The lab's findings are more relevant for sporting issues than for medical issues.
10 The initial impression created by the HPL lab is unfavourable.

Measuring the performance of the human body

The Human Performance Lab (HPL) in west London was built in 2013. The 18,000sq ft facility combines cutting-edge scientific research with the latest technology, to both push the limits of human performance and deepen understanding of health in general. The lab has worked with international athletes including racing driver Jenson Button, Paralympic Games gold medal winner David Weir, and world champion triathlete brothers Alistair and Jonny Brownlee. It can re-create any environmental, training or performance scenario under one roof, in high-altitude conditions or at temperatures of minus 20 degrees Centigrade. Both athletes and the general public are tested at the lab.

The elite athlete is the perfect case study to examine human function. By using such extreme subjects, who regularly undergo the most extreme physiological stress, we have a powerful model to enhance our understanding of the mechanisms that underpin health and performance. HPL has 15,000 scientists across the world representing a range of expertise, from neuroscientists looking at cognitive function, to performance scientists measuring physiology, and dieticians observing how diet changes health and performance. This expert community, which is growing rapidly, comes together on the HPL secure website.

The lab is justifiably proud of the work it does helping to translate the science of elite performance into the science of everyday health. The applications of its scientific findings are no less important for assisting a woman in her sixties with an arthritic hip walk five steps further each day than for helping an athlete reach their full potential.

The concept of marginal gains has revolutionised every kind of sport. Athletes know the tiniest change to their training and recovery regime or their diet can have a significant impact on their ability to perform, and can mean the difference between winning or losing. Having a purpose-built innovation centre designed to measure every inch of human body and brain performance, one step at a time, can be a game-changer. Some tests are as quick as 40 seconds on an iPad, to check what's happening to a person's cognitive function; at other times the tests can last for hours, and really push and stretch their subjects. This is especially the case when the lab is working with explorers who might be going to the South Pole, or rowing from the US to Australia.

At first glance, the lab is a fashionable, exclusive training centre, cleverly spotlit against orange and black walls, and furnished with the latest treadmills and bikes. And yet those same machines do far more than simply take your pulse or calculate how many calories you are burning. Although there is equipment that you'd see in an ordinary gym, the most important equipment consists of more technical machines which measure bone density, muscles, or the way our brain works in terms of making decisions. A huge range of tests measure all the different outcomes of activity, enabling scientists to understand what's happening to people in the brain and the body when they are exercising, either on the race track or in their daily lives. These findings also inform the work of pharmaceutical companies who are designing drugs, vaccines and other consumer healthcare products.

The lab is simultaneously engaged in a number of research projects. For example, one study is investigating whether rugby players can be trained to make quicker, better decisions during a match. When the right decisions are made, players can complete planned sequences, improve their field position and create scoring opportunities. One wrong decision could be the difference between winning and losing a game. The lab is working with Harlequins Football Club. As part of their training regime, the players watched a series of match videos. At a critical point, the video footage was frozen and players had to make a tactical choice about what should happen next from a list of options. Coaches then gave their feedback to the players on the best choice. Harlequins coaches were then asked to evaluate game footage recorded before, during and after training, for evidence of tangible improvements in the players' performance. The results of the study are currently being analysed by HPL.

One of the lab's original advisers, who helped to set up the facility and shape it in a way that would be meaningful to athletes, is Kelly Holmes, the double Olympic middle-distance running champion. Holmes' main role at the lab is to make sure that the scientists working with athletes know how to put data to good use: she helps them work out how to apply it to real-life scenarios. She works as a technical adviser, which means that when she sits down with a group of scientists and practitioners, experts in their own field, she can explain what happens down on the ground.

Mark Langley, the head of the lab, explains the aims of its work as follows: 'To a certain extent, if you are an athlete coming in and you have something that is not quite right and you want someone to help you fix it, the lab is a problem-solving business. But it's exactly the same for a medical patient. Taking away the pain caused by arthritis, for example, is in itself a real success, but actually what we want to do is to reduce the pain so that the person can move better. If they start moving better, it is good for their heart, good for their lungs, good for obesity etc. That person is healthier as a result, and actually that's what really gets the team excited. Helping athletes is great, but actually how we apply that to the broader population is really what we're about.'

Task analysis

5a Think about the first test task and answer the questions.

1 Were you able to locate the right section of the text quickly?
2 If you had a problem choosing the correct answer, what was the reason?
3 Are there any new words or phrases that you need to look up?

b In the second test task, have you got a mixture of *Yes*, *No* and *Not given* answers?

Vocabulary

➤ **COURSEBOOK** page 138

Vocabulary related to talent

1 Match the sentence beginnings (1–6) with the endings (A–F).

1 The Minister for Culture was congratulated for her commitment to
2 Providing that it has the support of employees, the company has the capability to
3 Although she was a good swimmer, the girl lacked the motivation to
4 Football requires close coordination between
5 One of China's early technological achievements was
6 A higher level of investment in playing fields is required to

A increase productivity.
B widening participation in the arts.
C the invention of paper.
D train for competitions.
E raise national standards in sports.
F members of the team.

EXPERT LANGUAGE

Motivation can either stand alone, or be followed by a verb or verb phrase.

---

2 Choose the correct option in *italics* to complete the text.

Educational standards

The country's **1** *investment / capability* to improve its economic output is dependent upon a steady supply of well-educated school leavers. So in spite of disappointing results in national tests, the government has stressed its **2** *capability / commitment* to raising levels of **3** *coordination / achievement* in schools. However, critics have blamed lack of **4** *investment / achievement* in wages and training, and pointed to the low levels of **5** *motivation / coordination* amongst overworked teachers whose pay has remained frozen for several years. They also claim that there is too little **6** *capability / coordination* between local education officials and head teachers.

---

3 Answer the questions using your own ideas and opinions.

1 Which do you think has more influence in the development of outstanding musicians, capability or motivation? (Why?)
2 Which do you think should be the priority, government investment in public sports facilities or in training for top-class sportspeople? (Why?)
3 Which is a more important target for teachers of young children, educational achievement or the motivation to learn about new things? (Why?)

Collocations for success and talent

4a Complete the collocations with the words below.

broad   concerted   desired   driving   pivotal   transferable

1 _____ force   4 _____ skills
2 _____ outcome   5 _____ spectrum
3 _____ effort   6 _____ role

b Complete the sentences with the phrases in Exercise 4a. You may need to change the order of the words.

1 Football enthusiasts represent a _____ of society.
2 A child's parents are often the _____ behind his or her achievements in music.
3 Changing jobs is not necessarily difficult, as many occupational _____ are _____ .
4 A cricket captain plays a _____ in matches by directing the team's strategy.
5 A _____ by parents and schools is required to help children achieve their full potential.
6 Ambitious actors need both drive and determination to achieve the _____ .

Describe personal qualities

5 Complete the sentences with a suitable adjective. The first and last letters are given.

1 By the age of six, Beethoven was already an a _ _ _ _ _ _ _ _ _ d musician.
2 Manufacturing companies need to be i _ _ _ _ _ _ _ e, as consumers are always looking for new products.
3 Despite their opponents' early lead in the match, the team made a t _ _ _ _ _ _ s attempt to score a goal.
4 In order to reach the highest levels of the profession, musicians need to have a s _ _ _ _ e- m _ _ _ _ d determination to succeed.
5 Television actors need to have e _ _ _ _ _ _ _ _ e faces, as the audience will see them close up.
6 I _ _ _ _ _ _ _ _ _ _ l teachers can have a big impact on children's personal and educational development.

6 Write a short description of a person you know who has been successful in their chosen field. Use some of the words from Exercise 5.

TEST STRATEGY

In Part 2 of the IELTS Speaking test you may be asked to give a description like this.

Language development

> COURSEBOOK page 141, EXPERT GRAMMAR page 181

Explain how something works

1   Match the descriptions (1–4) with the pictures (A–F). There are two extra pictures.

1 It is what people use to travel on snow.
2 It is the part which is used to steer.
3 This is the thing that protects you from rain or sun.
4 This is the thing that makes sailing safer.

2   Match the sentence beginnings (1–6) with the endings (A–F).

1 This is the bit that
2 This is the thing that you
3 It is the part which allows
4 They are what you press
5 This is the thing which is used
6 It is the part

A press to make the machine work.
B to select the kind of rice being cooked.
C you plug into an electric socket.
D to carry the machine around
E which opens the lid.
F hot air to escape.

3   Look at the diagram below of a rice cooker. Match the sentences in Exercise 2 with the parts of the cooker (A–F).

Rice cooker

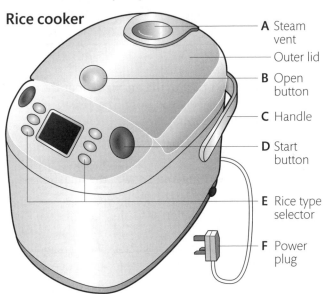

A Steam vent
   Outer lid
B Open button
C Handle
D Start button
E Rice type selector
F Power plug

Describe what something looks like

4   Look at the descriptions below (1–4) relating to the rice cooker in Exercise 3. Match them to the general descriptions (A–D).

1 It is approximately 35 centimetres long and 30 centimetres wide.
2 It consists of an outer case with a lid, and an inner rice bowl which is removable.
3 The outer case is made of metal and plastic, and the inner bowl is made of metal.
4 It is roughly rectangular, with rounded edges.

A structure   C material
B size   D form

> **EXPERT LANGUAGE**
>
> Use the present simple tense to describe what something looks like and how it works.

5   Describe the electric vegetable steamer in the diagram below. Say what it looks like and how it works.

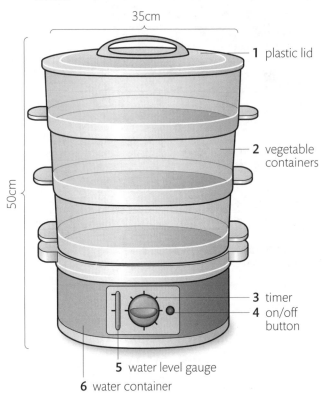

35cm

50cm

1 plastic lid
2 vegetable containers
3 timer
4 on/off button
5 water level gauge
6 water container

Writing (Task 1)

> **COURSEBOOK** page 142

Understand the task

1   Look at the writing task below and answer the questions.

   1   What do the diagrams show? What problem is the system designed to solve?

   2   What is the starting point for the process? What is the end point?

The diagrams below shows the system for moving a canal boat upstream, and how a swing bridge works on a canal.

Summarise the information by selecting and reporting the main features, and make comparisons where relevant.

Write at least 150 words.

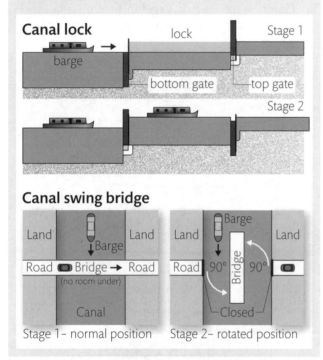

Work with unknown vocabulary

2   Look at the first diagram, which contains specialist vocabulary associated with canals. Match the words (1–3) with the definitions (A–C).

   1   lock   2   barge   3   gate

   A   A device for controlling the flow of water

   B   A device for lowering and raising boats between water of different levels

   C   A long, flat-bottomed boat for carrying passengers and cargo on canals and rivers, either powered or towed by something else

TEST STRATEGY

In diagram tasks, aim to use the visual clues to help you work out the meaning of specialist vocabulary.

Write about unknown processes

3   Look carefully at the processes involved in the first diagram and answer the questions.

   1   What is the position of the barge in Stage 1? What does the driver want to do?

   2   In Stage 1, is the lower gate open or closed?

   3   In Stage 2, where does the barge go?

   4   What happens to the gates in Stage 2?

   5   What happens to the water level in the lock in Stage 2?

4   Now look at the second diagram, which shows another device for canal boats – the swing bridge – and answer the questions.

   1   In Stage 1,

     A   In what position is the bridge?

     B   Can cars cross the canal to the road on the other side?

     C   What is the problem for the barge?

   2   In Stage 2,

     A   In what position is the bridge?

     B   What has happened to the roads on both sides of the canal?

     C   What can the barge now do?

5   Choose the correct option in *italics to* complete the first part of a sample answer to the task in Exercise 1a.

The two diagrams both show engineering systems used on canals. The **1** *one / first / beginning is a called a lock which is used when there is a difference in water level and boats need to be raised,* **2** *whereas / also / additionally the second is a swing bridge which enables cars to cross a canal until barges need to sail through. The lock* **3** *takes / uses /composes an arrangement of two gates. The barge wanting to move upstream waits in the lower area* **4** *until / while / once the lower lock gate is opened. It is then sailed through to the area between the gates. The upper gate is opened,* **5** *taking / breaking / allowing the water to flow through, which raises the level of the barge and* **6** *until / whereby / when the upper gate is opened, the barge sails through.*

Test practice

6   Write the next part of the answer about the swing bridge. Use ideas from Exercises 2–5 to inform your answer.

Assess and improve

7   Check your writing and answer the questions.

   1   Is the information logically ordered?

   2   Does the information accurately describe what is happening?

   3   Have you used the labels shown in the diagrams?

   4   Are all the verbs appropriate for the processes?

Listening (Section 3)

> COURSEBOOK pages 140 and 143

Before you listen

1 Look at the listening rubric and answer the questions.

You will hear two students discussing with a tutor their research project on one person who learns new languages easily: a good language learner.

1 What is the general topic?
2 What do you think might be the purpose of their discussion?

General and specific language

2a Look at the following extracts from an audio script on good language learners (GLLs). Make the underlined words more specific by choosing the most likely alternative in *italics*.

1 … we thought a/an *lively / quick / in-depth* comparison would give real substance to the study
2 … we had a couple of *tedious / informal / irrelevant* chats with her before we started the actual research
3 … we got a lot of *rich / pleasing / lively* data from her in this first interview
4 … she was very open about *person / personal / personnel* details of her life

b What other words could you use to make each of the underlined words more specific?

Deal with abstract ideas

3 In the listening task, the speakers discuss some of these topics. Which are more general and which are more specific?
• Core characteristics of GLLs
• The way the GLL uses her languages
• How the GLL records vocabulary when travelling
• The value of doing of a case study

Test practice

4a 🔊 9.1 Listen and complete the test task.

Questions 1–6
Choose the correct letter, A, B or C.

1 What was the main reason for choosing a case study?
   A It would be difficult to find a larger sample of appropriate learners.
   B It will be easier to analyse data from one single respondent.
   C It would shed light on the students' own language-learning abilities.

2 Anabelle and Rory were both surprised that their language learner
   A doesn't use her foreign languages when on holiday.
   B doesn't really enjoy language learning.
   C doesn't use languages in her job.
3 Anabelle and Rory decided to use only interviews because
   A their first interview yielded so much valuable information.
   B they felt other methods tend to be too intrusive.
   C they felt the GLL preferred this approach.
4 Anabelle feels the new recording equipment
   A is an improvement on previous technology.
   B needs improvement in one key aspect.
   C is unhelpful without special training.
5 The good language learner's most effective strategy for learning vocabulary is
   A drawing pictures to show the meaning of words.
   B using a dictionary frequently.
   C writing translations regularly in a notebook.
6 Anabelle is surprised that, when learning grammar, the GLL
   A practises patterns by repeating them many times.
   B waits a long time before producing structures.
   C varies her techniques according to the language she's learning.

> HELP

1 Listen for the word *opted* – this is a synonym for *chose* and will signal the reason for using a single case study.

Questions 7–10
Complete the sentences below.
*Write **NO MORE THAN TWO WORDS** for each answer.*

7 For the literature review, Anabelle and Rory agree to write more about learner _____ .
8 They worry that they aren't presenting a true picture of _____ .
9 For the Findings section, the tutor encourages them to reduce the number of _____ they use.
10 They ask the tutor for advice on how to set out _____ .

b Look at questions 7–10 again. Which questions deal with more abstract concepts and which with more concrete information?

Task analysis

5 Look at your answers to the test task. Which ones are you most sure of? Why? Did any of the questions deal with very abstract notions? Why do you think this is the case with Section 3 listening tasks?

Language development

> **COURSEBOOK** page 144, **EXPERT GRAMMAR** page 181

Estimation and indication

1 Look at the words/phrases below and answer the questions.

---
about   and so on   approximately   around   kinds of
more or less   types of

---

1 Which four words/phrases mean the same?
2 Which of the four synonyms in question 1 usually appears before an adjective or noun, rather than a number?
3 Which of the four synonyms in question 1 is least likely to be used in speech?
4 Which two phrases mean roughly the same as 'groups of'?
5 Which phrase is used at the end of a list?

2 Choose the correct option in *italics* to complete the text.

Fortnum and Mason

Fortnum and Mason is a very successful department store. It was founded in London **1** *around / more or less* 320 years ago, and has been in business ever since. Its core products are still **2** *about / more or less* the same: it sells all **3** *kinds of / types* high-quality groceries such as tea, coffee, biscuits, preserves **4** *and so on / more or less*. However, it has expanded considerably since it first opened. More recently, one of its most popular products has been souvenirs, because **5** *about / and so on* 70 percent of its customers are tourists. However, the current manager intends to attract more British customers too. In addition, the company gives annual awards to individuals who write books or articles about **6** *all kinds of / more or less* subjects relating to food and drink.

3 Complete the sentences with a word or phrase from Exercise 1. There may be more than one possible answer.

1 Grocer's shops, which have been largely replaced by supermarkets, used to sell all _____ dried food such as flour, sugar and eggs.
2 Greengrocers, as the name suggests, sell different _____ fruit and vegetables.
3 Hardware stores can still be found in towns, and they sell pots, pans, cutlery _____ .
4 These days, people like shopping in supermarkets, because they can find _____ everything under one roof.
5 In 2010, there were _____ 110 big supermarkets in London.
6 Nowadays, all _____ people do some of their shopping and banking online.

4 Match the questions (1–8) with the answers (A–H).

1 How many states are there in the USA?
2 Which is bigger, one third or 0.33%?
3 What is the population of Singapore?
4 What kinds of job do art graduates usually do?
5 What is the average summer temperature in Sydney?
6 What proportion of Chinese people live in cities?
7 What kinds of thing does Brazil export?
8 How big is the Sahara desert?

A more or less a half
B around five and a half million
C soya beans, engineered goods and meat, etc.
D about 50
E approximately 3.6 million square miles
F around 23 degrees centigrade
G they are more or less the same
H graphic design, clothing design, art education and so on

5 Answer the questions using some of the words from Exercise 1.

1 For how long have you been studying English?
2 For what kinds of reason do people in your country learn English?
3 What proportion of people in your country go on to higher education?
4 Which types of skills do you think people acquire by playing computer games?
5 Which types of skills do you think people acquire by doing team sports?
6 How many friends do you have on social media?
7 What kinds of people make the best leaders?
8 What kinds of thing do you like doing in your spare time?

TEST STRATEGY

You may be asked questions similar to these in Parts 1 or 3 of the IELTS Speaking test.

Vocabulary

> COURSEBOOK page 144

Replace *thing*

1a Match the categories below with the lists (1–8).

advantages   electronic equipment   ~~footwear~~
problems   qualities   raw materials   tools   workplaces

1 shoes, boots, sandals, slippers _footwear_
2 high costs, low income, risk of unemployment
   _____
3 honesty, ability, imagination, skill _____
4 office, farm, factory, hospital _____
5 good job, good health, happy family _____
6 scissors, screwdriver, brush, hammer _____
7 laptop, tablet, phone, satnav _____
8 steel, copper, wood, oil _____

b Complete the text below with words from Exercise 1a.

Success in business

Successful companies share a number of common characteristics. Firstly, they try to regard 1 _____ as the normal challenges which any organisation may face, and with a little creative thinking can be turned into 2 _____ . They also do their best to try and develop in their employees the 3 _____ which will be most useful for meeting the objectives of the organisation.

Leading businesses also try to ensure that their 4 _____ are comfortable and meet the workforce's needs, whether this means plenty of light and creative areas for graphic designers or hygienic workspaces for nurses. Providing the right resources is also important. Manufacturing companies which process 5 _____ , such as wood or cloth, take special care that their workers are provided with appropriate clothing, including comfortable 6 _____ , and also the best 7 _____ for the job. These may range from specialised 8 _____ to simple mechanical devices.

2 Replace *things* in the sentences with the words below.

activities   clothes   problems   products   qualities
services   strategies   tasks

1 Researchers have released a list of 14 things that successful people do in the mornings before breakfast.
2 Making a list of things to do helps people to manage their work more effectively.
3 Things like listening to customers, checking out the competition and having a flexible business plan are said to be good for new companies.
4 Farmers' markets are increasingly successful because there's a demand for local things like poultry, eggs, cheese, honey, bread and apple juice.
5 Singapore has a successful economy based on things like banking, legal services and advertising.
6 Many business are experiencing things such as rising costs, strong competition and currency fluctuations.
7 Employers are looking for things like conscientiousness, responsibility and creativity amongst job applicants.
8 Senior businesswomen wear things like trouser suits, smart dresses and high-heeled shoes for work.

3 Write sentences using the prompts.

1 many successful products / developed / result of / observing / animal characteristics
   _____

2 important / wear / appropriate clothes / attending / job interview
   _____

3 job applicant / personal qualities / as important / his / her qualifications
   _____

4 London / important centre / financial services / insurance / accountancy
   _____

5 one / most useful skills / work / ability / prioritise / different tasks
   _____

6 hotels / offer / outdoor activities / tennis and swimming / popular / tourists
   _____

7 one / biggest problems / businesses / face / today / competition / overseas
   _____

8 one / basic strategies / employed / football / a team / retain the ball / long / possible
   _____

4 Write five sentences about a successful product in your country. Use words from Exercises 1 and 2.

Speaking (Part 3)

➤ COURSEBOOK pages 139 and 145
EXPERT SPEAKING page 189

Develop topic-specific vocabulary

1 Match the phrases (1–6) with the meanings (A–F).

1 be a cut above
2 go to great lengths
3 have a hidden talent
4 put your mind to
5 set your sights on
6 stand out from the crowd

A focus on
B be different from the rest
C be better than the rest
D be good at something, although this isn't obvious
E have a goal
F do everything possible, however difficult

2 Complete the text with the phrases 1–6 from Exercise 1.

Applying for a job

Before you do anything else, you should **1** _____ getting information about the company that you want to work for. This is a fairly easy thing to do; a good starting place is the company website. When you write your application, remember that the company may receive hundreds of similar applications, so yours needs to **2** _____ , or it may be passed over quickly. Include information about previous work experience, as well as your education and skills. If you **3** _____ , such as singing or playing a musical instrument, mention that too.

If you are called for interview, practise answering questions with a friend beforehand. The better prepared you are, the more likely you will **4** _____ the other candidates. At the interview, try to relax, and just **5** _____ getting the job that you want. Good luck!

3 Complete the sentences using the words below.

corporation entrepreneur incentive lucrative
monopoly overheads redundant

1 Productivity generally increases when employees are offered an _____ to increase their output.
2 One well-known _____ who now owns several businesses started life as a journalist.
3 In the UK, rail companies have a _____ on particular routes, so customers have no choice.
4 Some individuals initially run a business from their own home, to reduce _____ .
5 Since the introduction of computers in the workplace, many employees have been made _____ .
6 As the elderly population continues to rise, companies regard the trend as a _____ business opportunity.
7 The board members of more than one _____ have been forced to resign due to mismanagement.

Create thinking time

4 Read the questions (1–4) about popular shops and consider how you might answer them. Use one of the phrases below for each answer.

1 What is one of the most popular department stores where you live?
2 Which group of people is the store most popular with?
3 How important do you think the sales staff are to the success of a store?
4 Some people say that traditional stores will soon disappear because of competition from the internet. Do you agree with that?

That's an interesting question ...
I've not thought much about this before, but ...
What I'm trying to say is ...
So, you're asking whether I think ...
I'm not sure if this is the right way to put it, but ...
You want to know my feelings on ...

5 🔊 9.2 Look at the strategies (A–D) for gaining thinking time in an interview. Listen to four speakers answering the questions in Exercise 4, and match what they say with one of the strategies.

A select key words (from the question) and repeat them
B reformulate the question
C use a thinking-time phrase
D signal the start of an explanation

Speaker 1 _____   Speaker 3 _____
Speaker 2 _____   Speaker 4 _____

Test practice

6 Answer the questions below about academic success, using the strategies in Exercise 5 to help you. If possible, record your answers.

1 How important do you think it is for an individual to be academically successful?
2 Which do you think is more important for academic success, ability or hard work?
3 Do you think that academic success will be more important or less important in the future?

Assess and improve

7 Answer the questions.

1 Which of the strategies did you find easiest to use? Why?
2 Did you know all of the words that you needed to answer the questions?
3 Did you use a dictionary to find out words that you didn't know?

Writing (Task 1)

> **COURSEBOOK** pages 148–149, **EXPERT WRITING** page 199

Understand the task

1a Read the instructions for the writing task. What are you required to do? Underline the key words that show the requirements.

The diagrams below show floor plans for a library in 2004 and in 2014.

Summarise the information by selecting and reporting the main features, and make comparisons where relevant.

Write at least 150 words.

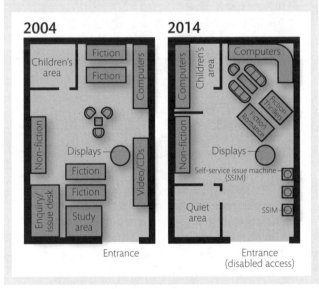

b Look at the list of areas/objects in the library (1–10) and identify what happened to them between 2004 and 2014. Put them in the correct column of the table below.

Removed	Changed (nature/ size/location)	Stayed the same

1 Enquiry/Issue desk
2 Fiction shelves
3 Displays
4 Computers
5 Children's area
6 Non-fiction shelf
7 Videos/CDs
8 Seating
9 Study area
10 Entrance

c Complete the sentences about the diagrams in Exercise 1a with the words below.

made   remained   removed   replaced

1 The issue desk was _____ with three self-service issue machines.
2 The children's area _____ in the top left-hand corner.
3 The room was _____ into an open area.
4 The video and CD area was _____ .

Language and content

2a What tense would you use to write about these diagrams? Why?

b Match the terms in Column A with the items in B to describe the changes in the library.

Column A	Column B
1 more pleasant	A seating area
2 larger	B fiction titles
3 significant	C video/CD section
4 extended	D enquiry desk
5 increased	E environment
6 replaced	F entrance
7 reorganised	G development
8 removed	H number of computers

Plan the task

3a Look at the different comparisons in Exercise 1b. Which of these do you think are most important?

b Which would be the best opening sentence of the report describing these diagrams? Why?

1 The plans show that the library was completely redesigned between 2004 and 2014, making it a much more pleasant environment for users.
2 The two plans show many changes occurred in this library between 2004 and 2014, particularly in the shelving and room design and use of self-service issue machines.

Write your report

4a Plan your comparison of the diagrams in Exercise 1a.

b Write your complete answer. Write at least 150 words.

Assess and improve

5 Check your writing and answer the questions.

1 Have you covered all of the requirements of the task?
2 Have you given an overview and summarised key changes and comparisons?
3 Is there some descriptive information for each key change from the diagrams to develop your answer?

Reading (Matching sentence endings; Multiple choice)

> **COURSEBOOK** pages 152–153

Before you read

1 Read the title and sub-title of the reading passage. What does 'affective' mean?

Paraphrase ideas

2a Look at the underlined words in question 1 of the test task below. In the first paragraph of the reading passage, identify the parts which relate to the underlined words.

 b Read the parts you identified carefully. What was the writer watching?

 c Look at options A–H in the test task below and choose the best ending.

Test practice

3 Follow the same steps as in Exercise 2 and complete the test task.

Questions 1–5

*Complete each sentence with the correct ending, **A–H**, below.*

*Write the correct letter, **A–H**.*

1 The writer's own face was monitored as he looked at

2 The lab where Rana el Kaliouby worked has designed things like

3 The attempt to create machines which can recognise feelings is called

4 International experts from various academic fields are trying to identify

5 In the 1990s, Picard was working on ways to expand

A affective computing.
B the food he was about to eat.
C computers' powers of recognition.
D a short video.
E emotional intelligence.
F an innovative motor vehicle.
G an academic journal
H physical expressions of emotion in people.

Test practice

4 Follow the same steps as in Exercise 3 and complete the test task.

Questions 6–10

*Choose the correct letter, **A**, **B**, **C** or **D**.*

6 What conclusion did Picard reach after reading a book?
 A The writer of the book had been mistaken.
 B Emotion and intelligence are two separate concepts.
 C Human cognitive abilities could never be matched by computers.
 D Computers should be programmed to recognise emotion.

7 Picard and her colleagues at Affectiva discovered that
 A fluctuations in heart rate are linked to a variety of emotions.
 B it is possible to match emotions to physical symptoms.
 C the physical signs of emotion are the same for all individuals.
 D facial expressions are the most reliable indicator of emotion.

8 What do we learn about Affectiva in the passage?
 A It was established by el Kaliouby.
 B It is currently short of funding.
 C It conducts research into health problems.
 D It specialises in the physical signals of emotion.

9 The Affdex database has shown that
 A women and men in the UK smile equally often.
 B age is not a significant factor in smiling.
 C people who smile often are happier than those who don't.
 D American women smile more often than French women.

10 Most recently, Picard's group have been designing software
 A for sale to private companies.
 B for use in industrial computers.
 C to allow an individual's health to be monitored.
 D to suggest the best response to a medical emergency.

Affective computing

From robots anticipating our wishes, to wristbands that help autistic children speak – the way we engage with technology is changing.

In a quiet breakfast cafe, on a sunny October morning in Boston, USA, I watched a 30-second clip of Pixar's film *Inside Out*, in which a gang of five animated emotions control the thoughts of a little girl called Riley. On the iPad screen I was holding, the green character called Disgust geared into action, making Riley overturn her plate of vegetables, and I gasped. When Riley's father tries to pacify her by pretending her spoon is an aeroplane, I laughed. All the while I was watching, the iPad was reading my emotions.

The emotion-sensing app I used had been developed over a ten-year period by an Egyptian-born computer scientist called Rana el Kaliouby at a laboratory in Massachusetts Institute of Technology – a place where designers, computer scientists, artists, architects and neuroscientists pool ideas. Its collaborations have led to products that belong firmly in the future – from foldable cars to social robots.

The idea behind the emotion-sensing app was to create a computer that could recognise a range of subtle human emotions, based on facial expressions. The lab's work is part of a growing field of research known as 'affective computing', the scientific efforts to give electronic devices emotional intelligence so that they can respond to our feelings and make our lives better. Now scientists all over the world, including physiologists, neurologists and psychologists, have joined forces with engineers to find measurable indicators of human emotion that they can teach computers to look out for. The field now has its own academic journal and groups devoted to its study around the world.

The term 'affective computing' was coined by a former colleague of el Kaliouby called Rosalind Picard. In the early 1990s, Picard was trying to give computers better perception by helping them process visual and auditory cues. While reading a book written by a neurologist, she came across the role of emotion in human intelligence. When she looked into this, she found emotion was one of the key ingredients of intelligent perception. She became convinced you couldn't build a truly intelligent computer unless it had emotional capabilities like humans. Picard decided to found her own lab called Affectiva, which was based on this principle, and she began to measure heart fluctuations, skin conductance, muscle tension, pupil size and facial muscles, in order to figure out which changes in our body consistently relate to emotions. She and

her colleagues found that within an individual there are consistent patterns that relate to several emotions. A wearable computer could be taught to recognise those patterns.

Affectiva is now one of the most successful companies in facial-expression analysis – it is backed by $20 million and has customers ranging from the BBC to Disney. Picard has since left the company to work on a new emotional computer that focuses on medical conditions such as autism and epilepsy, while El Kaliouby has become Affectiva's chief scientific officer. The software she uses now is called Affdex, an evolved version of what Picard and she had been building for years. When the software scans my face, it covers my image with a sprinkling of green dots. It has never seen me before, but it traces my eyebrows, lips, nose and eyes instantly. Based on a database of 3.4 million unique facial expressions sourced from 75 countries, it can pick up micro-expressions.

Tens of thousands of volunteers are recruited to watch video clips via webcam, and their emotional responses are aggregated to pick out the overall trends. With its huge database, Affdex has a measure of universal human emotion. It has found that women are more expressive in general than men – their smile intensities are larger, and they also smile for longer. And older people are more expressive than the young. Smiles also vary by culture. 'In the US, women smile 40 per cent more than men, in France and Germany it's 25 per cent more, and in the UK there is no difference. We don't know why!' El Kaliouby says.

While Affectiva has been focused on commercial applications, Picard decided to go back to the area that most fascinated her: emotion-sensing, wearable devices for healthcare. Picard's group has designed a range of such devices to pick up emotions – wristbands and cuffs for daily use that can track biometric data such as your pulse or electrodermal activity and motion. The newest device is known as the E4, and one of its primary uses is to predict dangerous medical conditions.

Affective scientists such as El Kaliouby and Picard all agree that emotionally intelligent devices will soon become a part of our daily lives. 'We are going to see an explosion of richness in this area,' Picard says. 'The age of emotional machines – it's coming.'

Vocabulary

> **COURSEBOOK** page 154

Nouns for hypothesising

1 Choose the correct option in *italics* to complete the sentences.

1 There is a widespread *assumption / insight* that house prices in the UK will continue to rise.
2 If global demand for energy does not slow down, there will be significant *implications / inferences* for the wider economy.
3 There is some *concept / speculation* that increasing automation will make lawyers and doctors redundant by 2050.
4 Even though surveys show that poverty and ill health are linked, the *inference / insight* that one causes the other is unproven.
5 The *implication / concept* of fairness is incompatible with big wage differences.
6 Techniques such as electronic tagging have given us *insights / assumptions* into the behaviour of wild animals.

2 Complete the sentences with the correct form of the words below.

assumption   concept   implication   inference
insight   speculation

1 There is some _____ that most conventional shops will have been replaced by online stores by 2030.
2 Government regulations allowing people over 65 to continue working challenged employers' _____ that old people are not fit to work.
3 It is to be hoped that the _____ of equal opportunity becomes a reality in the coming decades.
4 Global warming has _____ for agricultural practices in all parts of the world.
5 Space exploration will continue to provide _____ into the origins of the universe.
6 Recycling goods is better for the environment than discarding them. However, the _____ that people often draw – that this justifies increased consumption – is wrong.

Academic collocations

3a Underline the adjective on the left which collocates best with the word in bold.

1	deep	intense	hard	**speculation**
2	abstract	imaginary	unreal	**concept**
3	larger	longer	wider	**implications**
4	staple	primary	underlying	**assumption**
5	free	open	public	**perception**

b Complete the text using the words in Exercise 3a.

Arts funding

There is intense **1** _____ amongst the artistic community that the government is about to reduce levels of funding for the arts. Such a move would have wider **2** _____ for the future of theatre and cinema. The **3** _____ persists that the arts have little economic value, despite the role they play in boosting foreign tourism and other exports. And the **4** _____ of art as an enriching experience for individuals is unrecognised by bureaucrats who are simply juggling financial costs and benefits.

Phrases for speculation

4a Answer the questions about the words below.

chance confident guess impression likelihood surprised

1 Which of the words are adjectives?
2 Which of the words can be verbs or nouns?
3 Which of the nouns is always uncountable?
4 Is *guess* a regular or irregular verb?
5 Which of the nouns are sometimes uncountable, and sometimes countable?

b Complete the conversation with the words in Exercise 4a.

Anne: Hi, Helen. How are you?
Helen: Fine thanks. You?
Anne: I'm fine, well I **1** _____ so, sort of.
Helen: Oh, what happened?
Anne: Well, you know I compete in swimming competitions.
Helen: Oh yeah, so you're still doing that?
Anne: Yeah, I love it. But I fell off my bike a few months ago and hurt my arm. There was a slight **2** _____ I'd have to give up swimming for the rest of the year. I got the **3** _____ that my trainer was really worried.
Helen: Oh no!
Anne: Yeah, it was a bit worrying. Luckily it wasn't as bad as I thought. I've almost fully recovered now, and I've just started training for the next race.
Helen: Oh, that's great. What's the **4** _____ of you winning?
Anne: I'm fairly **5** _____ . At least, I'd be **6** _____ if I didn't come in the top three.
Helen: That's pretty impressive! I'll come and watch you race one day.
Anne: I'd love that!

5 Answer the questions about yourself.

1 What is the likelihood that you will visit another country next year?
2 How confident are you that you will get the IELTS score that you want?
3 Is there any chance that you will soon be invited to a wedding?

Language development

> COURSEBOOK page 157, EXPERT GRAMMAR page 181

Unreal conditionals, *wish* and *if only*

1a Some of the sentences below refer to an event that might happen, and others refer to an unreal event. Tick those which refer to an unreal event.

1 If I'd had the opportunity, I would have gone to Borneo on a biology field trip.
2 If I had more free time, I would learn to play a musical instrument.
3 I wish I'd been able to study medicine.
4 I'd go swimming more regularly if I could persuade my friend to come too.
5 I wish I had accepted the first job that was offered to me.
6 If only I'd worked harder, I would have got the qualifications I needed.
7 What other language would you study if you had the time?
8 If the plane had been on time, I would have arrived home in the afternoon.
9 My mother would have told me about the wedding if I had called her.
10 The price of the house would have come down if only I'd waited a few months.

b Underline the phrases in the sentences in Exercise 1a which refer to the hypothetical (unreal) past.

2 The sentences below all refer hypothetically to the past. Choose the correct option in *italics* to complete the sentences.

1 If you *hadn't studied / didn't study* English, what other language would you have studied?
2 Where *did you live / would you have lived* if you'd had a free choice?
3 I wish my cousin *didn't move / hadn't moved* to another part of the country, because I don't see him very often now.
4 If only you *had told / told* me about the problem, I could have helped you.
5 If I *hadn't had / haven't had* such a close family, I might have gone to live in a different country for a while.
6 I *could apply / could have applied* for promotion if I'd wanted to, but I'm happy in my current job.
7 If only we *haven't been / hadn't been* in such a hurry, we might have noticed that we were heading in the wrong direction.
8 If *I'd practised / I practised* more often, I could have entered for the national badminton competition.
9 Which airline *would you have used / would you use* if you had been flying to the USA?
10 If it *hadn't been / wasn't* for the cold weather, we would have enjoyed the trip.

Other hypothetical forms

3a Read the sentences and answer the questions (1–2).

A **Suppose** you'd had more money to travel, which countries would you have visited?
B **It's time** you started to think about the kind of job you'd like to do.
C **What if** you'd missed your train, how would you have got home?
D Take a snack **in case** your train is delayed and you have to wait a long time.

1 Which of the words/phrases in bold mean the same?
2 Which of the sentences refers to the hypothetical past?

b Complete the dialogue using the words in Exercise 3a.

Man: How was your holiday?
Woman: I really enjoyed it. I spent most of the time sitting on the beach and swimming. We were lucky, because the weather isn't always great at this time of year.
Man: Oh, really? And 1 _____ it had rained? What would you have done?
Woman: There were some museums in the town. And I'd taken plenty of books 2 _____ the weather was bad. But luckily the sun shone every day. How about you? Have you got any holidays planned?
Man: Unfortunately not. I haven't had a day off in six months, so 3 _____ I had a break. I feel like I need to recharge my batteries!
Woman: I bet you do! So then, 4 _____ you were very rich, and could choose to go anywhere in the world. Where would you go?
Man: I think I'd go to Australia, to dive in the Great Barrier Reef. They say it's shrinking and being damaged by pollution. I'd really like to see it now 5 _____ it disappears one day.
Woman: Good choice.

4 Complete the sentences using your own ideas and experience.

1 If the internet hadn't been invented, _____ .
2 Suppose space travel became cheaper, _____ .
3 If electricity hadn't been discovered, _____ .
4 I wish I'd been able to see _____ .
5 My holiday would have cost less if _____ .
6 It's time I started _____ .
7 Our football team would have been more successful if _____ .
8 World fish stocks wouldn't have declined so much if _____ .

Writing (Task 2)

> **COURSEBOOK** page 158, **EXPERT WRITING** page 200

Understand the task

1   Read the writing task. Which of the sentences below is the best paraphrase for the statement in the first line?

> *'Technology stifles human creativity.'*
>
> *To what extent do you agree or disagree with this statement?*

    1   Technology makes humans more creative.
    2   Technology should be used in creative ways.
    3   Technology makes humans less creative.
    4   Technology is not always used creatively.

Write about hypothetical alternatives

2a   Complete the sentences with the words below.

    can   had   may   wouldn't

    1   Imagine how much more creative the world would be if people _____ more free time allowing them to relax properly.
    2   If we had never invented the means to record images in the form of paintings, we _____ have been able to express ideas of beauty and value.
    3   I believe robots of the next century _____ be designed to perform tasks such as providing basic care for the sick and vulnerable.
    4   If we use this definition of technology, any tool, e.g. the simple pencil, _____ be viewed as an innovative technology.

b   Which of the sentences in Exercise 2a refer to the past, which to the present and which to the future?

c   Read the paragraph below from a sample answer to the task in Exercise 1. Underline the hypothetical situations mentioned. Do they refer to the past, the present or the future?

> Technology can be defined as the application of theories to the real world for practical functions. Using this definition, the stylus and clay tablet can be seen as the cutting-edge technologies of the ancient world, just as high-powered computers are today's. If we had never invented the means to write down our ideas, we would not have been able to communicate them to a wider community of readers. Consequently, we would have been deprived of the stimulus of feedback and any creativity would have been very restricted.

Develop a coherent argument

3a   Read the following paragraphs. Which one do you think is the most coherent?

> 1   Turning to the current era, some people are worried that humans are increasingly dependent on machines to do their thinking for them. They are particularly concerned that children no longer use their imagination in play because machines now create the worlds of their games. However, the same point might have been made about the printing press and imagine how much less creative the world would be without books. Just like a good novel, a good computer game can provide a springboard for richly imaginative thinking.

> 2   Turning to the current era, some people say that humans are dependent on machines and machines do the thinking for humans. Some people feel that children in the current era do not use their imagination. Computers do the imagining instead of children. People said that the printing press stopped people being imaginative and books are produced which help us to be creative. A computer game is like a book because it also helps us to be creative.

b   Analyse the more coherent paragraph and identify which structures/use of vocabulary help to promote a sense of linkage or coherence. Where relevant, draw an arrow to show how words link to other parts of the text.

Test practice

4a   Make a plan of your answer to the writing task in Exercise 1, using ideas and language from Exercises 2 and 3.

b   Write your answer. Focus on making the argument coherent and try to use some examples of hypothetical language to support your arguments.

Assess and improve

5   Leave your essay for a while, then re-read it. Analyse your answer using these questions.

    1   Have you included relevant summaries in your introduction and conclusion?
    2   Have you covered all aspects of the task?
    3   Have you used paragraphs and put them in a logical order?
    4   Have you clearly signalled the main points?
    5   Have you provided persuasive support for your points?
    6   Have you used some hypothetical alternatives to support your arguments?

Listening (Section 4)

> COURSEBOOK pages 156 and 159

Before you listen

1 You are going to hear a lecture about ways people might be helped to be more creative. Read the notes in the test task in Exercise 4 and match the four sub-headings with the phrases 1–4 below.

1 How to measure and identify creativity
2 Two studies on creativity
3 Explaining basic ideas
4 Ways to stimulate creativity

Metaphors and similes in lectures

2 Read the extract from a lecture on creativity. Underline the metaphors/similes the speaker uses. Why do you think he uses them?

How do we define creativity? It's actually a very abstract notion, hard to pin down. Many people say that a creative act is like a light bulb being switched on. Others talk about blue-sky thinking or thinking outside the box, but put simply, creativity is producing something new. For me, a crucial additional element is that something has to have value – so for this talk I'm defining creativity as when something novel but also worthwhile is formed. The created item may be intangible like a scientific theory, a symphony or even something more down to earth like a joke …

Hypothesising

3a Read the statements below. Most of these statements relate to something which has actually happened but two statements are hypothetical (they relate to what might happen). Which are the two hypothetical statements?

1 … today I'll discuss recent research studies which indicate that this quality of creativity is more fluid than had previously been thought.
2 a focus on *place* considers the setting or circumstances in which creativity thrives
3 … there are a wide range of approaches for measuring or gauging creativity but I'm just going to look at three.
4 A second technique is to ask them to conceive of what might happen in strange circumstances like a world where there is no gravity.
5 the participants who'd done the boring task beforehand performed significantly better
6 The research team suggest that parents shouldn't worry about their kids getting bored – if you had more bored youngsters, there would be more creative thinkers.

b Identify the language of hypothesis in the statements in Exercise 3a. Which statements
1 use a conditional?
2 ask you to imagine an unlikely situation?

Test practice

4 🔊 10.1 Complete the test task.

Questions 1–10
Complete the notes below.
Write NO MORE THAN TWO WORDS for each answer.

Enhancing creativity

Background
Many metaphors for creativity, e.g. a light bulb, thinking outside the box
Working definition: a phenomenon where something new and 1 _____ is created
Can be intangible, e.g. a theory or music composition or joke
Can be concrete, e.g. a machine or artwork such as a 2 _____

What makes someone creative: the 4Ps
Person: open to the new, curiosity and most importantly 3 _____
Product: number, detail and rarity
Place: where creativity flourishes, especially one where there are suitable 4 _____ and facilitators
5 _____ : main focus is on level of divergent thinking

Gauging creativity
Finding unusual uses for common everyday objects
Generate a list of consequences from hypothetical situations (e.g. loss of 6 _____)
Word association

Recent research

University of Maryland
Students were asked to imagine they were either an eccentric poet or a rigid 7 _____
Findings: creative thinking was higher among the 'poet' group

University of Central Lancashire
Experimental group: to write out 8 _____ before creativity test; control group – no boring task
Students were asked how many uses they could find for 9 _____ supplied in the experiment
Findings: 'Bored group' found more uses
Implication: allow kids to be bored: they might be more creative
Researcher does her most creative thinking whilst 10 _____

> HELP

1 The word *novel* is a synonym for *new*, so this is NOT the answer. You must write another factor which is mentioned by the speaker in his definition of creativity.

Language development

> COURSEBOOK page 160, EXPERT GRAMMAR page 182

Past modal verbs

1 Answer the questions about the modal verbs below.

could	may	should	would

1 Which verb is used to recommend something?
2 Which two verbs are used to express lack of certainty?
3 Which verb is used to express certainty?
4 With which verb can *not* not be contracted?

2 Tick the sentence (A or B) which expresses the meaning shown in brackets.

1 A Many more inventions could have been developed further if funding had been available.
  B Many more inventions would have been developed further if funding had been available.
  (The writer thinks this is a possibility.)

2 A The UK should have invested more money in wind-turbine manufacture, to provide jobs and export opportunities.
  B If the UK had invested more money in wind-turbine manufacture, there would have been more jobs and export opportunities.
  (The writer is of the opinion that this was the right course of action.)

3 A Silk textiles may never have been produced if the Chinese Emperor's wife hadn't accidentally discovered silk thread.
  B If the Chinese Emperor's wife hadn't accidentally discovered silk thread, silk textiles would never have been produced.
  (The writer feels sure that this is the case.)

4 A Malaria may have been preventable before now if medical researchers had made it a priority.
  B Malaria would have been preventable before now if medical researchers had made it a priority.
  (The writer thinks this is a possibility.)

3 Choose the correct option in *italics* to complete the text.

The importance of patents

Patents give entrepreneurs and inventors legal protection against copying. Without the protection of a patent, an invention **1** *might be* / *would be* copied and sold by any individual or company. Although patent laws vary from country to country, the protection they afford **2** *may* / *should* last for at least 20 years in countries which are members of the World Trade Organization. However, great care has to be taken that the right procedure for obtaining a patent is followed. The case of Mr X illustrates this.

Mr X applied for a provisional patent for a product that he had invented, and then started to approach companies who might be willing to manufacture it. However, he **3** *may have* / *should have* provided a lot more detail when he completed the patent application. When one of the companies he approached copied his idea, Mr X filed a complaint, but the complaint lacked validity because his patent application had been too imprecise.

If Mr X had employed a lawyer who specialised in patent applications, his application **4** *would have been* / *should have been* completed more appropriately and the U.S. Patent Office **5** *may have* / *would not have* supported his case. As it was, he failed.

Many other inventors **6** *would have* / *could have* failed to develop their ideas on account of patent problems too.

4 Complete the text with suitable words. There may be more than one possible answer.

The father of the microscope

Anthony van Leeuwenhoek was born in 1632 in the Netherlands. He had little education and began work at an early age in a shop selling cloth. If his family **1** _____ wealthier, or if he **2** _____ a different occupation, he certainly **3** _____ made the important discoveries he is credited with.

Cloth merchants often used magnifying glasses to examine the cloth they were buying, and Anthony naturally acquired one of his own. He began to take an interest in how magnifying lenses were made, and in 1671 he built his own microscope, and used it to observe the tiny plants and animals living in water. Eventually he discovered bacteria. At first scientists rejected Anthony's findings, but eventually they were accepted. If Anthony **4** _____ acquired a magnifying glass, the advances in biology and medicine that built on his work **5** _____ delayed by many years, and many more people **6** _____ victims of disease.

5 Rewrite the sentences in the past tense.

1 If more money is invested in medical research, many lives will be saved.
  If more money had been invested in medical research, many lives would have been saved.

2 The HIV virus will spread less quickly if national governments make health education a priority.

3 Scientists may find a way of storing solar energy sooner if the research is properly funded.

4 Governments should consider investing more in renewable energy so that climate change goals can be met.

5 People may make more effort to reduce waste if the government campaign is effective.

6 If trade barriers are relaxed, food producers in poorer countries will benefit considerably.

Vocabulary

> COURSEBOOK page 160

Verb patterns

1a Decide whether the words below are followed by an infinitive or the *-ing* form of the verb (gerund). Write them in the correct place in the table.

~~afford~~ avoid deny involve manage promise risk suggest

+ infinitive	+ -ing
afford,	

b Complete the dialogue with the correct form of the words in Exercise 1a.

A: How's the plan for your new business going? It's a coffee shop you want to open, isn't it?

B: Yes, that's right. I've just been trying to sort out the finance.

A: Have you **1** _____ to get a bank loan?

B: Yes. The bank's **2** _____ to lend me 60 percent of the capital I need. I'd rather **3** _____ asking anyone in my family to help me – family and business don't always mix – so a friend **4** _____ applying for a government loan as well.

A: Are you going to buy the premises?

B: No, I'm not. That would cost a lot, and if the business was unsuccessful, I would **5** _____ losing it. It's a chance I can't **6** _____ to take. So I'm just going to rent a place at first. I think that's the sensible thing to do.

A: Yes, and with a coffee shop there isn't the amount of stock you have to have if you're running a restaurant. So it doesn't **7** _____ stocking up on expensive food that you might not sell.

B: That's true.

A: Well, it sounds really exciting. I can't **8** _____ being a bit jealous. If you want any help, let me know.

B: Thanks!

2 Match the sentence beginnings (1–8) with the endings (A–H).

1 Inventors who don't apply for a patent risk
2 Starting a new business involves
3 Business consultants usually suggest
4 If their songs are freely copied, musicians cannot afford
5 Thanks to publicity from a popular TV series, several entrepreneurs have managed
6 Some enterprising individuals have avoided
7 As an aspect of their brand, some companies promise
8 Few successful company owners would deny

A drawing up a detailed plan.
B incurring high overheads.
C to invest time in creating new ones.
D having their ideas stolen.
E having had help from business consultants.
F to deliver their products according to certain standards.
G expanding a new company slowly.
H to obtain financial support for a business idea.

3a Complete the sentences with the correct form of the words below.

apply buy copy create develop face get replace

1 Obtaining legal protection for an idea involves _____ for a patent.
2 A formal letter, known as a Letter of Intent, is sometimes issued when a company promises _____ a certain number of an entrepreneur's products.
3 Inventors of new products can rarely avoid _____ help from experts to promote them.
4 Successful fashion designers often manage _____ new styles using traditional fabrics.
5 Many people who have good ideas cannot afford _____ them.
6 In the 19th century, engineers initially faced great opposition when they suggested _____ wind with steam to power ships.
7 Unscrupulous companies make small changes to a new design, and then deny _____ it.
8 The pioneers of vaccination risked _____ ridicule by the doctors of the day.

b Complete the text below with the correct form of the words in Exercise 3a.

Entrepreneurs and investors

A popular TV series, which runs in several countries across the world, features entrepreneurs describing a business idea to potential investors. The entrepreneurs range from fashion designers who have **1** _____ a new clothing range, to engineers who have **2** _____ a new tool.

Any entrepreneur who **3** _____ to appear on the programme **4** _____ an information pack detailing the 'rules' of the programme. He or she then prepares a 'pitch' before **5** _____ the investors in an interview room. If the investors are convinced that enough people would **6** _____ the product, they compete against each other to invest in it.

The series was first shown on Japanese television, but the format has been **7** _____ by TV companies around the world. The investors become celebrities, but every so often one of them leaves the show and is **8** _____ by a new investor.

4 Write about a product or discovery that you think is/was very useful or important. Use words from Exercises 1 and 3.

Speaking (Part 2)

> COURSEBOOK pages 155 and 161

Develop topic-specific vocabulary

1a Tick the adjectives below which have a similar meaning to *talented*.

artistic	competent	creative	gifted	imaginative
original	practical	realistic		

b Write the noun form of the adjectives in Exercise 1a.

c Which of the following people might take part in a talent show?

acrobats   musicians
businessmen   politicians
dancers   singers

2 Read the task card below. Think about how you might answer the question and make notes.

> *Describe a talented person that you would like to meet. You should say:*
>
>   *who the person is —①*
>
>   *what his/her talent is —②*
>
>   *how you know about him/her —③*
>
> *and explain why you would like to meet this person. —④*

3a 🔊 10.2 Listen and read what a student says about the topic in Exercise 2. Match the things he says with the points on the task card.

                            ①

'The person I'd like to meet is a <u>writer called Ian Rankin</u>. He's Scottish, and he writes crime novels that are centred around a detective called Inspector Rebus, and they're set in Edinburgh. His special talent is creating believable characters – his characters are very true-to-life, and his plots are full of suspense and drama, they're very exciting right up to the end. You can't really guess what the ending will be. He's written about 12 or 15 novels about Inspector Rebus. I'd like to meet him so I could ask him some questions. What I'd like to know is how he gets new ideas each time for the next novel. I'd also be interested in knowing how he develops the plot – whether he plans it all out first, and then follows that plan as he writes, or whether ideas just come to him as he starts writing. I'd like to know how he makes sure that all the characters stay true to life. And I would ask him if he has a map of Edinburgh in front of him to keep track of where the characters go, and where the crimes take place. Oh yes, and I'd like to ask him how he knows so much about police methods.'

b Which of the topics does the speaker not talk about?

> **TEST STRATEGY**
>
> When you do Part 2 of the Speaking test, make sure that you mention all of the topics on the card. It will help you to speak for longer, and to use a wider range of vocabulary.

Use speculation in your answers

4 The fourth part of the speaking card asks the speaker to speculate. Underline the language he uses to do this in Exercise 3a.

Test practice

5a Read the task card below and make notes about how you would answer it.

> *Describe a talent that you wish you had. You should say:*
>
>   *what the talent is*
>
>   *how common it is*
>
>   *what you would do with this talent*
>
> *and explain why you wish you had this talent.*

b 🔊 10.3 Listen to a student doing the task and complete the notes.

> *Would like to be able to _____*
>
> *_____ people can do it*
>
> *Would use the talent to _____ and to _____*
>
> *Would like to have the talent because _____*

c Listen again and write down any words or structures which you might like to use in your answer.

d Do the task in Exercise 5a and record yourself if possible.

Assess and improve

6 Assess your answer using these questions.

    1 Are there any words that you wanted to use but didn't know?

    2 Did you use the right grammatical structures for speculating?

Writing (Task 2)

➤ COURSEBOOK pages 164–165, EXPERT WRITING page 200

Understand the task

1a Read the writing task and answer the questions below.

> *'Curiosity, rather than necessity, is what drives invention.'*
>
> *To what extent do you agree or disagree with this statement?*
>
> *Give reasons for your answer and include any relevant examples from your knowledge or experience.*

1 What is the difference between curiosity and necessity?
2 Which of the following words relate more closely to *curiosity* and which to *necessity*?

need   inquisitiveness   interest   requirement   essential   fascination   desire to know

b Which is the best synonym for the word *drives* in the expression *drives invention*?

1 leads   2 analyses   3 motivates

Plan the task

2a Read some opinions which might be used in the essay task in Exercise 1a. Which opinions support the notion that curiosity is more powerful than necessity in driving invention (✓)? Which support the opposite view (✗)? Could any points be used both for and against (=)?

1 Anyone who wants to succeed in business must be able to predict what the market wants.
2 Inventors at heart are people who want to satisfy their thirst for knowledge.
3 If we want to preserve our security, we must constantly improve our weapons of defence.
4 People want to create devices which enable them to see the natural world in more detail.
5 It is difficult to say exactly what motivates the design of new inventions.
6 Without the innate desire to push boundaries, we would never have moved out of the caves.

b Which of the sentences in Exercise 2a include hypothetical situations? Underline the language of hypothesis.

c Identify at least two ideas from Exercise 2a which you will incorporate into your own answer.

d Make a plan for your essay. Ensure you include all the following:

- A meaningful introduction which does not simply repeat words from the exam task

- A clear statement of your own opinion – either close to the beginning or at the end
- Some examples to give substance to your points
- Clear links between points
- A satisfying conclusion which encapsulates a point or points you wish your reader to take from your essay

Language and content

3a Complete the sentences with the words below.

ground-breaking   original   perceived   role   trace

1 Many different factors play a _____ in the development of inventions.
2 It is widely agreed that the capacity for _____ thinking is the hallmark of creativity.
3 Einstein's Theory of Relativity was truly _____ : nothing like it had been thought of before.
4 We can _____ the origins of computers back to mathematicians such as Ada Byron in the early 19th century.
5 Engineers and other technologists develop new devices in response to a _____ need.

b Underline the discourse markers (link words/phrases) in the sentences. Choose one of these to continue points 1–5 in Exercise 3a.

A In turn, these products generate a whole new set of requirements.
B As a result, it revolutionised the way people thought about the world.
C Consequently, we must try to develop this quality from as young an age as possible.
D However, it is often one person's vision which triggers the process in the first place.
E Although these devices are often considered to be quintessentially 20th-century inventions.

Write your essay

4 Write your answer to the essay task in Exercise 1a. Use ideas from Exercise 2 and language from Exercises 3a and 3b. Write at least 250 words.

Assess and improve

5a Leave you essay for a couple of hours, then re-read it. Analyse your writing using these questions.

1 Was the introduction clear?
2 Did you argue your opinion effectively?
3 Did you organise your ideas in a logical way, with good use of paragraphs?
4 Were all the examples you gave equally effective? If not, what would you change?
5 Did you use any of the vocabulary you learnt from Exercises 3a and 3b?
6 Do any sections fail to make sense?
7 Did you conclude in a satisfying way?

b If you are not satisfied with any sections, rewrite them.

Answer key

Module 1

Reading

1a 1

1b Students' own answers

2 migration = when birds or animals travel regularly from one part of the world to another
navigational = allowing you to find out where you are or where you are going
genetic = relating to genes
compass = an instrument that shows directions and has a needle that always points north

3a
2	noun (or noun phrase)	5	adjective or noun
3	noun (or noun phrase)	6	noun or noun phrase
4	verb		

3b
1 The insects are typically found in …
2 Monarch butterflies migrate for two reasons.
3 … has been the subject of scientific interest …
4 Now at last, scientists believe they have cracked the secret …

4
1	single spot	6	(the) direction
2	freezing temperatures/winter	7	complex
3	milkweed plants	8	sun
4	learn	9	antennae
5	navigational	10	compass

5 Students' own answers

Vocabulary

1
1	acquire	5	retain	9	process
2	capacity	6	reaction	10	research
3	focus	7	focus		
4	process	8	method		

2 Students' own answers

3a
1	demonstrate	4	focus
2	acquire	5	conduct
3	process	6	trigger

3b
1	acquire a skill	4	process information
2	demonstrate intelligence	5	trigger a reaction
3	conduct research	6	focus attention

4 Students' own answers

5

6 Students' own answers

7a Students' own answers

7b Students' own answers

Language development

1a
1	get it in	3	talk you through
2	up-to-date	4	top up

1b
1 If you can't find the book you are looking for, the bookshop assistant can order it for you.
2 If you move house, you should make sure that the library has your current address.
3 If the online application form isn't clear, ring up and someone will explain it.
4 If the print on your photocopies looks faded, you probably need to refill the ink.

2a
1	E	3	B	5	C
2	A	4	A	6	D

2b
1	reorganise	5	inaccessible
2	unlikely	6	uninformative
3	enable	7	mismanagement
4	International		

3
1	international	5	likelihood
2	management	6	access
3	reorganisation	7	inadequate
4	enable		

4a
1	Digital	4	easily
2	valuable/invaluable	5	legal
3	variety		

4b
1	digital	3	variety
2	illegal	4	valuable/invaluable

Writing

1a
1 one country – vague
2 number (1000s)
3 2004 to 2016 – definite, with predicted figures for 2020
4 different science subject areas

1b
1 five
2 Biological sciences
3 Computer sciences
4 Physical sciences and Mathematical sciences
5 Agricultural sciences
6 That there has been a major change in popularity of certain sciences, particularly a growth in the number of graduates of Biological sciences and the decline in graduates of computer sciences.

2 A 2   B 4   C 3   D 1

3a 2 gives the best overview because it summarises an overall trend

3b 1 detail   2 trend   3 trend   4 detail

4a Students' own answers

4b Sample answer:
The graph shows significant variation in the number of students on different courses in one adult education college over 30 years, with predicted figures for 2025. The most striking change was in the popularity of Employability courses. In 1985 this group was only the third most popular but by 2015 it had risen to first position. There was a particularly large increase between 2005 and 2015, rising from 500 to 625 students with this figure set to rise to 800 by 2025. Fitness courses also saw noticeable improvement in subscription, growing by almost 200 between 1985 and 1995, though the rise became more gradual after this with only 50 added to the total by 2015. In contrast, the number of adults studying languages declined, with numbers dropping from 350 in 1985 to 300 in 1995 and 280 in 2005. However, the figures levelled off in the following ten years and they are forecast to remain the same in 2025. Art and design courses were the least popular throughout the period, with their numbers fluctuating slightly between 200 and 280.

Listening

1 Students' own answers

2a Suggested answers:
A   It was formed by combining two older institutions, e.g. joining, together, colleges, a date
B   It has changed its courses a lot over the last 20 years, e.g. alter, programmes, significantly, a date or number
C   It has not always been in its present location, e.g. current place, situation, change, move

2b C

3	1	C	3	C
	2	B	4	A

Audio script 1.1

N = Narrator   A = Andy

N: You are going to hear an introductory talk to students at a college open day. Listen and answer the questions.

A: Good morning, everyone. My name's Andy Gresham and I'm Director of Student Services here at Patterson College. It's great to see so many of you here today for the first open day of the year. We hope that you'll like what you hear and see today, and that you'll decide to come and study with us.

I'm going to start my talk by giving you a bit of background about the college. We've been on this current site for only 20 years, but we started in London, opening our doors to students in 1857. A decision was made to make the change when student numbers on all our courses grew considerably.

Now, we've always prided ourselves on the variety of subjects we offer – from sports science to teacher training to media and journalism. But we also offer different modes of study, not just the traditional full-time, face-to-face modes. We have a number of successful four-year sandwich courses with industry-based learning in the third year. Some students opt to study part-time, though this tends to be mainly mature students and their numbers are in decline. Takeup of our distance programmes is relatively small but it's been growing significantly in recent years.

What's the best thing about studying with us? Well, every year we get very high student ratings across the board. But for our students the key is the number of people getting jobs after they leave us – all our teaching staff keep this very much in mind in the design of resources and delivery of our courses.

And as you can see, our campus is a real asset, with its beautiful views and pleasant parkland. We've just confirmed plans to refurbish our library, going ahead imminently, and major investment has already gone into our sports facilities, and our complex is now state of the art. And of course there's our brand new student support hub, where we are now.

4a **Questions 1–4:** you must choose one correct option from three possible answers.
Questions 5–10: you must choose two correct options from five possible answers.

4b Suggested answers:
Which TWO things does Andy say about campus accommodation?
Alternative ways of expressing these: *staying on campus/college residences*
Which TWO things does Andy say about ways of getting to the college?
Alternative ways of expressing these: *transport or travel to college*
Which TWO things does the speaker say many people forget to include in their application?
Alternative ways of expressing these: *items people don't remember to send with their application forms*

4c 5/6 B/E (in either order)
7/8 B/D (in either order)
9/10 C/E (in either order)

Audio script 1.2

Later you'll have the opportunity to see the different types of campus accommodation we offer. About half of the accommodation is in separate rooms in Halls of Residence, and the rest in what we call 'village houses' where you can live in groups of five with a shared kitchen. Unfortunately, you can't book a particular room but we can arrange for you to specify who you want to be with, sharing a house. Of course you don't have to stay on campus – many students move into town in their second year – but the majority return for their last year. This is obviously strongly recommended for people wanting access to resources round the clock when they're up to their eyes in dissertations.

Now, transport to the college. Some of you have commented that it's quite a long journey from the city centre but it depends on how you travel. We have good bus services throughout the day, and students are entitled to discount fares. But evening services don't run as late as many people would wish. And since the railway station closed we rely heavily on buses. Walking is possible – it takes about 40 minutes – and cycling is popular because it's pretty flat, though there are no designated cycle ways. If you share a taxi between four, it actually works out as little as getting the bus.

As I say, I hope you'll enjoy the day and that you'll decide to apply to Patterson College. If you do put in an application, please remember to tell us how you'd like us to communicate with you – we want to make sure we do this efficiently. We often have difficulty getting hold of applicants if we need something at short notice, like copies of your qualifications. And we do need to have your full name as it appears on your passport or other form of official ID. You'd be surprised how many people don't supply us with this essential information.

Now does anyone have any questions …

Language development and vocabulary

1
| 1 | E | 3 | F | 5 | B | 7 | D |
| 2 | C | 4 | H | 6 | G | 8 | A |

2
2 I had studied Spanish.
3 I am going to study Spanish.
4 I studied Spanish.
5 I will study Spanish.
6 I have studied Spanish.
7 I was studying Spanish.

3
1 have got/have become
2 are falling
3 paint
4 have found
5 had seen
6 are appearing
7 see/have seen
8 have become
9 will talk/'m going to talk

4
| 1 | C | 2 | B | 3 | E | 4 | A |

5 Suggested answers:
1 I might cut spending.
2 I might visit Australia.
3 I might shop somewhere else.

Speaking

1a
1 ambitious
2 dedicate
3 dedicated
4 demand
5 demanding
6 disheartening/disheartened
7 inspiration
8 inspired/inspirational
9 talent

1b
1 talented
2 ambitious/dedicated
3 demanding
4 inspired
5 dedicated
6 disheartened

2
| 1 | D | 3 | F | 5 | A |
| 2 | B | 4 | E | 6 | C |

3 Students' own answers

4 Students' own answers

5 Students' own answers

Writing

1
1 The popularity of different modes of non-traditional study
2 Under 25-year-olds, over 25-year-olds
3 Vague – one unnamed university
4 Number of students
5 The time period is 1985 to 2015, with predicted figures for 2025.

2a The two graphs show changes in the number of students at a given university taking courses following non-traditional modes of study, from 1985. The first shows figures for under-25s and the second gives statistics for more mature students.

2b B, C, A

2c Students' own answers

3a Simple future *will* or *is predicted to*

3b
1 students under 25 – younger students/learners, under-25s
2 students over 25 – more mature students, older learners, over-25s
3 predict – forecast, set to
4 rise – increase, grow
5 fall – decline, drop, go down, decrease

4 Sample answer

The graphs show the percentage of loans of different types of books and other material in two libraries between 1980 and 2010, with predictions for 2020. There are clear differences in borrowing habits between the two locations. In Library A there was a steady rise in the proportion of loans of fiction from 41 percent in 1980 to 54 percent in 2010, with the growth set to continue, reaching 65 percent by 2020. At the same time non-fiction loans declined from 52 percent to 35 percent in 2010, though these are predicted to decline less dramatically over the coming years. The pattern is reversed for Library B: fiction loans fell from 65 percent in 1980 to 50 percent in 2010, with figures forecast to decline even more sharply by 2020. There was an increase of approximately 20 percent in non-fiction loans and an even more marked rise is forecast for 2020. DVDs and CDs in both libraries had a similar pattern of growth from 1980 to 1990 but whereas in Library A these held steady for 20 years, in B they declined. These non-print loans are predicted to decline in both, each reaching 4 percent in 2020.

5 Students' own answers

Module 2

Reading

1 Students' own answers

2a urban solutions

2b 3

2c 1

3 Students' own answers

4a Figures show that in future a greater proportion of people will live in cities.

4b By 2050 that figure will have risen to 70 percent.

4c
| 1 | T | 3 | T | 5 | NG |
| 2 | F | 4 | NG | | |

5a 1, 3, 4, 6

5b
6 air quality
7 wheelchair users
8 transport systems
9 Heathrow/the airport
10 insurance companies

6 Students' own answers

Vocabulary

1a
| 1 | C | 3 | B | 5 | A |
| 2 | F | 4 | E | 6 | D |

1b
1 transformed
2 settling
3 disappearing
4 emerging
5 enabled

2a 1 D   2 B   3 C   4 A

2b The more formal expressions are single words, and the less formal expressions are phrases.

3 Students' own answers

4a
2 the transfer of plant diseases from one country to another
3 rotates around the sun in just over 365 days
4 can be affected by heat
5 an internet connection
6 Construction of a new hydro-electric power station
7 rise in penalties for pollution has succeeded in reducing factory emissions
8 The extraction of natural gas from rock cavities

4b Students' own answers

Language development

1 1 has   2 were   3 were   4 was

2
1 was held
3 was taken down
3 have been devastated
4 was inhabited
5 had been found/was found
6 are, known

3a
1 In 2008 the Kalka-to-Shimla railway, which <u>had been constructed</u> more than a century earlier, was granted World Heritage status.
2 By 1899, while a railway <u>was</u> still <u>being constructed</u> to transport gold prospectors in Canada, the Gold Rush was almost over.
3 Before work begins at the site of a new railway line in the UK, archaeologists <u>may be allowed</u> time to search for evidence of earlier occupation.
4 When people visit Gleisdreieck Park in Berlin they <u>will be impressed by</u> the peacefulness of this former railway junction.
5 In many parts of the world, rail transport <u>is being upgraded</u> in an attempt to reduce road traffic.

3b 1 C   3 A   5 E
     2 D   4 B

4
1 is situated
2 was partly built
3 (was) partly carved
4 is surrounded
5 are riddled
6 has been inhabited
7 to be damaged
8 were resettled
9 will be placed

5 Students' own answers

Writing

1
1 How fruit is prepared and processed through canning
2 It starts with the fruit being harvested.
3 Four main stages
4 The process finishes with transport to shops and cafés.
5 You do need to mention all the steps in the process but some can be grouped together in one sentence.

2 1 D   2 A   3 C   4 B

3 2

4 1 C   2 A   3 B

5a In the factory the fruit undergoes stringent quality control. To enable this <u>to be done</u> properly the fruit needs to <u>be</u> thoroughly <u>washed</u>: workers can only see if there are any marks or bruises when the fruit is clean. The fruit <u>is then weighed</u> and <u>graded</u> into different sizes. Only fruit of the right quality and size <u>is used</u> for canning: rejects <u>are sent</u> for animal feed and other uses. The next phase is preparation for canning. The fruit <u>is peeled, cored</u> and <u>cut</u> into pieces. These pieces <u>are poured</u> into tins, which <u>are</u> immediately <u>sealed</u>. It is only at this stage that the fruit <u>is cooked</u>, which also has the effect of sterilisation.

It's difficult to use the active voice in such process descriptions because in almost every case we don't know the 'agent' (who does the action) or we would be forced to use bland repetition, e.g. *people/workers harvest the fruit/drive the lorries*, etc.

5b the fruit then undergoes, workers can only see
Sometimes it is helpful to name the agent, e.g. that workers inspect the fruit (rather than this being done by machine), so we use the active voice *workers can only see*. The first sentence also uses the active voice – *the fruit undergoes*. This is used because the verb *undergo* conveys the notion of something being done to the subject.

6 Sample answer
There are essentially four main phases in processing fruit for canning. Firstly, the fruit is harvested by hand from orchards and then loaded onto lorries for transportation to the canning factory. In the factory the fruit undergoes stringent quality control. To enable this to be done properly the fruit needs to be thoroughly washed: workers can only see if there are any marks or bruises when the fruit is clean. The fruit is then weighed and graded into different sizes. Only fruit of the right quality and size is used for canning: rejects are sent for animal feed and other uses. The next phase is preparation for canning. The fruit is peeled, cored and cut into pieces. These pieces are poured into tins, which are immediately sealed. It is only at this stage that the fruit is cooked, which also has the effect of sterilisation. Once cooled, the cans then have labels stuck on them and are stacked for storage before being despatched to different outlets such as shops or cafés.

Listening

1a One word and/or a number

1b Suggested answers:
1 Surname
2 A date (NB you can write the date in any acceptable form, e.g. 22.01.94 or 22nd Jan 1994)
3 Name of a country
4 An activity/occupation, e.g. cooking, painting
5 A type of media or person

2a 1 Spiro   4 teaching
     2 22/06/94   5 TV/television
     3 Ireland

Audio script 2.1

N = Narrator   V = Volunteer   R = Receptionist

N: You will hear a receptionist at a wildlife sanctuary talking to a volunteer. Listen and answer the questions.

V: Hello, I'm a new volunteer. I spoke on the phone to your colleague in the main office and she told me to report here.

R: Yes, you've come to the right place. Welcome to Branscombe Otter Sanctuary!

V: Thanks.

R: I'll just need to take down a few details. What's your full name?

V: Brian Spiro.

R: Is that S-P-I-R-O?

V: That's right, yeah.

R: That's straightforward – thanks. And if you don't mind, what's your date of birth? I just need it for our records.

V: 22nd of the sixth, 94.

R: Lovely. And how long will you be volunteering with us?

V: Well, just for a couple of weeks, while I'm on vacation ... if that's OK?

R: That's great. And what's your nationality? Is that a Scottish accent I can hear?

V: Actually I'm from Ireland. Although everyone says I've lost most of my accent.

R: Right. Now, can I take some contact details?

V: Do you want my home address?

R: Well, I presume you're staying locally?

V: Yeah – at the Youth Hostel.

R: In Branscombe?

V: Yep ... do you need my room number? ... I don't think I've got it with me.

R: No, that's fine – we normally contact you by phone, anyway, if we need to get hold of you for whatever reason.

V: Yeah, that's easiest.

R: So can I take your mobile number?

V: It's 0706 549 870.

R: Great, thanks. Now, as you know, there are various areas where we need volunteers and we try to draw on any particular skills or experience you have. For example, if you have any experience of catering you might want to ...

V: ... work in the café ... afraid not ... I'm hopeless at cooking!

R: Not to worry ...

V: I have done some teaching, if that's any use ... one-to-one with primary school kids.

R: Definitely ... I'll put that down if I may?

V: Yes, of course ... in fact, I was wondering whether you needed any help in the Visitor's Centre?

R: Absolutely ... that was what I was thinking. We've actually just lost one of our long-time volunteers from there so it'd be good to slot you in! In a moment I'll send you over there and you can talk to the leader – his name's Pete.

V: Great. I presume he'll show me what to do?

R: Definitely – he's very helpful. Right, just one more question – how you found out about the sanctuary ... was it through the Tourist Office?

V: It was actually something I saw on TV ... it was on last week.

R: Oh yes, great.

2b Students' own answers

3a Suggested answers:
B is behind the Cub pool.
C is near the end of the main path, on the left.
D is in the middle of park, before where the paths cross.
E is in front of Enclosure 1.
F is between the small pond and Enclosure 2.
G is in front of Enclosure 2.

3b You must label five places. Two places will not be labelled.

4 6   G   8   F   10   C
     7   D   9   B

Audio script 2.2

R = Receptionist   V = Volunteer

R: Now, you'll need to find your way around the sanctuary so let me just explain where the key places are. I've got a very simple map here ... I'll talk you through it.

V: Thanks, that'd be really helpful.

R: We're now in the Reception area. You'll be based at the Visitor's Centre, which is the large building at the opposite side of the sanctuary park area.

V: Yes, I can just see it.

R: Good. Now, visitors often ask for the Animal feeding area 'cos it's quite difficult to find. It's actually quite near here – between the large pond and Enclosure number two.

V: OK.

R: And you'll also need to explain where people can buy feed for the animals. They don't often realise we have a designated kiosk for this.

V: Oh, OK.

R: For various reasons we've recently moved the kiosk. It used to be to the left of the Visitor's Centre, but we found it wasn't doing very well, so we've moved it right next to where the two paths cross, from the café and from the Visitor's Centre.

V: I can imagine you get more traffic that way.

R: Yeah.

V: And what about toilets?

R: We've actually got two sets – one is next door to the café, as you'll have guessed ... and the other is on the opposite side of the park, just behind Enclosure 2.

V: Got that.

R: And another crucial place is the First aid hut. We put this close to the Cub pool, the other side from the Reception, so it's accessible from the café, but it obviously needs to be quiet and secluded.

V: I've made a note of that. Can I just ask – I imagine you have quite a few families get separated, so is there a meeting point?

R: Yes, good question – it's very close to the Visitor's Centre, just to the side of the café toilets.

V: Right.

R: Good well, if you ...

5   Students' own answers

Language development and vocabulary

1 1   A all   2   A all
         B some   B some

2 1   Archaeology is particularly important for learning about prehistoric societies, for whom there are no written records.
     2   There is no single approach to archaeological theory which has been followed by all archaeologists. (no comma necessary)
     3   The cuckoo, whose calls used to be regarded as the first sign of spring, is now absent from many of its former breeding grounds.
     4   There are no other languages related to the Basque language, which is spoken in parts of Spain and France.

5 Aerial photographs can detect many features which are not visible at ground level. (no comma necessary)

6 Olympic athletes who receive financial support from their governments are able to train full time for their events. (no comma necessary)

3
1	where	3	which	5	which
2	who	4	whose	6	why

4
2 It was computers that/which seriously affected the print business of encyclopaedia.
3 Teachers and students from around the world have contributed more than 88,000 new articles, for which they were not paid, to Wikipedia./Teachers and students from around the world, who were not paid, have contributed more than 88,000 new articles to Wikipedia.
4 Wikipedia, which has to focus on being accurate and relevant in this modern age, is constantly being updated.
5 Our method of getting information has switched from PCs to other devices which are smaller and more mobile.
6 Billions of new internet users who come online for the first time will use a mobile device first.
7 Many new internet users, who speak languages other than English, will come from the developing world.
8 Wikipedia needs to reach out to people in the developing world, who will benefit greatly from its educational materials.

5 Students' own answers

6a
1	during	3	when	5	while
2	Before	4	After	6	As/While

6b
1	during	3	When	5	during
2	when	4	while	6	after

6c Students' own answers

Speaking

1

Period	Materials	Location	Style
at the end of the last century five years ago in 2005 recent in the 21st century	stone wood steel glass concrete	in the city centre by the river on a hilltop overlooking a park	irregular plain ornate symmetrical rectangular futuristic bold circular unusual tall traditional

2 Students' own answers

3
1 No
2 He omits to describe what the building is used for.

Audio script 2.3
One building that I don't like is in the centre of London. Most people call it the Gherkin, because it's shaped like one of those vegetables. It's very tall, you can see it from a long way off, but I'm not sure what its exact height is. It's this unusual shape, which I mentioned, and it's made of steel and glass. The glass reflects the light and it makes the building look black. It's very shiny, and futuristic looking. It was built at the beginning of this century, around 2002 as far as I remember. And … it's won quite

a few architectural awards, most people seem to think it's great. But I don't like it. I'm not really sure why, except that it doesn't fit in with any of the other buildings around it – it's much taller, and its shape and style is completely different. So I think it spoils the harmony of the area.

4
1	stunning	3	bustling	5	unique
2	remote	4	unspoilt		

5 Suggested answers:
2 want to visit the ancient temple there
3 there's no danger of flooding
4 you often see in tourism adverts
5 tourists from Europe are around

6 Students' own answers

7 Students' own answers

Writing

1
1 Water treatment. It starts with water collected in a river and finishes in individual homes/businesses, etc.
2 Five/5
3 What the process is designed to do and what the main features are.

2a Sentence 2 is more effective because it summarises the whole process more effectively, including how many major stages are involved and what the essential purpose is.

2b
1	is called	4	passed through
2	is taken	5	being cleaned
3	via		

2c Students' own answers

3a
1	pumped	4	added
2	pressed	5	stored
3	returned		

3b Suggested other verbs: *make, take, clean, remove, extract, lift*

4a Students' own answers

4b Sample answer
There are essentially five main stages involved in the processing of natural rainwater to make it of good enough quality to drink safely. The first stage is called abstraction, where the water is taken out of a river via a pumping station and passed through to a reservoir. The next major stage is clarification, with the water being cleaned by passing it through a flash mixer. However, this is not sufficient to remove finer particles so it must be pumped through a centrifuge which removes remaining debris. The extracted material is pressed into a thick sludge to make it more manageable. It is then lifted by conveyor belt onto lorries and taken away for disposal, with any remaining water being returned to the mixer for further cleaning. The fourth disinfection stage involves the addition of chorine to the water, before it is sent to the final distribution phase, being stored in a smaller reservoir until required. From here it is pumped on to the consumer, whether in homes, schools or workplaces.

5a Students' own answers

5b Students' own answers

Module 3

Reading

1 1 B   2 B   3 A

2a 2

2b iv

2c Suggested answers:
B The increase in MS in Europe
C A link between birthdays and MS
D A link between vitamin D and autoimmune diseases
E The government's response to scientific findings

3 1 iv   2 vi   3 i   4 vii   5 ii

4a Which two statements does the writer make about birthdays?
C

4b Scientists have long recognised the significance of birthdays in relation to MS.
… when evidence first emerged, almost two decades ago, that people born at the end of winter were more likely to get MS, and those born in autumn less so, many scientists found it hardly credible.

4c Not correct

5 C, E

6 Students' own answers

Vocabulary

1 1 danger   4 test   7 outcome
2 issue   5 Methods   8 problems
3 threat   6 challenge

2 1 find   3 tackle   5 pose
2 face   4 make

3 2 make, priority   4 find, solution
3 poses, threat   5 challenge, face

4 1 D   3 B   5 G   7 C
2 F   4 E   6 A

5 Suggested answers:
1 Next year I intend to make swimming a priority as a way of remaining healthy.
2 Some of my friends do rock climbing because they enjoy facing a challenge.
3 For me, going to the gym as a method of keeping fit would be a last resort.
4 Doing yoga is probably one of the best methods of exercising the joints.
5 In my opinion, the biggest issue for people who work long hours is having insufficient time for friends and family.
6 One of the consequences of taking up gardening is that I feel more relaxed.

Language development

1 1 real   3 real   5 unreal
2 unreal   4 real

2a 1 unlikely   2 possible

2b 1 would get   3 raised   5 used
2 worked   4 would be

3 2 If there were more organic farms, fruit and vegetables would be safer to eat.
3 If children got more sleep, they would make better progress at school.
4 If people washed their hands more often, infections would spread less quickly.
5 If people had better health education, the cost of healthcare would be reduced.

4a 1 unless   4 Supposing that
2 as long as   5 otherwise
3 Provided that   6 As long as

4b 1 As long as/Provided that   3 Supposing
2 unless   4 otherwise

5 Suggested answers:
1 take up badminton   4 we'll waste time talking
2 go to the gym later   5 I keep studying hard
3 I get up earlier

Writing

1a A problem-solution essay

1b The core problem is the fact that so many people choose to eat unhealthy food. The two elements you must write about in the essay are a) why people do this and b) what measures can be taken to address these causes.

2 1 E   3 B   5 C
2 D   4 A

3a Correct order: C 1   B 2   E 3   D 4   A 5

3b D   1   B   5   C   2   A   4   E   3

4 Sample answer:
It has long been known that eating certain kinds of food – processed meat, greasy hamburgers, sugar-laden cakes – causes a wide range of problems, from obesity to heart disease. However, many people choose to ignore warnings and eat large amounts of unhealthy food. Why do they do this and what can be done to prevent it? Firstly, processed food is generally cheaper than fresh food because it tends to be mass produced and often also contains chemicals to preserve it for longer. The solution to this is therefore to make the food more expensive and consequently less attractive. It is common to impose massive taxes on cigarettes and the same levy should be put on things like sugar or trans-fats.
A second reason why many people choose unhealthy foods is because there are numerous temptations to buy and consume them. For example, many fast food outlets are owned by large corporations and they promote their products through expensive promotional campaigns and slick adverts, many of them specifically designed to 'hook' children to their products early on. These adverts make no mention of the high number of calories the food contains or of the amount of fat used in its preparation. Many people feel that this issue can best be handled by banning advertising of unhealthy food to children, for example to prohibit commercials on children's TV or other media and on mainstream channels before the 9p.m. watershed. In addition, advertising and texts like menus should also be required to show clearly how much sugar and fat is in each meal.
As can be seen, there are a number of ways to tackle the problem of unhealthy eating, but they all require action by governments as well as the willpower of individuals.

Listening

1 1 Allergic reactions to food   3 One/1
    2 Three/3

2 widespread: common
cause: result in
symptoms: reactions
milder: minor
temporary: short-term, quickly disappear
problems: difficulties
severe: serious
adulthood: later life

3a Students' own answers

3b What are the <u>two main risk factors</u> for allergies?
What are the <u>names</u> of the <u>two main techniques for</u>
<u>identifying</u> allergens?
• <u>turned</u> the <u>seeds into</u> 8 _____
• the treatment <u>doesn't change</u> the seeds' 9 _____ or taste
• unsure of reason for success – believed to be <u>affected by</u>
<u>changes</u> to the 10 _____ inside the molecules

4 4 family history   8 liquid
    5 shortage of vitamins   9 colour
    6 skin test   10 pressure
    7 elimination diet

Audio script 3.1

N = Narrator   S = Student

N: You will hear a presentation by a biology student on the topic of food allergens – substances in food which cause an abnormal reaction in some people.

Listen and answer the questions.

S: Good morning everyone. I've chosen as the topic for my presentation the issue of allergic reactions and the foods which cause them. Before I talk in detail about a particular research project, I'll start with a bit of background information on allergies.

As many of you know, allergies appear to be becoming much more common in many parts of the world. In the developed world generally, 4 percent to 8 percent of people are estimated to have at least one food allergy and the figure rises to 25 percent in certain countries, such as the UK.

Allergic reactions to food can cause a variety of symptoms – from the very mild to severe, for example a mild reaction would be a slightly itchy rash on the skin, to moderate breathing difficulties which disappear very quickly and don't have a major effect. There are, however, some far more serious reactions than these, for instance, fainting. So, clearly it's very important to establish the degree of severity of reaction a person has to a particular food. Also, it's interesting to note that allergies to certain foods tend to be suffered mainly by children. For example, by the time they're adults, many people stop being allergic to eggs, milk and soy. By contrast, nut and shellfish allergies almost always go on right through people's lives.

Now, how can people manage allergies to reduce their effects? Well first of all, it's important to find out whether they have certain risk factors. The principle factors are twofold – there's family history which can give a strong indication. In addition to this, another trigger for an allergic reaction can be a shortage of vitamins.

But above all it's crucial to identify which foods are causing the problems. It's not always obvious and of course individuals may be allergic to more than one type of food. There are various techniques of doing this. One method is to do what's known as a skin test where you make a small prick with a needle tipped with a small amount of the substance and see whether there is a local reaction. Another technique is called an elimination diet, where you gradually withdraw foods and monitor levels of improvement. Another approach, less widely used, is to have a blood test – to determine whether immunoglobin E antibodies are present.

Alongside all these techniques for managing allergies is ongoing research which attempts to neutralise the effects of the allergens, in other words trying to reduce their power to harm. I'm going to report on a particular research project which focused on one allergen – in sesame seeds. Scientists recognised that allergies occur when a certain substance, part of the body's immune system, binds to proteins in the food molecules. This binding triggers the release of harmful chemicals which cause the allergy symptoms.

The team took the sesame seeds and reduced them to liquid. This change was necessary for the next stage of the process, because solids are less responsive to the treatment. The scientists then passed a series of electric pulses through the fluid, and this altered the structure of the protein in the food.

The results were extremely positive. Firstly, it was found that 95 percent of the proteins' allergic qualities vanished. And what's more the treatment appeared to have no harmful effects on the enjoyment of the food because the taste and colour of the product remained more or less the same.

However, the research team admits they still don't know exactly why the treatment works. They have found that between pulses of electricity, a very high pressure of up to 1,200 atmospheres is created inside the protein molecules and they think it is this which is the key to successfully neutralising of the allergen.

Language development

1a 1 can't not   4 must to finish
    2 don't must   5 should
    3 need spend   6 needn't

1b 1 can't   4 must finish
    2 don't have to   5 shouldn't
    3 need to spend   6 shouldn't/mustn't

2 1 could   4 have to   7 have to
    2 may   5 have to   8 would
    3 can   6 must   9 shouldn't

3 1 could/might   4 won't
    2 will   5 would
    3 could/might   6 could/might

4 1 died of typhoid, he might not have been motivated to cure infectious diseases
    2 suggested that infections were caused by micro-organisms, other scientists wouldn't have developed antiseptic methods for surgery
    3 could develop new treatments
    4 the smallpox vaccine in the nineteenth century, thousands of people would have died of the disease
    5 shouldn't keep unused medicines when they have passed their expiry date
    6 need to make sure that there aren't any holes in them
    7 people don't have to take vitamin supplements
    8 must be registered with the General Medical Council before they can practise medicine

5 Suggested answers:
1 will go to Canada to study
2 I'll take it again
3 might visit my brother in Hong Kong
4 need to have very good English

Vocabulary

1a apparently, evidently, naturally, unfortunately

1b apparently, evidently; undeniably, undoubtedly

1c undeniably, undoubtedly

1d

| 1 | A | 3 | B | 5 | B |
| 2 | B | 4 | D | 6 | C |

2

1	Evidently	5	Naturally
2	Unfortunately	6	undoubtedly
3	Naturally	7	unfortunately
4	Apparently		

3 Suggested answers:
1 Naturally, swimming is good for health as well as being enjoyable.
2 Unfortunately, eating chocolate isn't very good for your weight.
3 Naturally, just because a person has money it doesn't mean they're happy.
4 Listening to music is undeniably one of the best forms of relaxation.
5 Evidently, taking vitamin supplements has little effect on health.
6 Walking undoubtedly helps to strengthen bones.
7 Apparently memory deteriorates with age.
8 Yoga is undoubtedly good for reducing stress.

Speaking

1a 1

1b

Positive	Negative	Neutral
cheerful	anxious	attitude
contented	pessimistic	outlook
optimistic	worried	therapy
		treatment

1c Suggested answers:
1 If a person has a happy childhood, with a lot of opportunity to meet people and try different activities, that person might be very confident and sociable as an adult.
2 I think this is very likely. People with a positive attitude are likely to achieve more because they have self-belief, which may be just as important for success as ability.
3 I think the key to happiness is more likely to be good relationships with others than status or material possessions.
4 Probably adults, because they face a lot of pressures like exams, work, childcare and money problems.
5 Both may be important, but I think if therapy works, it is a better treatment because there will be fewer, if any, side effects.

1d

| A | 3 | C | 5 | E | 4 |
| B | 2 | D | 1 | | |

1e Students' own answers

2a Suggested answers:
1 May have been brought up in big family, or family with lots of visitors. Or may have inherited a sociable personality.
2 Very important. Social skills are valuable in all spheres of life, e.g. the workplace, the neighbourhood.
3 Yes – opposites attract, and people with similar personalities might be antagonistic, e.g. two assertive people who like to dominate might not get on well.
4 Definitely. People in general respond to others' behaviour and opinions – there is a tendency to converge.
5 Positive, assertive people. Good listening skills. Physical characteristics may be important too, e.g. height, voice quality.
6 Probably different, but not too different. Need a mix of skills and personalities.

7 The general attitude. Someone who has a positive attitude and is keen to learn is more valuable than someone with the correct exam results.

2b Speaker 2 uses more adjectives.

Audio script 3.4

1 Well, some individuals just enjoy being with others, and maybe they don't like being alone. That's just how they are, from childhood even. Other people are the opposite. Their nature is like that, it's not something that they choose. So the reason is I think that it's from birth, the difference.

2 I think individuals who are sociable are more confident than others. It could be because they grew up in a large family, so they feel very comfortable mixing in large groups. That's what they're used to. And it's also possible that they feel insecure when they're alone. Some people don't like being alone. Also, people who are outgoing may need the stimulus of other people's company, they might feel bored when they're by themselves.

2c Students' own answers

3a Students' own answers

3b Students' own answers

Writing

1 The core problem is the increase in mental health problems amongst the young.

2a Suggested answers:

Column 1: lack of employment opportunities for the young, leading to a sense of low self worth; problems with new technologies – young people sharing ideas about self harm

Column 2: increase worthwhile volunteering opportunities for the young, help to lead into paid employment; monitor social networking sites/forums for damaging messages, etc.

2b Students' own answers

3 Students' own answers

4a Because of improvements in care and in living conditions, many people in different parts of the world are living longer and healthier lives. However, there are certain problems which <u>appear to be</u> resisting this trend. In particular, <u>it is believed that</u> mental ill health is on the rise, especially amongst younger people. The reasons for this are many and varied. Perhaps the most powerful cause <u>could be</u> that some young people feel alienated from wider society. Nowadays, communities <u>tend to be</u> less multi-generational than they used to be and young people have fewer role models to look up to or respected older figures they can ask for advice and guidance.

4b 1 appear to be/tend to be   3 it is believed
     2 could be   4 appear/tend

5 Sample answer

Because of improvements in care and in living conditions, many people in different parts of the world are living longer and healthier lives. However, there are certain problems which appear to be resisting this trend. In particular, it is believed that mental ill health is on the rise, especially amongst younger people.

The reasons for this are many and varied. Perhaps the most powerful cause could be that some young people feel alienated from wider society. Nowadays, communities tend to be less multi-generational than they used to be and young people have fewer role models to look up to or respected older figures they can ask for advice and guidance. These days the role might be taken by counsellors or mental health-care professionals but, for many, there is a stigma attached to this form of treatment. If you have a physical illness, it is acceptable to go to a doctor but people feel less comfortable going to a psychiatrist. One solution is to make every effort to talk openly and honestly about mental health so that gradually people will see how common it is and that it is nothing to be afraid of.

Another possible cause of mental ill health in the young is a reduction in the amount of physical activity they do. The link between physical and mental health has long been understood and spending long hours in front of a screen instead of doing sport or playing outside can trigger depression. It is therefore important to invest in sports for young people, to make sure recreation grounds are kept open and that sports clubs for young people are maintained.

It would be short-sighted to ignore this burgeoning problem and we should aim to bring about improvements in mental well-being to match the achievements in physical health care.

6a Students' own answers

6b Students' own answers

Module 4

Reading

1 Students' own answers

2a 1

2b Students' own answers

3 1 Paragraph A: movies; the internet; the music industry; schools; clothes; TV
    2 Paragraph B: 'There are a few exceptions to this.'; 'Some ... but most ...'

4 1 B   3 B   5 D
    2 G   4 A

5a paragraph E

5b nouns

5c 1 technology   2 consumption

6 6 growth
    7 durability (also possible: sustainability)
    8 unemployment

Vocabulary

1 1 define   4 acknowledge
    2 assume   5 convince
    3 conceive   6 speculate

2 1 C   3 A   5 B
    2 F   4 D   6 E

3a 1 It is formally acknowledged
2 There is a common misconception
3 There is a widespread belief
4 There is an underlying assumption

3b Suggested answers:
1 There is a widespread belief that supermarket prices are higher than necessary.
2 It is formally acknowledged that discarded packaging from consumer goods is polluting the oceans.
3 There is an underlying assumption that it is always better to buy locally produced goods than imported goods.
4 There is a common misconception that glass bottles are more environmentally friendly than plastic ones.
5 There is a widespread belief that some companies pass on information about our shopping preferences without our knowledge.

4a 1 take   3 have   5 be
2 resign   4 pass

4b 1 resign themselves to   4 are open to ideas
2 have little faith   5 take into consideration
3 passing judgement on

Language development

1 1 D   3 F   5 C
2 A   4 B   6 E

2 1 C   3 G   5 H   7 A
2 D   4 E   6 B   8 F

3 1 unless
2 if   6 Although
3 whereas/while   7 While/Whereas
4 Whenever   8 Whether
5 as

4 Students' own answers

5a 1

5b 1 It is widely believed **that** shopping is good for the national economy.
2 It is my belief **that** people shop when they are bored.
3 A lot of people think **that** supermarket prices are too high.
4 There is a common misconception **that** food should not be eaten after its 'Best Before' date.
5 It seems to me **that** having a wide choice of products is unnecessary.
6 Children should be taught to recognise **that** adverts are designed to persuade them.

6 Students' own answers

Writing

1a 2

1b 3

2a Students' own answers

2b 1 ✓   4 ✓   7 ✓
2 ✓   5 ✗   8 ✓
3 ✗   6 ✗   9 ✗

2c 1 Ac   4 Ac   7 P
2 P   5 Ac   8 Ac
3 P   6 Ac   9 P

2d 2 Advertising is an essential means of communicating to consumers distinctive features of products.
3 Adverts are, by definition, designed to present a positive view of products, disguising less attractive aspects.
7 Adverts can be miniature works of art, portraying ideas in a witty, original way.
9 Many people feel oppressed by the constant exposure to adverts, across all types of media.

3a Students' own answers

3b 1 most of which   4 In addition
2 Firstly   5 Although
3 lead to   6 particularly

3c Type 4

4a Students' own answers

4b Sample answer

There are a number of convincing arguments against advertising, most of which portray adverts as a blight on society. Firstly, our constant exposure to commercial images is said to lead to poor mental health. Nowadays especially, there is hardly a moment when we are free of adverts in one form or another, whether it be an animation at the side of an email page, or roadside hoardings, or incessant radio jingles. In addition, adverts are considered to misrepresent the truth. Although they are often glossy and humorous, they deliberately give false information and fool people into believing that they must have a particular product, forcing them to spend money they can ill afford to part with. Another claim is that advertising is responsible for persuading young people to adopt bad lifestyle choices, for example to start smoking or drinking heavily. Adverts, it is asserted, deliberately 'hook' people, particularly youngsters, ensuring they will be addicted to certain products for the rest of their lives.

I accept that many of these points are true. However, I also recognise that adverts are an essential feature of any free economy. If advertising were banned, consumers would have no way of knowing the full range of items on offer. There would be little incentive for innovation because the only way of selling new products would be through word of mouth. I also feel that adverts are often extremely well crafted and witty, even sometimes very moving. It is true adverts are all around us but this can actually be a good thing.

On balance, I feel that advertising has the potential to do harm but that it is possible to control it in such a way that the damage is limited and the benefits outweigh the disadvantages.

Listening

1a Two/2

1b Devices related to health and fitness. Three gadgets are described.

1c 1 noun   6 noun/gerund
2 plural noun   7 noun/gerund
3 noun/gerund   8 noun
4 noun   9 noun
5 adjective   10 verb

2a Information will be given across the rows, left to right, rather than down the columns, i.e. all the information will be given about the UV Bracelet before moving onto information about the Vibrapower Disc.

2b 1 a)   3 b)   5 a)   7 a)
2 b)   4 a)   6 b)

2c 1 B   2 C   3 A

3

1	weather forecast	6	motivation
2	colours	7	noise
3	sport	8	laptop
4	battery life	9	doctor
5	enjoyable	10	carry

Audio script 4.1

R = Radio presenter   C = Carrie

R: Now to *Consumer Matters*. It should be easier than ever to get fit – there are countless gadgets and apps out there dedicated to helping with just that. This week Carrie Foster's been trying out three of the latest gadgets on the market designed to help you keep fit and healthy. Carrie …

C: The first item I looked at is called UV Bracelet. The bracelet is linked to a phone app designed to monitor how much ultra violet or UV radiation you're getting when you're sunbathing. It's basically a sparkly rock on a band worn around your wrist that contains hundreds of tiny sensors. The app gives a live UV index, and warns when there are dangerously high levels of radiation. In addition it provides a weather forecast for your current location with plenty of in-depth information. You hook it up to your smartphone and it delivers its data via a sleek app. It's got a lot of great features. It's free to download and it comes in a variety of colours – taupe, platinum, or gunmetal – it has a very flexible strap so you can have it working whilst you're doing sport, of whichever kind.

On the downside, though it was fully charged and meant to last for a month, it had much poorer battery life than I'd thought. It lost connectivity with my phone but there was no warning. The result? A lobster-red 'tan' which could be pretty dangerous. I'd give it a rating of 7 out of 10.

The second gadget I trialled was very different. It's called the Vibrapower Disc and the idea is that you do various stretches and exercises on top of the plate as it vibrates, toning your body much more than ordinary exercise alone. There are lots of positives – I have to say I did find it enjoyable to do exercise on it. Research shows that it can increase the rate of fat loss pretty efficiently, which I can believe. Also, as someone who doesn't exercise regularly, it did help me keep up my motivation, especially as you can only do it for 20 minutes max. The sensation takes a bit of getting used to, but it's worth persevering.

The main shortcoming is that the Vibrapower Disc is huge – so it's difficult to know where to put it. Also it's pretty hard to get a suitable place to set it up because of objections about noise – which may irritate anybody who happens to be around. My rating? Again, pretty positive – 7 out of 10.

The last of the three gadgets is an app to keep an eye on your blood pressure – the Smart BP Monitor. It consists of two parts – a band or sleeve which you wrap round your arm, which links to an app on your smart device. It's quite flexible – if you don't have a smartphone, there's a USB charger so it can also function on your laptop. The app has several snazzy functions – you can use your phone's camera to check your pulse and it also tracks how many steps you take on a daily basis. If you're really worried about your blood pressure, and you want to monitor it regularly, this could be a useful app for you because it has a facility to email a doctor automatically with your stats.

The negatives are that I found the readings inconsistent – one minute it insisted I had a problem and the next minute I was normal. Another thing is that while it's easy to monitor, the actual sleeve is hard to carry because it's rather bulky – not exactly handbag ready. I'd rate it as 5 out of 10.

4 Students' own answers

Language development

1

A	3	C	1	E	6
B	5	D	2	F	4

2

1	these	3	it	5	which	7	it
2	which	4	they	6	where	8	it

3

1	which/that	3	when	5	their
2	which	4	which/that	6	they/these

4 Students' own answers

Vocabulary

1

1	However	5	On the contrary
2	whereas	6	Initially
3	However	7	In particular
4	For instance	8	Nevertheless

2

1	While	5	As a result
2	In particular	6	Furthermore
3	At first	7	On the contrary
4	Nevertheless		

3

A	5	C	8	E	6	G	3
B	2	D	4	F	7	H	1

4 Students' own answers

Speaking

1

1	brand	4	necessities	7	symbol
2	goods	5	local		
3	luxury	6	Imported		

2a

1	goods	4	necessities	7	status
2	brand	5	local		symbol
3	luxury	6	Imported		

2b Students' own answers

3

1	C	3	A	5	B
2	F	4	E	6	D

4a Students' own answers

4b Students' own answers

5 Students' own answers

Writing

1a
1   The social effects of online shopping
2   You don't have to write about both sides of the argument – but you can if you wish.
3   'Shift' refers to the change from shopping in traditional stores to buying online.

1b Students' own answers

2a Suggested answers

Ideas	Support/Illustration
3 Can't see the item before buying	Especially problematic for clothes – frequently have to send things back
4 Against the point of view in the statement, i.e. pro online shopping Online shopping offers much more choice	The world is your shopping mall – consumers are not restricted to what is in the local warehouse

2b Students' own answers

3a
1	high street	4	squeeze out
2	no-go areas	5	outsource
3	thriving	6	far-reaching

3b It is true that online shopping seems to benefit individual ~~shopper~~ **shoppers** by offering wider choice and lower prices. However, it is important to look more ~~deeper~~ **deeply** at the range of consequences for society as a whole. Firstly, because of the ~~raise~~ **rise** of internet shopping, many high-street stores have been ~~force~~ **forced** to close down. A large proportion of town centres have numerous empty spaces where shops once were, and the ~~absent~~ **absence** of a thriving commercial centre makes these places dangerous, no-go areas.

3c shopper – C plural
deeply – A adverb
raise – E wrong word
force – D verb form
absent – B noun

4 Sample answer

It is true that online shopping seems to benefit individual shoppers by offering wider choice and lower prices. However, it is important to look more deeply at the range of consequences for society as a whole. Firstly, because of the rise of internet shopping, many high-street stores have been forced to close down. Many town centres have numerous empty spaces where shops once were, and the absence of a thriving commercial centre makes these places dangerous, no-go areas. Another problem connected to shop closures is a decline in social cohesion. Stores have traditionally been the hub of local communities: going shopping is as much a social as a commercial encounter. For disabled or elderly people or parents looking after young children, shopping provides the chance to get out of the house and to meet people. Related to this issue, it is important to recognise that in many parts of the world there is tremendous inequality of access to the internet. In particular, older people and people on low incomes do not have the same level of access to the benefits of internet shopping.

A second major problem is that the rise of internet purchasing is squeezing out smaller businesses. It tends to be the case that only large retailers have the capital and organisational capacity to offer cheap and speedy online shopping and home delivery services. Also, as online shoppers demand lower and lower prices, retailers often outsource to low-cost suppliers, using, for example, poorly paid workers in less-developed countries.

To sum up, I believe that the transition from shopping in stores to buying online has been one of the most significant changes in society in recent years, and one that has serious and far-reaching effects.

5 Students' own answers

Module 5

Reading

1 Students' own answers

2a
1	a house
2	(energy-saving) gadgets and materials
3	orange
4	(conventional opaque, blue-coloured) solar collectors
5	the conservatory roof

2b This

3a the paints used on its walls have insulating properties

3b F

4
1	F	2	D	3	A	4	E

5a paragraph 8 and the beginning of paragraph 9

5b a noun

5c pumps

6
5	pumps	7	roof
6	leaves	8	gravity

7a In <u>future</u>, all <u>homes and offices</u> will have <u>glass panes</u> which are <u>orange</u>.

7b 'orange-coloured panes of glass. Very soon ... every office, and ... every home' (paragraph 4)

7c F (they will be colourless)

8
9	F	11	T	13	T
10	F	12	NG	14	NG

Vocabulary

1a
1	experimentation	4	innovation
2	automation	5	intelligence
3	controversial	6	accessible

1b Suggested answers:
1 natural gas should be obtained by fracking
2 reduced the cost of goods
3 a suitable topic for fictional books
4 encourage children to think of new ideas in school
5 appear on the market
6 Health care

2a
2	both	4	few
3	three quarters	5	a third

2b
1 three quarters/the majority
2 Both
3 few
4 third
5 majority
6 most

2c Suggested answers:
1   Both my parents own a smartphone.
2   About three quarters of my friends own a laptop computer.
3   Few of my friends own a car.
4   About a third of my friends own an Xbox.
5   Few of my friends own a pet.
6   Most of my friends own an electronic activity tracker.

3a 1   B   3   A   5   B
       2   A   4   B   6   A

3b Students' own answers

Language development

1   1   argued   4   explained   7   suggested
       2   explained   5   promised   8   said
       3   mentioned   6   told

2   1   The scientists explained that buildings technology was developing very quickly.
       2   He suggested that the reporter should go and see their eco-house.
       3   When they entered the house, he told the reporter to look closely at the conservatory roof.
       4   The reporter argued that the light coming through the orange glass is like street lighting.
       5   The scientists promised the reporter that before long they'd all be able to produce electricity in their homes using colourless glass panes.
       6   The reporter mentioned that the temperature inside the house was very comfortable.
       7   The scientist said that technology was developing so fast that houses soon become outdated.
       8   The official promised that the government's target was for all new houses to generate their own energy by 2025.

3a Suggested answers:
2   I asked the shopkeeper whether (if) he/she had any tinned fish or not.
3   I asked one of my friends if he/she would/to pick me up from my house.
4   I asked my cousin whether we should meet at the cinema or at the car park.
5   I asked the teacher if I could borrow the book.
6   I asked the taxi driver to go to the station.
7   I asked the police officer where the central market was.
8   I asked my friend if he/she wanted to eat noodles or rice.

3b 1   instruction   4   question   7   question
       2   question   5   request   8   question
       3   request   6   instruction

3c 2   I asked Lisa whether (if) she would like tea or coffee.
       3   I asked the clerk if I could borrow a pen.
       4   I asked the police officer where the bus station is/was.
       5   I asked the customer whether he/she used gas or electricity for cooking.
       6   I asked my girlfriend what time she would be ready.

Writing

1   1   Percentage of household income spent on different household items
       3   Seven items plus one miscellaneous 'Others'
       4   The y axis shows percentage of household income

2a 1   F Approximately one third of spending was on housing costs.
       2   T
       3   F The smallest percentage of total spending was on clothes.
       4   F Only 5 percent of total spending was on entertainment.
       5   T
       6   T

2b 1   12 percent
       2   8 percent
       3   17 percent and 11 percent
       4   3 percent
       5   transport and food

3a 1   The chart shows the proportion of expenditure on different items in an average household in one country in 2015, according to educational level.
       2   Three different educational levels
       3   Six areas plus one micellaneous (unspecified) 'Others'

3b 3

3c 1   -   3   -   5   +   7   +
       2   +   4   -   6   +

3d travel abroad and food at home

4   Sample answer

The chart shows that having a more advanced educational level made a small but significant difference in the way people spent their income, in a given European country in 2015. Firstly, although housing costs accounted for by far the largest percentage of outgoings, it was much higher for householders with school education only: 35 percent compared with just 30 percent for those with further education and declining to 25 percent for university graduates. It was also noticeable that school leavers chose to eat in the home more than those with other educational levels (14 percent compared with 8 percent and 5 percent for those completing further education and university graduates respectively). University graduates spent proportionately much more than school leavers on pension provision (17 percent compared with 10 percent). Transport spending showed a notably different trend – with further education-educated householders spending a higher percentage of their income (25 percent) than either of the other two groups. Correspondingly, spending on Other items was lower for this group (11 percent) than for school leavers (15 percent) and university graduates (17 percent).

Listening

1   For agreement about actions

2a Extract 1
       A   we'll obviously need something really striking for the introduction, it's helpful to start with something simple like the meaning of the word 'television'
       B   Sure; of course, we could start with that; Simple but clear – great
       C   no disagreement

       Extract 2
       A   Could we say something about how he set up a telephone exchange in his bedroom … act out how it worked?, What about focusing on him studying at Glasgow University, which had a world-renowned engineering facility? I think it'd be good if we could give the audience some idea of what the laboratories were like.

B   OK … fair enough.; Then let's go for that.
C   That'd be great … but only if we had another 30 minutes!, Hmmm … I'm not sure how easy it would be to get video footage.

2b 7 stages, 9 actions
A   show <u>pictures</u> of <u>Baird's colleague</u>
B   <u>compare TV</u> with <u>other gadgets</u>
C   read out a <u>quotation</u>
D   show a short <u>video</u>
E   <u>act out</u> a scene
F   show a <u>picture of a lab</u>
G   explain using <u>a diagram</u>
H   discuss the <u>meaning of a word</u>
I   ask the <u>audience to give their opinion</u>

3 1   H   3   B   5   C   7   I
       2   F   4   G   6   D

Audio script 5.1

N = Narrator   L = Leo   K = Kerry

N: You will hear two Engineering students – Leo and Kerry – discussing a presentation they are planning on the inventor of the television, John Logie Baird.

L: Hi, Kerry. Glad we could meet today … we've only got a week before the presentation.

K: No problem, Leo. I've got the notes we made about what the various stages of the talk will be, but we ought to agree on what we include in each part.

L: Sure. Well, we'll obviously need something really striking for the introduction.

K: I always think it's helpful to start with something simple like the meaning or derivation of the term 'television'.

L: We could explain that it's made up of two parts – *tele* from Greek and *vision* from Latin … so that's 'far sight' … of course, we could start with that on the first slide.

K: Simple but clear – great. Now, we've already said we'll tell the audience something about the inventor himself – Baird – and his early years …

L: Set the scene of how he started out in engineering. He came from a small town in Scotland and was always fascinated by electronics.

K: Could we say something about how he set up a telephone exchange in his bedroom … act out how it worked?

L: That'd be great, but only if we had another 30 minutes!

K: OK … Fair enough! What about focusing on him studying at Glasgow University which had a world-renowned engineering faculty? I think it'd be good if we could give the audience some idea of what the laboratories were like.

L: Hmm … I'm not sure how easy it would be to get video footage.

K: I saw some stills photos on the university website – they're just rooms, not his colleagues, but I still think they'd work well.

L: Then let's go for that.

K: The next part is about the first experimental demonstration of a TV.

L: In 1924. Should we show a simple diagram of how the TV worked?

K: Well … most of the people in the audience will be non-specialists so I think we want to ground it in something they're familiar with … like a smartphone.

L: We could get people to bring out their phones and we could make a quick comparison with what that prototype TV could do.

K: Or more accurately … what it couldn't do!

L: That's a better idea … good.

K: And then we've got the second experiment in 1926 – the one everyone talks about … where Baird managed to transmit a picture of his business partner.

L: Which, very surprising for the time was a woman … which we could emphasize.

K: I know … but I think that would be a bit distracting – let's stick to important stuff.

L: You mean this is where we try to talk through how the prototype TV worked … using a graphic.

K: OK … it's not that complex really …

L: Yeah.

K: Right, so, then we have Developments, from 1927 onwards …

L: When he moved onto things like colour TV. Wasn't that when the newspaper editor came out with the famous words about 'a madman who says he's got a machine for seeing by wireless!'

K: Should we share what he actually said in this section?

L: Why not? I think it stresses how disbelieving people were about the possibilities of TV.

K: Great. And then we've got Baird's other inventions. I really want to get something in about the development of radar.

L: Now this is something we do have video footage on …

K: I think it'd be brilliant in that stage … when there's something really worth looking at …

L: Exactly … but just 5–10 seconds-worth.

K: No problem. And that brings us to the last section which is Baird's legacy …

L: I was wondering whether we really should ask people for their views on this.

K: You mean encourage the others to join in with a brief discussion about what Baird means to us today?

L: Yes, I think it's good to have that level of interaction. You know, it would give the audience the opportunity to share.

4   Students' own answers

Language development

1   3

2   Nearly half of <u>Britons who have not managed to buy a house by their mid-thirties</u> doubt they will ever be able to do so, a report has found.

<u>The research from Yorkshire Building Society</u> found <u>49 percent of people aged 35 to 40 who are not homeowners but would like to be</u>, think it is now 'unlikely' or 'very unlikely' they will ever own a property.

<u>The survey, carried out by NatCen Social Research</u>, found that <u>more than two thirds (69 percent) of young adults aged 18 to 40</u> felt owning their own home was <u>a source of social and financial security</u>.

<u>Nearly a third (31 percent) of non-homeowners aged 35 to 40</u> have completely given up even trying to buy a home due to <u>affordability issues</u>, the research found.

The situation is unlikely to change unless there is <u>a dramatic downward shift in house prices</u>.

3 1 switches on the wall
  2 People who have a disability
  3 Central heating systems
  4 Smart homes
  5 almost two thirds of people
  6 the recommended minimum size
  7 Children under the age of six months
  8 Buildings designed in the 1960s

4 Suggested answers:
  1 of recycled materials is increasing
  2 price of raw materials means that they will soon be more affordable
  3 simplicity of the house design makes it cost-effective
  4 in the efficiency of all new homes is a major part of the government's policy
  5 first ice hotel was made over 20 years ago in a Swedish town
  6 the first exhibition of manufactured goods from all over the world

5a Students' own answers

5b Suggested answers:
  1 The place where I'd most like to live in future is Maine in the USA.
  2 Being able to buy a house which is in good condition interests me.
  3 Reducing household bills is one of the most important things for me.
  4 Cutting down on waste and energy consumption is a top priority.
  5 I'd like to buy an energy-efficient house made from recycled building materials.

Vocabulary

1a

The original speaker/writer	Reporting verbs
made a positive statement	claim, highlight, illustrate, point out, prove
made a negative statement	deny
made a hesitant statement	indicate, suggest
made a statement about danger	warn

1b

The person reporting a statement	Reporting verbs
is unsure whether the statement is correct or not	claim, deny, indicate, suggest, warn
accepts the truth of the statement	highlight, illustrate, point out, prove

2 1 warned   4 suggested   7 point out
  2 pointed out   5 warned   8 indicate
  3 claim, deny   6 highlighted

3 1 C   3 D   5 E
  2 F   4 A   6 B

4 1 Engineers claimed that the domestic water supply is completely safe.
  2 Estate agents denied saying that the house was suitable for a family.
  3 A government spokesperson pointed out that there are insufficient houses to meet current demand.
  4 A housing officer suggested that families with young children should have priority over single adults.
  5 An urban planner warned that the housing shortage was going to get worse over the next five years.
  6 A local resident claimed that bus services in that area were inadequate.

5 Suggested answer:

The government has said that local councils have to provide more houses to meet growing demand. The local council has pointed out that building firms are only willing to build larger houses, which yield a bigger profit. But local people warn that many people who are currently living with their parents cannot afford to buy these larger houses.

Speaking

1 1 C   3 F   5 E
  2 D   4 A   6 B

2a 1 Which is more labour-saving: a brush or a vacuum cleaner?
  2 Which is more outdated: a candle or a torch?
  3 Which was more revolutionary when it was first produced: paper or silk?
  4 Which is more state-of-the-art: robotic surgery or gene therapy?
  5 Which is more user-friendly: a driverless car or a conventional car?
  6 Which is more versatile: a piece of cloth or a pair of scissors?

2b Suggested answers:
  1 a vacuum cleaner   4 gene therapy
  2 a candle   5 a driverless car
  3 paper   6 a piece of cloth

3a 4/four

3b 1 No
  2 The speaker omits point 2

Audio script 5.2

I've got a sewing machine that I only use occasionally. It sits in a room upstairs and it gets quite dusty! I use it for different things, but mainly for mending or altering things. For example, whenever I buy trousers or tops the legs and the sleeves are nearly always too long. So I need to take them up. Or if I have a quilt cover and it tears I mend it. My friends laugh at me, because they just buy new things when they tear, but I don't believe in doing that. I think people throw too much away actually. But also, although they laugh, my friends and people in my family often ask me to alter things for them – clothes usually. I'm the sort of official sewing person, none of them even know how to use a sewing machine!

The other thing I use my machine for is making clothes. I really enjoy that, it's a kind of hobby. I used to do a lot more than I do now, but I'm just too busy these days. That's why I only use my machine occasionally. But hopefully some time in the future I'll be able to use it more often.

3c 1 Yes
2 She could have described the sewing machine (e.g. age, make, type).

4a Yes

4b 1, 2, 3, 5, 6, 7, 8

4c Suggested answers:
1 I only use
2 I've had
3 changed
5 that you put food in/that I use the blender for
6 dieticians said there was too much sugar in some of them
7 a paste with nuts and fat
8 longer

5 Students' own answers

6 Students' own answers

Writing

1 1 50 years – 1910–1960
2 Food by 13 percent; clothing by 2 percent
3 Housing by 5 percent; entertainment by 2 percent; Others by 8 percent
4 Healthcare
5 Decline in percentage spent on food

2 A 1   C 3   E 4
    B 5   D 2

3a 1 rising – increased/increase
2 falling – fell, declined, dropping
3 staying the same – remained constant, held steady, remained exactly the same
4 large – significant, notable
5 small – slight, fairly
6 percentage – proportion (priority/importance)

3b Students' own answers

4 Sample answer:
The two charts show that there was a significant difference in the proportion spent on different items over the 50 years between 1960 and 2010, in an average household in one country. The most noticeable change was in the order of importance of the different items: in 1960 the largest percentage was spent on food (30 percent) with housing accounting for the second largest portion (28 percent). By 2010 this had reversed, with food down to just 13 percent of the budget and housing increasing markedly to 33 percent. However, the largest proportion was spent on miscellaneous 'other' items: rising from 21 percent in 1960 to 39 percent in 2010. The percentage spent on clothing went down considerably – from 12 percent to 4 percent. The two remaining items – healthcare and entertainment – remained very similar: both of these areas of expenditure rose by 1 percent to 6 percent and 5 percent respectively.

5 Students' own answers

Module 6

Reading

1a 3

1b Students' own answers

2a 2

2b 1 'against' or 'opposite'   3 'bad' or 'wrong'
2 'again' or 'back'

2c/d contradicts: to disagree with something, especially by saying that the opposite is true
misleading: likely to make someone believe something that is not true
recall: remember
retrieve: to get back information that has been stored in the memory

3a 1 one/1
2 1 noun   7 noun
     2 quantifier/number   8 noun
     3 noun   9 noun
     4 adjective/noun   10 adjective
     5 noun   11 noun
     6 noun

3b Students' own answers

3c 1 shooting   7 video
2 13/thirteen   8 schemas
3 questions   9 game
4 accurate   10 conventional
5 stress   11 ghosts
6 juries

4 Students' own answers

Vocabulary

1a 1 concluded
2 facilitated
3 identify
4 contribute/have contributed
5 involves
6 derive/are derived

1b 1 identified   3 facilitated   5 contributes
2 involves   4 concluded   6 derive

2a 1 G   3 A   5 B   7 D   9 C
2 I   4 J   6 E   8 H   10 F

2b Students' own answers

2c Students' own answers

3a 1 rejected   3 supports   5 line of
2 flawed   4 sides   6 convincing

3b Suggested answers:
1 In my opinion, the argument for longer prison sentences is flawed, because studies show that crime does not decrease when sentences are longer.
2 I accept the argument for raising the legal driving age because young people are often too immature to drive responsibly.

3 Some people argue that everyone should be allowed to own a gun in case they need to defend themselves. However, the other side of the argument is that people may use guns aggressively rather than defensively.

4 It is sometimes argued that social problems are the real cause of crime. I support this view, because there is a proven link between poor early experiences and crime.

5 Studies showing a link between drug abuse and crime support the argument for harsher penalties for drug use.

6 Lawyers are trained to present a line of argument which is logical, and which can help jurors and judges to reach a fair decision.

Language development

1a conjunctions: although, whereas, while
adverbs: conversely, likewise, similarly
prepositions: despite

1b different: although, conversely, despite, whereas, while
the same: likewise, similarly

1c different sentences: conversely, likewise, similarly
the same sentence: although, despite, whereas, while

2 1 Despite   4 while   7 Conversely
2 Likewise   5 whereas
3 Although   6 although

3 2 the Japanese legal system is based on civil law, the U.S. legal system is based on common law

3 there are many differences between the legal systems of the two countries, a number of U.S. law firms have opened successful offices in Japan

4 law-makers try to write laws that are as clear as possible, there will always be occasions when this is difficult to do

5 in some countries it is the responsibility of an accused person to prove their innocence, in others it is the responsibility of the accusers to offer proof

6 Lawyers have to spend a long time training. Conversely, jurors have no training at all

7 In the USA, the legal powers of the federal government are limited. Similarly, in Germany some legislation is enacted by the country's member states

8 In ancient Rome, justice was symbolised by a picture of a woman holding scales and a sword. Similarly, the scales are used in many modern cultures/many modern cultures use the scales

4a 1 either   2 neither   3 both

4b 1 Convicted criminals are either sent to prison or made to pay a fine.
2 Both community police officers and people living in the area can help to prevent crime.
3 Keeping people in prison for a long time is not cheap, and neither is it effective.
4 Prisoners can choose either to study for a qualification, or to learn a new skill.

Writing

1 It is proposed that young offenders should not be treated in the same way as adult offenders.

2a Supporting points: 1, 4, 5, 6
Opposing points: 2, 3

2b This paragraph is 'against' the proposal. Points 2 and 3 are mentioned.

2c 1 D   3 A   5 B
2 E   4 C

2d 1 view   3 delinquency
2 opportunity   4 enlightened

3a 1 whereas   3 While
2 Despite   4 Although

3b 1 offender   3 accepted
2 committed   4 disadvantaged

4 Sample answer

However, there are many who take the opposite view. They claim that teenagers have much vaguer ideas about morality than adults do. It is also said that during the teenage years, people experience hormonal changes which make them act irrationally, for example, by taking far more risks than they would otherwise do. A second argument relates to prisons and that being imprisoned is the quickest way to turn youngsters from being petty offenders into serious criminals. It is suggested that a better approach to dealing with teenage law breakers is to require them to do community service, possibly even working in the neighbourhood where the crime was committed, thus helping them to understand the effect on their victims and ways they can make amends.

I am persuaded by the view that teenagers should be given a chance to redeem themselves before they are set on a life of crime. For this to happen we need more enlightened methods of dealing with young offenders.

Listening

1 3

2a Students' own predictions. Suggested answers:
1 a noun – an institution
2 adjective or noun
3 verb – action

2b 1 University
2 clothing/clothes
3 read

2c … [Elizabeth Fry] was born Elizabeth Gurney … in 1780 in Norwich, in East Anglia, a relatively remote area of Southeast England. She was born into a prosperous family of bankers and the family home was a large mansion – Earlham Hall – which now forms a section of the University of East Anglia. It was a large family and when her mother passed away, when Elizabeth was just 12, she spent much of her youth educating her younger brothers and sisters. When she was 18, Elizabeth attended a lecture by a charismatic preacher, whose words inspired her to take an interest in those less advantaged than herself. She began to look beyond the walls of her privileged home and to see the plight of the poor and the sick. She arranged to make collections of clothing for the poor, visited the sick in the villages nearby and invited local people to a small building in the grounds of her home, where she taught them to read. It was during this period that she met Joseph Fry, a banker. In 1800, when she was 20 years old, they married and moved to London. The couple went on to have 11 children.

3 1 overcrowding   5 homeless
2 cook   6 nurses
3 school   7 C
4 inspectors

Audio script 6.1

N = Narrator   S = Student

N: You will hear a talk, given by a first-year Criminology student, on Elizabeth Fry, a prison reformer from the early 19th century.

S: Good morning. I've chosen to give my presentation on Elizabeth Fry, a woman who had a major impact on the way prisons developed in Britain. She worked tirelessly to help improve conditions in prisons and was instrumental in bringing about major penal reform. Her work is still remembered today, in the UK and around the world.

In this talk, I'll explain the major turning points in her long and distinguished career, starting with her early life. She was born Elizabeth Gurney towards the end of the 18th Century – in 1780 – in Norwich, in East Anglia, a relatively remote area of Southeast England. She was born into a prosperous family of bankers and the family home was a large mansion – Earlham Hall – which now forms a section of the University of East Anglia. It was a large family and when her mother passed away, when Elizabeth was just 12, she spent much of her youth educating her younger brothers and sisters.

When she was 18, Elizabeth attended a lecture by a charismatic preacher, whose words inspired her to take an interest in those less advantaged than herself. She began to look beyond the walls of her privileged home and to see the plight of the poor and the sick. She arranged to make collections of clothing for the poor, visited the sick in the villages nearby and invited local people to a small building in the grounds of her home, where she taught them to read. It was during this period that she met Joseph Fry, a banker. In 1800, when she was 20 years old, they married and moved to London. The couple went on to have 11 children.

Soon after their arrival in the city, Fry visited the notorious Newgate Prison. She was profoundly shocked by what she saw. She was especially appalled to see the overcrowding in sections of the prison occupied by women and the children in their care. She found it horrifying that there was no special provision for these vulnerable people. The female prisoners were exposed to diseases of all kinds because they had to cook in their cells.

The family banking business suffered a decline which meant that Fry was not able to do any work in the prison for a number of years. But she never forgot what she'd seen in Newgate and went back in 1816 to establish a school for the imprisoned children. She also found a way for women to earn money by doing needlework.

Fry became a tireless advocate for prisoners' rights and her work had an impact all over the country. In 1817 she formed the ARFP – the Association for the Reformation of the Female Prisoners. She was also a persuasive writer as well as a speaker and produced a seminal book – *Prisons in Scotland and the North of England*. Wealthy and influential people rallied to support her – one such supporter was Prime Minister Robert Peel, who passed a number of Acts of Parliament, inspired by her research and advocacy, including the Gaols' Act of 1823. Although this Act failed to live up to its promise, because no inspectors were put in place to monitor change, conditions did eventually improve significantly, both for male and female prisoners.

Fry didn't just confine her work to gaols – after the bitterly cold winter of 1819 to 1820, she also helped homeless children and adults, establishing a 'nightly shelter' in London. Towards the end of her life, in 1840, Fry opened a training school for nurses. Florence Nightingale was inspired by her innovations, and used her ideas when caring for soldiers in the Crimean War.

Following her death in 1845, Fry was given many memorials, from glorious stained glass windows in Manchester to beautiful tapestries. The most well known is that between 2001 and 2016, her image featured on banknotes in Britain. The image shows the design of a key to a cell in Newgate which was awarded to Fry – a powerful symbol of all she achieved.

Language development

1a The first sentence follows a standard structure and has no particular emphasis; the sentences in Exercise 1b begin with cleft clauses, which add emphasis.

1b 1   C   2   B   3   A

1c 1   It was in the story called *His Last Bow* that Sherlock Holmes had retired to a small farm in the country and taken up beekeeping.
2   It was at a hospital in Edinburgh that the author of the Sherlock Holmes stories was a clerk.
3   It is for his tales of mystery that the American writer Edgar Allan Poe is best known.
4   It was the novel *Miss Smilla's Feeling for Snow* that probably prompted the current wave of Scandinavian crime stories and films.
5   It was Keigo Higashino who wrote the popular crime story *The Devotion of Suspect X*.
6   It was Maigret who was the fictional detective in *The Man in the Eiffel Tower*.
7   It was a Spanish author who originally wrote *The Depths of the Forest*.
8   It was a woman called Candice Fox who wrote the Australian crime novel *Eden*.

2 1   D   3   B   5   F   7   G
       2   H   4   E   6   A   8   C

3 Suggested answers:
1   if there were more public sports fields and sports facilities
2   if there were more community police officers
3   put locks on all their windows and doors
4   having a personal mentor who could give them support
5   the general public
6   the police
7   decide whether a person is innocent or guilty
8   function of parliament

Vocabulary

1a 1   It   3   there   5   there   7   It
        2   It   4   There   6   It

1b 1   G   3   A   5   B   7   F
        2   E   4   C   6   D

2 1   There   3   There   5   it
       2   It   4   It   6   there

3 1   E   3   A   5   B
       2   C   4   F   6   D

4 2   is illegal to download music and films without consent
3   are various hi-tech devices which can be used by the police to catch criminals
4   there is a maximum sentence of five years in prison for sending spam
5   is a federal crime to use the internet for betting on a sports match
6   has been a sharp increase in the number of email accounts which are hacked recently

5 Suggested answers:
1 It's unfair that the government has reduced the budget for giving legal aid to people on low incomes.
2 There are some lawyers who give their services without receiving a fee if the client cannot afford to pay.
3 It takes at least six years of study to become a lawyer in the USA.
4 There isn't a jury in courts in my country.
5 It's more than 60 years since the death penalty was abolished.

Speaking

1a
1	F	3	D	5	E	7	C
2	B	4	A	6	G		

1b
1	crime hotspots	5	facial recognition
2	drones	6	social media
3	suspects	7	prediction
4	data sources		

2a Suggested answers:
- Learn and practise new words (3)
- Learn and practise new grammatical forms (4)
- Practise listening to oral questions (2)
- Practise speaking, by yourself and with others (1)

2b 1 No   2 Yes   3 Yes

3a Suggested answers:
1 Some people think that if <u>more people</u> are <u>sent</u> to <u>prison</u>, <u>crime</u> will be <u>reduced</u>. What do you think about that?
2 Which is <u>more common</u> where you live, <u>people stealing</u> on the <u>street</u>, or people stealing from <u>houses</u>?
3 What <u>kinds of things</u> do you think people can do to <u>protect themselves</u> from <u>crime</u>?
4 Do you think having <u>more police</u> would help to <u>reduce crime</u>?

3b Students' own answers

3c Students' own answers

4a A = Q3   B = Q1

4b A Well, they can avoid going to areas which are known to be crime hotspots, <u>for one thing</u>. I mean, if that's possible of course – if they live in one of those areas, it's not. <u>Also</u> they can avoid going out late at night, especially if they're alone. <u>And thirdly</u>, people can carry alarms. They're easy to put in your pocket or bag and they're not very expensive. <u>And the last thing is</u>, I've read somewhere that people who look frightened are more likely to become victims of crime. <u>So</u> if possible, people should try and appear confident even if they're scared.
B I don't really agree with that, because it's a well known fact that spending time in prison can create so-called 'career criminals'. <u>For example</u>, when they go in for the first time, often after committing some minor crime, petty criminals meet and spend time with criminals who've committed more serious crimes, or who've committed a lot of crimes, and it's like being in a school – they're influenced by those people. <u>So</u> when they finally leave prison, they've got a lot of criminal contacts and they're less likely to give up crime. <u>On the other hand</u>, if petty criminals received some other kind of punishment, they'd be more likely to change their behaviour.

5a Students' own answers

Audio script 6.2

Let's talk now about crime.
1 How do you think the police might use social media to solve crimes?
2 What kinds of new technology help the police to do their job?
3 Some people say there's a connection between poverty and crime. Do you agree or disagree?
4 If we understood the causes of crime better, we may be able to prevent it. Do you think that's true?

5b Students' own answers

Writing

1a It is proposed that sometimes it is not criminal to break the law if it is for a good reason. The opposite view is that all acts which are against the law should be regarded as criminal acts.

2a 1 C   2 A   3 B

2b D, C, A, B

2c
1	moral	3	flawed	5	legislation
2	awareness	4	reversed	6	allow

2d 1 is the better option because it gives a pithy, memorable conclusion. It also does more than just repeat the task statement.

2e The writer is using structure 3

3 Students' own answers

4 Students' own answers

Module 7

Reading

1 Suggested answers: architecture, construction, modern, roof, site, structure

2
1 stalls, restaurants, apartments, car park
2 a mural
3 People really like it.

3a B, E, F, G, H

3b transformation, industrial, is (often) attributed to

3c the opening of the Guggenheim Museum Bilbao

3d D

4
1	D	3	G	5	A
2	H	4	E	6	C

5a
7	poor condition	9	mixed reaction
8	uniform	10	symbol

5b
7	E	8	I	9	b	10	F

Vocabulary

1a
1	distribution	5	parameters
2	maintenance	6	expansion
3	investment	7	construction
4	integration	8	co-ordination

1b
1	Construction	5	initiatives
2	parameters	6	infrastructure
3	compensation	7	maintenance
4	implementation	8	investment

1c Suggested answer:
Although environmental campaigners agree that train travel is less harmful than car travel, the government does not invest enough money in the system, so ticket prices are high. Also, since the services were privatised, there have been various accidents due to poor maintenance. A further problem is that expansion of the service has not been quick enough to cope with rising passenger numbers.

2
1	maintained	5	expansion
2	investment	6	invested
3	constructed	7	initiative
4	coordinating		

3a draw up, go ahead, oppose, put forward, shelve, unveil

3b
1	draw up/put forward	4	oppose
2	put forward	5	shelve
3	unveil/put forward	6	go ahead

Language development

1a Emirates Aviation Experience

The Emirates Aviation Experience, one of London's newest attractions, is the first of its kind globally. <u>Is located next to the Greenwich Peninsula terminal.</u> The exhibition gives visitors information about the operations and modern achievements of commercial air travel. <u>Using state-of-the-art technology, interactive displays, and life-size aircraft models, something for people of all ages.</u>

<u>So we've included a new on-board 'tour' as part of the Discovery experience.</u> The audio-guide commentary complements the 'visual' journey with a series of fascinating stories about East London. The tour presents a selection of our most famous London landmarks including the Thames Barrier and Royal Docks. <u>Also gives information about East London's exciting plans for the future.</u>

1b Emirates Aviation Experience

The Emirates Aviation Experience, one of London's newest attractions, is the first of its kind globally. **D** Is located next to the Greenwich Peninsula terminal. The exhibition gives visitors information about the operations and modern achievements of commercial air travel. Using state-of-the-art technology, interactive displays, and life-size aircraft models, **A** something for people of all ages.

C So we've included a new on-board 'tour' as part of the Discovery experience. The audio-guide commentary complements the 'visual' journey with a series of fascinating stories about East London. The tour presents a selection of our most famous London landmarks including the Thames Barrier and Royal Docks. **B** Also gives information about East London's exciting plans for the future.

2a 2, 4, 5, 8

2b 2 It is sponsored by Emirates Airline // that is why it is called the Emirates Air Line.

4 The cable cars leave each terminal every few seconds // the normal journey time is 5 minutes.

5 From 10a.m. to 3p.m. the journey time is longer, // visitors can have more time to enjoy the view.

8 Passengers can buy a '360' trip which enables them to stay on and go back to the original terminus // this costs the same price as a return trip.

3a 1 There are three major airports in the Washington DC region, Ronald Reagan Airport, Washington Dulles Airport and Washington Thurgood Marshall Airport.

2 Sydne<u>ys</u> airport is the oldest commercial international airport in the world.

3 Flights from Tokyo to Sydney depart at 19.25<u>;</u> 22.00 and 22.10.

4 <u>t</u>ravelling by cargo ship can be a good alternative to travelling by cruise ship, as cargo ships travel to more destinations.

5 There are several reasons why people prefer travelling by public transport, including lower costs compared to car or taxi<u>,</u> the reduced impact on the environment<u>,</u> and the convenience of not needing to find a parking space.

6 As Singapore is a small city, it uses sophisticated computer programmes to maximise the capacity of <u>it's</u> roads.

3b
A	4	C	5	E	3
B	1	D	6	F	2

3c 1 There are three major airports in the Washington, DC region: Ronald Reagan Airport, Washington Dulles Airport and Washington Thurgood Marshall Airport.

2 Sydney's airport is the oldest commercial international airport in the world.

3 Flights from Tokyo to Sydney depart at 19.25, 22.00 and 22.10.

4 Travelling by cargo ship can be a good alternative to travelling by cruise ship, as cargo ships travel to more destinations.

5 There are several reasons why people prefer travelling by public transport, including lower costs compared to car or taxi; the reduced impact on the environment; and the convenience of not needing to find a parking space.

6 As Singapore is a small city, it uses sophisticated computer programmes to maximise the capacity of its roads.

4 Suggested answer:
I regularly use trains, buses and my car. Occasionally I travel by plane too. I don't like using my car unnecessarily, but there are two reasons why I use it quite often: I live in the country so bus services are poor, and I have small children who can't walk very far yet.

Writing

1
1	car ownership
2	No – the name of the country is not stated
3	1995–2025
4	Figures for 2025

2a *x* axis = percentage, *y* axis = years

2b
1	three: people with no car, people owning one car, people owning two or more cars
2	people with no car
3	people with two or more cars
4	people with one car
5	the downward trend in percentage of people with no car (this will go up) and the stable figures for people with one car (this will go down)

2c 1   trends   2   between   3   reversal

3a Students' own answers

3b By <u>compare</u>, the figures for those moving because they were seeking work <u>arose</u> steadily <u>about</u> the same period – from 22 percent to 35 percent. The <u>percent</u> of migrants moving in order to accompany a spouse or family member was the highest in 1980 and <u>remains</u> steady during the 30 years, only varying <u>at</u> 2 percent in the whole period.

3c compare = 1 vocabulary choice
arose = 1 vocabulary choice
about = 3 preposition
percent = 2 word form
remains = 4 tense/aspect
at = 3 preposition

3d By ~~compare~~ **contrast**, the figures for those moving because they were seeking work ~~arose~~ **rose** steadily ~~about~~ **over** the same period – from 22 percent to 35 percent. The ~~percent~~ **percentage** of migrants moving in order to accompany a spouse or family member was the highest in 1980 and ~~remains~~ **remained** steady during the 30 years, only varying ~~at~~ **by** 2 percent in the whole period.

4a Suggested answer: ✓
The table shows a number of distinct patterns in the reasons stated for urban migration in a given country over 30 years. The most striking trend is a drop in the percentage of people moving to take up a specific job: in 1980 this accounted for 28 percent and this dropped steadily down to just 12 percent in 2010. By contrast, the figures for those moving because they were seeking work rose steadily over the same period – from 22 percent to 35 percent. The percentage of migrants moving in order to accompany a spouse or family member was the highest in 1980 and remained steady during the 30 years, only varying by 2 percent in the whole period. The figures for formal study fluctuated, starting at 13 percent in 1980, dropping noticeably by 1990 to 7 percent but then rising again in 2000 (10 percent) and 2010 (12 percent). The proportion of migrants moving to cities for no clear reason was very low in 1980 (just 4 percent). This saw a massive rise in 1990 (to 18 percent) falling again to 9 percent in 2010.

4b Students' own answers

Listening

1 1   What is Alex most <u>worried</u> about for the lesson?
   2   Which group of members is <u>increasing fastest</u> in the club?
   3   What does the <u>receptionist enjoy most</u> about gliding?

2a A   3   B   1   C   2

2b <u>underline</u> = answer   circle = distractors
Beth: It's two hours long and essentially what we do is start by giving a short talk to explain the basics, then you go up. It's a two-seater plane, (with an instructor behind you (A)) and dual controls ... so the (learner actually flies on her own for part of the time (B),) though of course the instructor takes off and lands.
Alex: Yes, but <u>I'm amazed that you go straight up in the plane without trying it out beforehand</u>, on a machine, even (though it's with an instructor (A).)
Beth: We have very experienced teachers and it's very safe.

3a 2   1 the lesson 2 most worried about
   3   1 group of members 2 fastest increase
   4   1 gliding 2 enjoy most

3b 1   A   2   C   3   A

Audio script 7.1

N = Narrator   R = Receptionist   A = Alex

N: You will hear a man, called Alex, telephoning to enquire about gliding school lessons.

R: Good morning, Zest Gliding Club.

A: Oh, hello. I'm interested in booking a beginner's gliding lesson for my wife and I'd like to ask a couple of questions.

R: Of course. How can I help?

A: Well, could you explain what happens in the lesson?

R: It's two hours long and essentially what we do is start by giving a short talk to explain the basics, then you go up. It's a two-seater plane, with a teacher behind you and dual controls ... so the learner actually flies on her own for part of the time, though of course the instructor takes off and lands.

A: Yes. But I'm amazed that you go straight up in the plane without trying it out beforehand, on a machine, even though it's with an instructor.

R: We have very experienced teachers and it's very safe.

A: OK. That's helped a lot but I do have a couple of worries ...

R: If it's about the weather, I need to tell you that good conditions are especially important for the first lesson, so if it's very windy or pouring with rain, we let you rearrange it and come back on another day.

A: That's fine, I read that on your website – very sensible – and it's not a problem because we don't live far from the club. I did want to ask, I understand you offer different types of flight?

R: Yes, we offer a faster flight and a slower, less adventurous version.

A: I know Rosie will prefer a gentle experience for the first time – thanks.

R: Yes.

A: And another thing – I wanted to find out about your membership. We've recently moved into the area and if things work out, we'd both be interested in joining the club.

R: We have 140 on our books at the moment, from all walks of life. Because gliding's usually an all-day commitment people often think of it as an older person's hobby, for retired people with time on their hands. But most of our members are middle aged. But we're trying hard to get under-25s involved and it is the biggest growth area, though it's still only about 10 percent of the membership, it's on the rise.

A: Sounds a good mix. My wife and I've always wanted to try gliding ... it must be an amazing feeling.

R: Well, I've been gliding for over ten years and I have to say each time I go up I learn something new about the sport. It's not really about the thrill of being so far above the ground, for me the great thing is the silence and freedom from stress ...

A: Sounds marvellous.

4a Students' own answers

4b 4   Faulkner
   5   25th August 1970 / 25.8.70/8.25.70
   6   1m/1 metre 72 cm/1.72m/metre
   7   neck
   8   (the) regular
   9   Bank Road/Rd
   10 radio

Audio script 7.2

R = Receptionist   A = Alex

A: So, if I may, I'd like to go ahead and make the booking.

R: Great. I'll just take a few details. It's for your wife you say?

A: Yes … that's correct

R: So I'll start by getting her name.

A: It's Rosie Faulkner.

R: How do spell that?

A: F-A-U-L-K-N-E-R

R: Thanks I've got that. Now her date of birth – I presume she's over 18?

A: She's 46. Her birthday's 25th August 1970.

R: Lovely, thanks. Now I hope you don't mind but I need to get a bit more information about your wife so we can make appropriate preparations. How tall is she?

A: She's one metre seventy-two centimetres.

R: Just writing that down … lovely, thanks. And does she have any medical conditions which would be helpful to know about – for example problems with her ears or her back?

A: The main thing is her neck … she had an injury 12 months ago – it's pretty much healed but …

R: Certainly worth mentioning. I'll put that on the form – thanks.

    And a contact number?

A: I'll just get that … OK it's 07753 42136.

R: And you mentioned it was a special event. Now, we offer different kinds of package. For example we have the Gold package which includes flowers and dinner in our restaurant after the flight. Or we have what we call the Regular.

A: I'll go for that latter one, please. My wife is someone who likes things simple.

R: Of course, quite understand.

A: Yes.

R: And what address should I send the voucher to?

A: It's Northbrook House.

R: Yes.

A: And that's in Bank Road.

R: Yes.

A: In Sandbrook – the postcode's BL2 4PD.

R: And do you have a date in mind for the lesson?

A: Well it'd be great if we could have the 25th of August.

R: Just checking the diary. Yes, that's possible.

A: Great.

R: We can offer either 10.00 a.m. or 3.00 p.m..

A: Oh the afternoon, please … so she can have a lie in.

R: Lovely – I'll put her down for 3 o'clock. And one final thing we like to know for our records is how you found out about the club – for example, was it from a friend?

A: Now, let me think … it was on the radio, someone talking about beginner's lessons.

R: Oh yes, we did run a series …

5 Students' own answers

Language development

1
| 1 | The | 3 | walk | 5 | travel |
| 2 | a | 4 | comes | 6 | arrive |

2a
| 1 | ✗ | 3 | ✗ | 5 | ✗ |
| 2 | ✓ | 4 | ✗ | 6 | ✓ |

2b 1 There is only one Department of Transport in a country.
   3 The subject is 'One', so the verb should be singular.
   4 There is only one 'main' mode of travel.
   5 The subject is plural (*most … schoolchildren*), so the verb should be plural.

2c
| 1 | the | 3 | was | 4 | the | 5 | go |

3
1	found	4	go/went	7	is/was
2	are/were	5	give/gave		
3	one	6	it		

4 Suggested answers:
   1 One solution to traffic congestion near schools is to ban cars from the area.
   2 Children's safety is more important than adults' convenience.
   3 The best way for children to get to school is to walk.
   4 Pedestrian crossings are an inexpensive way of increasing safety.
   5 Both parents and children benefit from getting exercise.
   6 Air pollution is one of the problems caused by traffic congestion.

5 Students' own answers

Vocabulary

1 Rules <u>for</u> Cyclists (enforceable <u>by</u> law)

The speed limit is 15km <u>per</u> hour <u>on</u> footpaths, and 25km <u>per</u> hour <u>on</u> cycle paths.

Bicycles must be equipped <u>with</u> lights which are visible <u>from</u> the front and rear. They must be used during hours <u>of</u> darkness (<u>between</u> 7p.m. and 7a.m.).

A maximum <u>of</u> two people cycling side <u>by</u> side is allowed <u>on</u> roads where there are two or more lanes going <u>in</u> the same direction, except <u>on</u> roads <u>with</u> bus lanes.

2
1	for	5	to	9	at
2	of	6	in	10	through
3	for	7	with	11	on
4	between	8	of	12	in

3a 1 <u>Among</u> 1990 and 2015, global airline passenger numbers rose from 1 billion to 3.5 billion.
   2 In 2016, the two largest markets <u>of</u> domestic airline passengers were the USA and China.
   3 Every tonne <u>in</u> aviation fuel burned produces between 3.15 and 3.18 tonnes of CO_2.
   4 The efficiency of aircraft and engines has significantly improved <u>after</u> the early 1960s.
   5 Jet aircraft today are <u>above</u> 80 percent more fuel efficient than the jets of the 1960s.

3b
1	Between	4	since
2	for	5	over (more than)
3	of		

4
1	For/Over	6	within/in
2	around/across	7	in
3	Since	8	to
4	of	9	with
5	with	10	about/on

5 2 between 4 by 6 amongst
3 to 5 from

6a 1 through 3 In 5 Between
2 After 4 through 6 During

6b 1 Atlanta
2 John F. Kennedy, a former president of the USA
3 Japan
4 e.g. China, Persia, Turkey
5 Atlantic, Pacific
6 19th century

Speaking

1 1 C 3 G 5 H 7 B
2 E 4 A 6 F 8 D

2 Students' own answers

3 1 I'm usually only travelling by bus when my car breaks down. Maybe once or twice in a year.
I usually only travel by bus when my car breaks down. Maybe once or twice a year.
2 It depends when you want to go in a bus with air conditioning or not. The fare on those buses is three times as much as the fare on ordinary buses.
It depends whether you want to go on a bus with air conditioning or not.
3 Not really. The buses where I live are quite frequent, especially over peak times. Maybe every five minutes.
The buses where I live are quite frequent, especially at/during peak times.
4 They are very comfortable. Before five years the city council ordered many new buses, so they are clean and they have more space than the old ones.
Five years ago the city council ordered many new buses, so they are clean and they have more space than the old ones.
5 I wear my earphones and I hear music on my phone, so the journey passes very quickly.
I wear my earphones and I listen to music on my phone, so the journey passes very quickly.
6 Some of buses have a special low step that the driver can operate. It makes it easy if you can't walk well.
Some buses have a special low step that the driver can operate.

4a Students' own answers

Audio script 7.3

Now let's talk about getting to work or college.

1 How do you usually get to work or college?
2 How long does it take?
3 Do you go with anyone else?
4 Do you enjoy your journey to work or college?
5 How often do you arrive late at work or college?

4b Students' own answers

Audio script 7.4

E = Examiner   S = Student

E: Now let's talk about getting to work or college. How do you usually get to work or college?

S: I usually walk to the station – that's about a mile – and then I get the train. Then I walk again – it's very close.

E: How long does it take?

S: It depends really. On average it probably takes me about an hour and ten minutes altogether, but sometimes the train is delayed so it can be longer.

E: Do you go with anyone else?

S: No, I go by myself. I don't know anyone else in my office who lives where I do.

E: Do you enjoy your journey to work or college?

S: I can't say I enjoy going to work, the train's often crowded with commuters and you have to stand all the way. But coming home is enjoyable! I feel more relaxed then.

E: How often do you arrive late at work or college?

S: Very rarely, because I always set off in good time. But unexpected things can happen – the train can break down or even get cancelled. But it doesn't matter too much if I'm late – my boss is very understanding, and I can do extra work at lunchtime if that happens.

4c Students' own answers

5 Students' own answers

Writing

1a the length of delay experienced by commuters in different-sized cities

1b 1 the average number of hours' delay experienced per commuter per year
2 by the size of their population
3 1985–2025
4 Column 6 – for 2025

1c 1 1985–1995
2 2005–2015
3 the small cities (<500,00 people), most notably 1985–1995

1d Ticked items: 2, 4, 5

1e Students' own answers

2a 1 F 3 T 5 T 7 T
2 F 4 F 6 T

2b 1 The table shows the total hours of delay per commuter.
2 The figures for 2025 are predicted.
4 There was a steady increase and then a fall in congestion over the 30 years 1985–2015.

3a simple past and future – because most of the data refer to past events but some (for 2025) are predictions for the future

3b Large change: significant, major, noticeable, serious, striking
Small change: slight, small, minor, relative

3c Students' own answers

4 Students' own answers

5a Sample answer:
The table shows figures for congestion in different-sized cities in one country over 30 years as indicated by the average delay experienced by individual commuters per year. Unsurprisingly, the larger the city the bigger the average delay, with mega cities of over 3 million people having 60 hours of delay per person in 2005. In terms of increase across the years, the most striking

growth occurred between 1985 and 1995. This affected all four categories of city but was most noticeable in small cities (those with under 500,000 inhabitants) with delays multiplying by a factor of three (from 7 to 21 hours). From 1995–2015 the figures held relatively steady with only a slight rise and fall, though 2005 saw a peak in delays for all sizes of city. Figures declined in 2015. It is predicted that there will be a significant reduction in congestion in coming years in the three larger city types: only the small cities will continue to experience the same amount of delay with only 1 hour difference forecast between 2015 and 2025.

5b Students' own answers

6 Students' own answers

Module 8

Reading

1 A

2a new urban developments, social cohesion, existing residents

2b Yes, it expresses an opinion which is the same as that in 2a (it talks of a 'challenge').

3	1	Y	3	NG	5	Y
	2	N	4	N	6	Y

4 7/8 B/D   9/10 C/D

5 Students' own answers

Vocabulary

1a	1	a scheme	5	resident
	2	network	6	policy
	3	sector	7	neighbourhood
	4	community	8	structure

1b	1	scheme	3	policies	5	community
	2	network	4	sector	6	structure

2	1	ethnic	3	rural	5	wider
	2	local	4	virtual		

3	1	national	3	economic	5	social
	2	key	4	current		

4a	1	of	5	by/with
	2	with/by/about	6	to/about
	3	to	7	about
	4	by/about		

4b

+	-	+/-
appreciative, delighted, devoted, sympathetic	outraged, dreadful	overwhelmed

4c Students' own answers

Language development

1	1	is awarding	5	was going to be
	2	will have finished	6	will be
	3	will be held	7	will have been holding
	4	will be singing	8	organises

2	1	C	3	E	5	G	7	H
	2	F	4	A	6	B	8	D

3	1	are predicting/predict
	2	will have, doubled/ will, double
	3	will be
	4	will have been integrated/will be integrated
	5	will be/is
	6	will overwhelm
	7	will be/are
	8	will, evolve
	9	will be able

4	1	75%	2	90%	3	100%	4	35%

5 Suggested answers:
In 2025 I will be doing a different job.
In 2025, I am likely to be married.
In 2025, I might have two children.
In 2025, my friend is bound to be a famous singer.

Writing

1 2

2a B, C, A, D

2b	1	T
	2	T
	3	F The function of the fourth sentence is to describe the second possible reason for the change.

2c Suggested answer:
People are living longer and younger generations are less able and/or willing to look after older relatives.

3a	A	1	Trade union membership is falling.
		2	c) both cause and effect
		3	Fewer workers nowadays are choosing to join a trade union.
	B	1	Unemployment
		2	a) causes
		3	People without paid employment tend to suffer in social as well as financial terms.
	C	1	women's employment compared to men's
		2	c) both cause and effect
		3	On average, women tend to have lower-paid jobs than men.

3b	1	This could be due to
	2	this decline can have negative consequences
	3	A further possible cause
	4	Another factor could be

4a Students' own answers

4b Students' own answers

4c Students' own answers

Listening

1 Suggested answers:
1 a reviewer/critic. You might hear him/her speaking on radio
2 A humour = comedy, discussion = debate
  B honest = trustworthy, true
  C technical terms = jargon, complex language
  D technology = computers
  E choice = selection, topics = subjects
  F expectations = predicted
  G multilingual = international
  H searching = probing/difficult

2 B, C, A, D

3a
1	E	3	A	5	C
2	B	4	H	6	D

Audio script 8.1

N = Narrator   P = Presenter   J = Jake

N: You will hear a radio interview with media expert Jake Gittis talking about different podcasts.

P: On today's show we're happy to welcome back Jake Gittis, who's going to start by talking about some of his favourite podcasts.

J: Yes, I've been having a great time listening in to some of this year's most popular podcasts – some taken from mainstream radio and others independently produced. Starting with one of the most respected and widely praised, *Object Lessons.* This basically follows the progress of humankind from its earliest beginnings to pieces of modern technology like the credit card. I really like the way the items and themes have been selected. So for instance, the high point of modern technology is not the space shuttle but a simple solar-powered lamp. My second choice is in complete contrast. Now surely the best thing about podcasting is that it lets anyone with basic equipment become a broadcaster. One of my favourite independently produced pieces is *Sky Stories.* Once a month, air stewardess Jane tells charming stories from life on board her planes – the great thing is that they're completely truthful so we get a very authentic picture of what goes on. Another independent podcast is *Football Focus,* which goes out weekly and has analysis of every game and lively chat. I love it because it manages to be both funny and factually correct – not surprising that it's been hugely popular since it started nearly ten years ago. Going back to a piece which also goes out on radio is *Team Science.* This podcast communicates latest research in an engaging way. You sometimes have to work hard to follow what the scientists say but it's well worth trying because the programme digs deep to get answers to some of the biggest mysteries in the universe. On the lighter side is *The Daily,* which sells itself as an 'audio newspaper for a visual world'. This comedy news show is co-hosted by presenters in London and New York and has been going strong since 2007. It's extremely clever but it doesn't exclude by using language which only a few people'll understand. Finally there's *Radio Headways* – an American radio documentary series with a mix of high-quality clever journalism and up-to-date sound equipment which means a really imaginative style.

3b Students' own answers

3c Students' own answers

4a
7   main reason – primary/major reason; preferring – liking best
8   learnt – gained/understood; crisis – very difficult situation
9   surprised – amazed; current position – present condition
10   well suited – appropriate

4b
7	B	8	B	9	B	10	A

Audio script 8.2

P = Presenter   J = Jake

P: Thanks, Jake … you're obviously a big fan of audio.

J: Definitely. I think we're going through a really exciting time across all the media, but I have a particular affection for radio. Unlike television, which makes us conform to other people's views of the world, it requires us to interact with what we hear. But above all, I feel it allows greater freedom to choose. For example, it doesn't have to broadcast a story simply because there's a striking photograph. Instead the broadcaster can make its editorial choice based on which stories are the most interesting and meaningful.

There's another thing about radio: when we all went through difficult economic times, the budget for radio was cut much more than for other media, and it was forced to work more effectively. Radio stations took the time to get the views of its audience about the things they actually want to know about – what's relevant and interesting for them. All this means that radio finds itself in a surprising position. I'm not surprised radio is popular with the usual loyal band of listeners but I'm astonished at how glamorous it's become. It annoys me how other media – like TV – look down on radio but the real experts know radio is the medium with the greatest potential. And one final thing … lots of people overlook how well suited radio is to the digital age. Although we now have the more expensive hi-tech digital radios they're still pretty portable and that means you can have radio wherever and whenever you want it.

P: Well thanks so much …

5 Students' own answers

Language development

1
1   as, because, since
2   as a result, consequently, therefore
3   as a result, consequently
4   all of them
5   as a result, consequently

2
1	As a result	5	since
2	because	6	because of
3	Consequently	7	Therefore
4	Due to	8	Due to

3
1	D	3	A	5	G	7	E
2	F	4	H	6	B	8	C

4 Suggested answers:
1   there is a shortage of houses
2   the fact that their families no longer live nearby
3   fans get too competitive
4   getting good marks in tests
5   they have been brought up to think of engineering as a male area
6   social media and computer games,
7   I've lost touch with some of my friends
8   I'll apply to do the IELTS test very soon

Vocabulary

1
1   increasing meat consumption
2   caring for an elderly population
3   acute housing shortages
4   national health campaigns
5   the nuclear family
6   physical punishment
7   free nursery education
8   lowering the voting age

Answer key

2 1 D   3 F   5 E
    2 A   4 C   6 B

3 2 The problem of youth unemployment has not been addressed properly by the government.
    3 The exact cause of autism is currently not yet known.
    4 The topic of animal communication is a common choice for psychology research.
    5 The issue of how to control children's use of social media has not yet been resolved.
    6 The cause of antisocial behaviour may be a chemical imbalance in the brain.

4 1 justice system
    2 the criminal
    3 criminal behaviour
    4 crime prevention schemes
    5 programmes
    6 rehabilitation
    7 prisoners

5 Suggested answers:
    1 problems experienced during childhood
    2 make those responsible do unpaid work in the community
    3 low wages
    4 treat staff unfairly
    5 is secure for life
    6 set appropriate boundaries

Speaking

1a 1 down-to-earth, larger-than-life, tongue-tied
    2 see eye to eye
    3 force of nature
    4 tongue-tied

1b 1 force of nature   4 larger-than-life
    2 tongue-tied   5 see eye to eye
    3 down-to-earth

2 Speaker 1: tongue-tied
    Speaker 2: force of nature
    Speaker 3: down-to-earth
    Speaker 4: see eye to eye
    Speaker 5: larger-than-life

Audio script 8.3

1 This friend of mine is normally very chatty and confident, and she knows a lot about different subjects, but for some reason when we're in a bigger group of people she hardly says a thing. She just can't seem to express herself.

2 When my mother decides to do something – I mean anything, from getting the local council to mend the road, to helping one of us to apply for a job and then get it – she just puts all her energy into it, and she won't be put off by anything.

3 My sister is a good person to run ideas by. I can be quite impulsive and make plans that aren't very realistic, I easily get carried away. But she's sensible and level-headed, and she usually makes me see that my idea is impractical. In a very nice way.

4 It's funny, I've got one friend who nearly always has the same opinions as me. We usually agree with each other on a lot of different subjects – we seem to think in the same way. It can be quite boring at times, we can't have a heated discussion!

5 This friend of mine always makes a big impression on people. For a start he's very tall and confident, and he's got a loud voice. And then he's funny – he's always telling funny stories and making people laugh. As far as I know his stories are true as well – he just seems to have an exciting life.

3a 1 modest   4 tolerant
    2 attentive   5 conscientious
    3 generous   6 sensitive

3b 1 tolerant   4 conscientious
    2 modest   5 generous
    3 attentive   6 warm-hearted

4a Students' own answers

4b Students' own answers

5 Students' own answers

Writing

1 1 professions and occupations
    2 the situation today and in the past, the relative importance of communication skills and specialist technical skills
    3 the importance of communication skills nowadays

2 1 A   4 B
    2 D   5 C
    3 E   Correct order: 5, 3, 2, 1, 4

3a 1 convey, accessible   3 technical
    2 Specialists   4 convince, impact

3b Nowadays it is very <u>difficultly</u> (difficult) to succeed in any occupation if you do not have the ability to communicate <u>effective</u> (effectively) with others. This is very <u>large</u> (largely) because today there is such a wealth of information technology which is playing an <u>increasing</u> (increasingly) important role in almost all aspects of our lives and people in all walks of life can no longer choose to ignore it: they have to be able to use it well.

All the errors relate to the use of adjectives and adverbs.

3c See answers in 3b

4a Students' own answers

4b Sample answer:

Nowadays it is very difficult to succeed in any occupation if you do not have the ability to communicate effectively with others. This is very largely because today there is such a wealth of information technology which is playing an increasingly important role in almost all aspects of our lives and people in all walks of life can no longer choose to ignore it: they have to be able to use it well.

A good example of this is the field of scientific research. It was once the case that scientists could work for most of their lives in a laboratory, seldom needing to connect with the world outside. Other people were given the task of communicating research findings. However, nowadays this is not enough: scientists themselves have to be able to bid for their own funding by writing and speaking in an accessible way to lay people, and they have to know what elements to emphasize and which to clarify. Very often they also have to explain findings of their investigations to the public – as their status and further funding is so dependent on the impact of their work on the wider community.

A second reason for the importance of communication skills is the fact that many people nowadays believe that knowledge belongs in the public domain. Everyone wants to get as much information as possible so they can make up their own minds on crucial issues rather than allowing others to do it for them. This means that communication is no longer just done by specialists in communication, for example public relations experts.

So all in all, although it is important for professionals in any field, from lawyers to doctors, to have a thorough grounding in the technical aspects of their discipline, the really successful ones are the good communicators.

5a Students' own answers

5b Students' own answers

Module 9

Reading

1 Suggested answers:
measure, test, scientist, mechanic, technician, equipment

2 1 top athletes, the general public
2 mainly positive

3a 1 <u>What</u> does the writer <u>say</u> about 'marginal gains'?
The concept of marginal gains has revolutionised every kind of sport. Athletes know the tiniest change to their training and recovery regime or their diet can have a significant impact on their ability to perform, and can mean the difference between winning or losing. Having a purpose-built innovation centre designed to measure every inch of human body and brain performance, one step at a time, can be a game-changer.

2 B (Athletes know that making very small changes to their behaviour can mean the difference between winning and losing.)

3b 1 B   2 A   3 B   4 D   5 A

4 6 Y   8 NG   10 N
7 Y   9 N

5a Students' own answers

5b Students' own answers

Vocabulary

1 1 B   3 D   5 C
2 A   4 F   6 E

2 1 capability   4 investment
2 commitment   5 motivation
3 achievement   6 coordination

3 Students' own answers

4a 1 driving   3 concerted   5 broad
2 desired   4 transferable   6 pivotal

4b 1 broad spectrum   4 pivotal role
2 driving force   5 concerted effort
3 skills, transferable   6 desired outcome

5 1 accomplished   4 singled-minded
2 innovative   5 expressive
3 tenacious   6 inspirational

6 Students' own answers

Language development

1 1 D   2 A   3 B   4 F

2 1 C   3 F   5 D
2 A   4 B   6 E

3 A 3F   C 5D   E 4B
B 6E   D 2A   F 1C

4 1 B   2 A   3 C   4 D

5 Suggested answer:
The electric vegetable steamer is made of clear plastic, with a silver metal base. It consists of a water container and three vegetable containers stacked on top. It is 35cm wide and 50cm high, and it is oval shaped.

The part which contains the water is filled to the required level. It is necessary to monitor the marks that show the minimum and maximum level of water, called a gauge, and then turn a knob which sets the time. The thing that switches the steamer on is a button next to this. Finally, there is a lid which is placed on the highest container to keep the steam in.

Writing

1 1 Diagram 1: A system for raising and lowering canal boats, Diagram 2: a system for moving canal boats under low bridges
2 Diagram 1 = The starting point is a boat on the lower side of a lock, wanting to go upstream. It ends with the boat having been raised and ready to sail on the higher level. Diagram 2 = The starting point is that the boat is waiting before the bridge. The end point is that the boat has moved past the bridge.

2 1 B   2 C   3 A

3 1 It's in the lower canal and the driver wants to go to the upper canal.
2 open
3 into the lock
4 the bottom gate is closed, the top gate is open
5 it rises

4 1 A across the canal, linking the two sides of the road (closed/down)
B Cars can cross when the bridge is in this position.
C The barge can't pass under the bridge – there isn't enough room.
2 A parallel to the banks of the canal (open/up)
B The roads on both sides have been closed, so no cars are in danger of driving into the canal/they cannot go across the bridge.
C The barge can now sail on past the bridge.

5 1 first   3 uses   5 allowing
2 whereas   4 until   6 when

6 Sample answer
The canal swing bridge uses a rotating mechanism. The normal position is with the bridge crossing the canal, allowing cars to drive from one side to another. However, when a barge wants to move through, the bridge is moved round by 90 degrees. The new position is with the bridge in the middle of the canal, parallel to the banks of the canal. This allows enough room for the barge to sail through. When this is done, the bridge is rotated back to its original position.

7 Students' own answers

Listening

1 1 learning languages
2 Perhaps to discuss problems the students are having with their research.

2a 1 in-depth   3 rich
2 informal   4 personal

2b Students' own answers

3 Core characteristics of GLLs = general
The way the GLL uses her languages = specific
How the GLL records vocabulary when travelling = specific
The value of doing of a case study = general

4a 1 A   6 B
2 C   7 identity
3 A   8 motivation
4 B   9 quotes
5 A   10 internet sources

Audio script 9.1

N = Narrator   R = Rory   T = Tutor   A = Anabelle

N: You will hear two students discussing with a tutor their research project on one person who learns new languages easily: a good language learner.

R: Dr Redfern?

T: Rory. And Anabelle ... do come in. You wanted to talk about your research project?

A: Yes. Our supervisor's away and we wanted your advice. We're doing a case study on good language learners.

T: Interesting topic. Why did you choose it, and in particular, why did you go for a case study?

A: We chose the topic 'cos we were fascinated by what we'd read on people who learn other languages very quickly. Rory picks up languages easily – he speaks Japanese, Arabic and Malay, but I have to work very hard to get even to intermediate level.

R: And what mainly prompted us to go for a case study was we thought an in-depth comparison would give real substance to the study.

A: Yeah. We thought of getting hold of a sample of, say, five good language learners and comparing them with five learners who had difficulty with languages. But we realised we'd have trouble finding that number of true good language learners and in the end we opted to look at one.

R: So we identified a friend of my parents who we thought fit the profile. We had a couple of informal chats with her before we started the actual research, which was really enlightening.

A: Really interesting.

R: Yeah, she speaks seven languages fluently but although she studied languages at university, she hardly ever uses them for work purposes, which I found hard to believe.

A: I couldn't believe it! But she does travel widely for holidays, and so keeps up her proficiency that way.

R: Yeah.

T: Interesting ... so all this emerged before the formal data-gathering stage?

A: Yes ... then we drew up questions to find out how our good language learner actually goes about learning a new language. And we conducted a semi-structured interview.

R: In the end we only used interviews. We'd asked the participant whether later we could get data using other methods, to keep a diary and perhaps take a language aptitude test. She said she'd like to try these ...

A: But we got so much rich data from her on this first interview that we stuck with this method throughout, and did three more interviews. She was very open about personal details of her life, so much so that we thought we were intruding upon quite private areas ... but she seemed happy to talk.

T: As long as she didn't mind.

A: No, she didn't.

T: So, you got a lot of data. Did you record video or just use audio?

A: Only audio. We tried out the new recording equipment the department's just bought.

R: We missed the training session on how to use it, which is a pity, but we managed to work it out on our own.

A: It's the first time either of us has used technology like this but I'm not sure it's worth the investment. It really needs some hands-free mechanism to speed things up.

T: OK, what did the data tell you about how your GLL learns languages?

R: Well, a lot about the specific techniques she uses, especially about learning vocabulary. When she's travelling to a new country she actually avoids buying a dictionary. She listens and reads and writes key words in a notebook but doesn't use translation that often; what seems to work best is doodling visuals representing what words mean ... she says this helps fix the word in her mind.

A: And I was surprised, by her approach to learning grammar. In whichever language she's learning, she avoids actually practising new structures in conversation for quite a while. She prefers to listen to locals talking and tries to recognise patterns being repeated in what she hears.

T: You've obviously got some interesting findings emerging ... but how would you like me to help?

R: Well, we're having problems with our literature review.

A: We've read a lot, about things like the GLL personality, but we think we need more discussion about identity and how the learner feels about herself as a user of new languages.

R: We thought it'd take up too much space but we still want to include something on this

T: I think it's crucial that you do.

A: Good.

R: That's reassuring, thanks. But it's worrying because that'll mean making room by reducing other sections.

A: We'll need to keep the stuff on motivation.

R: Absolutely, what we've written on this issue so far is rather simplistic. And what we've found is really interesting so we need to portray the issue in all its complexity.

T: I think you're right to do this. Because you have limited words, I think you have to make these choices.

A: OK, thanks.

R: Yes, thanks.

A: And we also wanted to ask about the Findings section. Should we include lots from our GLL?

T: Well, the advice I always give is to choose only the really memorable quotes. Readers don't want to wade through too many, and you can always refer them to the appendices.

R: Oh right, that's good to know.

A: And we want one last piece of advice from you, if you don't mind.

T: Sure.

R: We're still not sure how to cite internet sources.

T: The library has an excellent section about how to cite them – it's

4b Questions 7 and 8 deal with more abstract concepts, questions 9 and 10 deal with more concrete information.

5 Students' own answers
Section 3 listening tasks require you to listen to two or more people discussing complex academic issues, many of which are abstract.

Language development

1a 1 about, approximately, around, more or less
2 more or less
3 approximately
4 kinds of, types of
5 and so on

2 1 around 3 kinds of 5 about
2 more or less 4 and so on 6 all kinds of

3 1 kinds of/types of 4 more or less
2 kinds of/types of 5 about/approximately/around
3 and so on 6 kinds of/types of

4 1 D 3 B 5 F 7 C
2 G 4 H 6 A 8 E

5 Students' own answers

Vocabulary

1a 2 problems 6 tools
3 qualities 7 electronic equipment
4 workplaces 8 raw materials
5 advantages

1b 1 problems 5 raw materials
2 advantages 6 footwear
3 qualities 7 tools
4 workplaces 8 electronic equipment

2 1 activities 4 products 7 qualities
2 tasks 5 services 8 clothes
3 Strategies 6 problems

3 Suggested answers:
1 Many successful products have been developed as a result of observing animal characteristics.
2 It is important to wear appropriate clothes when attending a job interview.
3 A job applicant's personal qualities are just as important as his/her qualifications.
4 London is an important centre for financial services such as insurance and accountancy.
5 One of the most useful skills at work is the ability to prioritise different tasks.
6 Hotels which offer outdoor activities such as tennis or swimming are popular with tourists.

7 One of the biggest problems that businesses face today is competition from overseas.
8 One of the most basic strategies employed in football is for a team to retain the ball for as long as possible.

4 Students' own answers

Speaking

1 1 C 3 D 5 E
2 F 4 A 6 B

2 1 put your mind to
2 stand out from the crowd
3 have a hidden talent
4 be a cut above
5 put your mind to/set your sights on

3 1 incentive 5 redundant
2 entrepreneur 6 lucrative
3 monopoly 7 corporation
4 overheads

4 Students' own answers

5 1 B 2 A 3 C 4 D

Audio script 9.2

E = Examiner S1 = Speaker 1 S2 = Speaker 2
S3 = Speaker 3 S4 = Speaker 4

E: Let's talk now about department stores. What is one of the most popular department stores where you live?

S1: So … you're asking me which store most people like going to? I live in a big city and there are a lot of department stores, but one that's very popular at the moment is one that only opened recently. Because it has other facilities, like a nursery and a restaurant. It's called Mella.

E: Which group of people is the store most popular with?

S2: Which group is it popular with? I'd say young adults, say people between 16 and 25. But older people like it too. It's just that there's a room with computer games, and also a lot of the clothes are more suitable for younger people.

E: How important do you think the sales staff are to the success of a store?

S3: Oh, I haven't really thought about that before … but I suppose they're very important. Perhaps not as important as the goods themselves, but having a sales assistant who's polite and helpful makes a big difference to whether you go back to the same store again. They have to be well trained.

E: Some people say that traditional stores will soon disappear because of competition from the internet. Do you agree with that?

S4: Well no, I don't really agree with that. And why I don't agree with it is because … a lot of people, especially young people, like going shopping. They enjoy trying clothes and shoes on, it's almost like a leisure pursuit for them, a hobby. And also, it's much safer to try things on than order them online, because even if they're your size you can never really tell if they'll fit.

6 Students' own answers

7 Students' own answers

Answer key

Writing

1a <u>Summarise</u> the information by <u>selecting</u> and <u>reporting the main features</u>, and make <u>comparisons</u> where relevant. Write at least <u>150 words</u>.

1b

Removed	Changed (nature/size/location)	Stayed the same
Enquiry/Issue desk Videos/CDs Study area	Fiction shelves Computers Children's area Seating Entrance	Displays Non-fiction shelf

1c
1	replaced	3	made
2	remained	4	removed

2a past simple tense – the changes are all completed actions in the past (2014)

2b
1	E	3	G	5	H	7	B
2	A	4	F	6	D	8	C

3a Students' own answers

3b 1 The sentence summarises the extent of the changes and their impact.

4a Students' own answers

4b Sample answer:
The plans show that the library was completely redesigned between 2004 and 2014, making it a much more pleasant environment for users. The most significant developments were the reduction in the number of shelves to make the area feel more spacious and the introduction of features more suited to a modern resource centre. The Enquiry and Issue desk was removed and replaced with three self-service issue machines, while the number of computers increased. The small entrance was extended into a disabled access point. The seating area was made larger with more comfortable chairs and the small Study area was extended and relocated to a separate Quiet area. Another significant change was in the design of the Children's area: this remained in the top left-hand corner but instead of being a closed room, it was made into an open area. Finally, there was an important change in the library content: the number of shelves devoted to books was reduced and the organisation was according to genre. The video and CD section was removed altogether.

5 Students' own answers

Module 10

Reading

1 relating to or having an effect on the emotions

2a I watched a 30-second clip of Pixar's film *Inside Out* … All the while I was watching, the iPad was reading my emotions.

2b a 30-second clip of Pixar's film *Inside Out*

2c D

3
1	D	2	F	3	A	4	H	5	C

4
6	D	7	B	8	D	9	A	10	C

Vocabulary

1
1	assumption	3	speculation	5	concept
2	implications	4	inference	6	insights

2
1	speculation	3	concept	5	insight(s)
2	assumptions	4	implications	6	inference

3a
1	intense	3	wider	5	public
2	abstract	4	underlying		

3b
1	speculation	3	perception
2	implications	4	concept

4a
1	confident, surprised	4	regular
2	chance, guess	5	chance, impression
3	likelihood		

4b
1	guess	4	likelihood/chance
2	chance	5	confident
3	impression	6	surprised

5 Students' own answers

Language development

1a Ticked sentences: 1, 3, 5, 6, 8, 9 and 10

1b 1 <u>If I'd had</u> the opportunity, I <u>would have gone</u> to Borneo on the biology field trip.
3 I <u>wish I'd been able</u> to study medicine.
5 I <u>wish I had accepted</u> the first job that was offered to me.
6 <u>If only I'd worked harder</u>, I <u>would have got</u> the qualifications I needed.
8 If the plane had been on time, I <u>would have arrived</u> home in the afternoon.
9 My mother <u>would have told me about the wedding</u> if I had called her.
10 The price of the house <u>would have come down</u> if only <u>I'd waited</u> a few months.

2
1	hadn't studied	6	could have applied
2	would you have lived	7	hadn't been
3	hadn't moved	8	I'd practised
4	had told	9	would you have used
5	hadn't had	10	hadn't been

3a 1 *Suppose* and *what if*   2 A and C

3b
1	what if/suppose	4	suppose/what if
2	in case	5	in case
3	it's time		

4 Suggested answers:
1 communication would have been much slower
2 a lot of people would want to visit the moon
3 people would have continued to use oil lamps or candles
4 the Pyramids
5 I'd travelled by boat instead of by plane
6 thinking about the kind of career that I want
7 they'd trained more regularly
8 there'd been better international cooperation

Writing

1 3

2a
1	had	3	may
2	wouldn't	4	can

2b 1 present 3 future
2 past 4 present

2c Technology can be defined as the application of theories to the real world for practical functions. 1 <u>Using this definition,</u> the stylus and clay tablet <u>can be seen</u> as the cutting-edge technologies of the ancient world, just as high-powered computers are today's. 2 <u>If we had never invented</u> the means to write down our ideas, <u>we would not have been able</u> to communicate them to a wider community of readers. 3 Consequently, <u>we would have been deprived</u> of the stimulus of feedback and any creativity <u>would have been</u> very restricted.

1 present
2 past
3 past

3a Paragraph 1 is more coherent

3b They – some people
no longer – increasingly
now – increasingly
the same point – dependent on machines to do their thinking for them
without books – printing press
a good novel – books
imaginative – imagination

4a Students' own answers

4b Sample answer:

Technology can be defined as the application of theories to the real world for practical functions. Using this definition, the stylus and clay tablet can be seen as the cutting-edge technologies of the ancient world, just as high-powered computers are today's. If we had never invented the means to write down our ideas, we would not have been able to communicate them to a wider community of readers. Consequently, we would have been deprived of the stimulus of feedback and any creativity would have been very restricted.

Turning to the current era, some people are worried that humans are increasingly dependent on machines to do their thinking for them. They are particularly concerned that children no longer use their imagination in play because machines now create the worlds of their games. However, the same point might have been made about the printing press and imagine how much less creative the world would be without books. Just like a good novel, a good computer game can provide a springboard for richly imaginative thinking.

Of course we cannot predict where technology will take us in the future. If we build robots with the characteristics of humans, then it is possible that we shall have to re-examine this question. However, it is my belief that robots will be designed which can perform tasks such as household chores or driving cars but that this will actually have a positive effect: instead of depriving humans of creativity it will have the liberating effect of freeing up time for humans to exercise our inventiveness even more.

To conclude, I view technology as a crucial element of human creativity and far from holding back new ideas, I believe technology acts as a catalyst for them.

5 Students' own answers

Listening

1 How to measure creativity = Gauging creativity
Two studies on creativity = Recent research
Explaining basic ideas = Background
Ways to stimulate creativity = What makes someone creative: the 4Ps

2 How do we define creativity? It's actually a very abstract notion, hard <u>to pin down</u>. Many people say that a creative act is <u>like a light bulb being switched on</u>. Others talk about <u>blue-sky thinking</u> or <u>thinking outside the box</u>, but put simply creativity is producing something new. For me, a crucial additional element is that something has to have value – so for this talk I'm defining creativity as when something novel but also worthwhile is formed. The created item may be intangible like a scientific theory, a symphony or even something more <u>down to earth</u> like a joke.

The speaker is possibly using these metaphors to make abstract ideas more concrete and thus to provide a sound foundation for the lecture.

3a Sentences 4 and 6 include hypothetical language.

3b 1 6: The research team suggest that parents shouldn't worry about their kids getting bored – <u>if you had more bored youngsters, there would be more</u> creative thinkers.

2 4: A second technique is to ask them to <u>conceive of what might happen</u> in strange circumstances like a world where there is no gravity.

4 1 worthwhile 6 gravity
2 sculpture 7 librarian
3 autonomy 8 phone numbers
4 resources 9 plastic cups
5 Process 10 commuting

Audio script 10.1

N = Narrator S = Student

N: You will hear a lecture on the topic of creativity and research on ways to make people more creative.

S: Good morning. The topic I've chosen for my presentation is enhancing creativity. Now, most of you will think of yourself as either being a creative person or not, but in my talk today I'll discuss recent research studies which indicate that this quality of creativity is more fluid than had previously been thought.

But first I'll start with some background to the topic. How do we define creativity? It's actually a very abstract notion, hard to pin down. Many people say that a creative act is like a light bulb being switched on. Others talk about 'blue-sky thinking' or 'thinking outside the box', but put simply creativity is producing something new. For me, that's not enough – for this talk I'm defining creativity as when something novel but also worthwhile is formed. The created item may be intangible like a scientific theory, a symphony or even something more down to earth like a joke. Or it can be something concrete – an object, such as a newly invented machine, or it could be a work of art, for example a sculpture.

Some of the most interesting work on creativity relates to what makes one person creative and another not. Theorists focus on a variety of aspects but the most commonly cited ones are known as 'the four Ps'. Starting with person, someone who's creative is deemed to have openness, showing curiosity and above all autonomy. Secondly, a focus on product looks at attempts to measure creativity and encompasses the number and detail of ideas as well as how rare or unusual they are. Meanwhile, a focus on place considers the setting or circumstances in which creativity thrives, particularly access to resources and the presence of facilitators. These are considered essentials in creative places. Creative lifestyles are characterised by being nonconformist as well as having flexibility. Finally, a focus on process tries to describe the ways people achieve – the mechanisms and techniques for it but mainly on how divergent the thinking is.

Now there are a wide range of approaches for measuring or gauging creativity, but I'm just going to look at three here. Firstly, in creativity studies, participants are often given some everyday object like a brick and asked to dream up the widest variety of different uses. A second technique is to ask them to conceive of what might happen in strange circumstances like what would happen in a world without gravity. And finally, a very common method is word association – what springs to mind when I say *horse* or *keyboard*, for example.

Turning now to two very interesting recent research studies on creativity. The first was done at the University of Maryland, where researchers wanted to explore the effect of identity on creativity and they asked students to imagine themselves as one of two stereotypes: the 'poet' which was considered eccentric and the 'librarian' which was considered rigid. It wasn't that the researchers themselves endorsed these labels but that they found that they were stereotypes frequently held by undergraduates. The study found that the participants who had imagined themselves as stereotypically imaginative poets performed better on tests of creativity. That requirement to project themselves into a particular identity enhanced their creativity.

A second study, at the University of Central Lancashire, looked at the role of boredom in creativity. Now, most people think that doing boring tasks shrinks and stultifies the mind but this study found otherwise. Researchers divided participants into an experimental group who were given a tedious task of copying phone numbers and a control group who were not given any humdrum task to do. They then asked both groups to come up with unusual ideas for what you can do with plastic cups: basically they wanted them to think of as many uses for them as possible. The findings were surprising: the participants who'd done the boring task beforehand performed significantly better, indicating that boredom can catalyse creativity. The research team suggest that parents shouldn't worry about their kids getting bored – if you had more bored youngsters, there would be more creative thinkers. They also suggest the same for adults. The lead researcher says she does her best creative thinking as she's commuting to and from work. And more of us should … if only we would value our times of boredom, we would be more creative.

Now does anyone have any questions? If so, I've got about 10 minutes now that I can spare …

Language development

1 1 should   3 would
    2 could/may   4 may

2 1 A   2 A   3 B   4 A

3 1 might be   4 would have been
    2 should   5 may have
    3 should have   6 could have

4 Suggested answers:
    1 had been
    2 had chosen/followed
    3 would not have
    4 had not
    5 might/would have been
    6 would have been/become

5 2 The HIV virus would have spread less quickly if national governments had made health education a priority.
    3 Scientists may have found a way of storing solar energy sooner if the research had been properly funded.
    4 Governments should have considered investing more in renewable energy so that climate change goals could be met.
    5 People may have made more effort to reduce waste if the government campaign had been effective.
    6 If trade barriers had been relaxed, food producers in poorer countries would have benefitted considerably.

Vocabulary

1a

+ infinitive	+ -ing
afford, manage, promise	avoid, deny, involve, risk, suggest

1b 1 managed   4 suggested   7 involve
     2 promised   5 risk   8 deny
     3 avoid   6 afford

2 1 D   3 G   5 H   7 F
    2 A   4 C   6 B   8 E

3a 1 applying   4 to create   7 copying
     2 to buy   5 to develop   8 facing
     3 getting   6 replacing

3b 1 created/developed   5 facing
     2 developed/created   6 buy
     3 applies   7 copied
     4 gets   8 replaced

4 Suggested answer:

Velcro is now a very common product – these days it is very difficult to avoid having items which contain it. It is more effective than many other types of fastening, and it is inexpensive, so most people can afford to buy clothing with Velcro. In addition, it is easier to use than other fasteners, so even young children can usually manage to open and close it.

Velcro was modelled on the characteristics of a small lizard, and its development involved analysing the way in which the lizard managed to climb vertical surfaces.

Speaking

1a artistic, creative, gifted, imaginative, original

1b art/artist   imagination
     competence   original/originality
     creativity/creation   practicality
     gift   reality

1c acrobats, dancers, musicians, singers

2 Students' own answers

3a 'The person I'd like to meet is 1 <u>a writer called Ian Rankin</u>. He's Scottish, and he writes crime novels that are centred around a detective called Inspector Rebus, and they're set in Edinburgh. 2 <u>His special talent is creating believable characters</u> – his characters are very true-to-life, and his plots are full of suspense and drama, they're very exciting right up to the end. You can't really guess what the ending will be. He's written about 12 or 15 novels about Inspector Rebus.

4 <u>I'd like to meet him so I could ask him some questions</u>. What I'd like to know is how he gets new ideas each time for the next novel. I'd also be interested in knowing how he develops the plot – whether he plans it all out first, and then follows that plan as he writes, or whether ideas just come to him as he starts writing. I'd like to know how he makes sure that all the characters stay true to life. And I would ask if he has a map of Edinburgh in front of him to keep track of where the characters go, and where the crimes take place. Oh yes, and I'd like to ask him how he knows so much about police methods.'

3b how you know about him/her (3)

4 I'd like to meet him so I could ask him some questions. What I'd like to know is how he gets new ideas each time for the next novel. I'd also be interested in knowing how he develops the plot – whether he plans it all out first, and then follows that plan as he writes, or whether ideas just come to him as he starts writing. I'd like to know how he makes sure that all the characters stay true to life. And I would ask if he has a map of Edinburgh in front of him to keep track of where the characters go, and where the crimes take place. Oh yes, and I'd like to ask him how he knows so much about police methods.

5a Students' own answers

5b Would like to be able to sing
A lot of people can do it
Would use the talent to join a choir/do choral singing, and also to sing for herself
Would like to have the talent because singing is therapeutic

Audio script 10.3

The talent I really wish I had is singing. If I were granted any wish for myself, that would be the thing I'd ask for. Lots of people are able to sing, and obviously really enjoy it, and it's unusual to have no singing ability. If I had the talent, I'd probably join a choir and do choral singing. But most of all I'd sing to myself – around the house and so on. The reason I'd like to have the talent is that I think singing is therapeutic – I mean that it makes people feel happy and relaxed. You don't need any special equipment or training, so it's something that you can do spontaneously whenever you feel like it.

5c Students' own answers

5d Students' own answers

6 Students' own answers

Writing

1a 1 curiosity relates to a natural interest to find out more about something; necessity relates to need
2 need – necessity
inquisitiveness – curiosity
interest – curiosity
requirement – necessity
essential – necessity
fascination – curiosity
desire to know – curiosity

1b 3 motivates

2a 1 ✗   3 ✗   5 =
2 ✓   4 ✓   6 ✓

2b 3 <u>If we want</u> to preserve our security, <u>we must</u> constantly improve our weapons of war.
6 <u>Without</u> the innate desire to push boundaries, <u>we would</u> never have moved out of the caves.

2c Students' own answers

2d Students' own answers

3a 1 role   4 trace
2 original   5 perceived
3 ground-breaking

3b A <u>In turn</u>, these products generate a whole new set of requirements.
B <u>As a result</u>, it revolutionised the way people thought about the world.
C <u>Consequently</u>, we must try to develop this quality from as young an age as possible.
D <u>However</u>, it is often one person's vision which triggers the process in the first place.
E <u>Although</u> these devices are often considered to be quintessentially 20th-century inventions.
1 D
2 C
3 B
4 E
5 A

4 Sample answer:

There is no question that curiosity plays a major role in all kinds of innovation. We can see that some inventions were developed out of a desire to satisfy a thirst for knowledge and to push the boundaries of the unknown. Let us take as an example the ground-breaking invention of the telescope. People had always used their naked eyes to gaze at the planets and to chart their passage across the sky, but I suggest that it was sheer curiosity which made them create a telescope which enabled them to discern detail: the features of Jupiter's surface, or the rings of Saturn for instance.

However, for machines such as the canon or the rocket, necessity is more likely to have provided the impulse for invention. If people with wealth and power perceive the need for a particular type of armament to defend their country or to invade another, then it is likely that appropriate backing will be provided to scientists and engineers to design and develop the weapon. Another dimension of need is commercial. The design of a radically new hand-held computer is likely to be borne out of the desire to beat the competition and sell more merchandise.

However, in reality it is difficult to identify the exact impetus behind the design of any device or theory and my own view is that virtually all successful inventions are the product of a mix of inquisitiveness and perceived necessity. It is likely that an invention that is initially designed to satisfy curiosity is soon picked up by others and developed to fulfil a particular need. Equally, necessity might be the prime driver in some inventions but they are developed in new ways because of humans' innate desire to explore.

5a Students' own answers

5b Students' own answers

Pearson Education Limited
Edinburgh Gate, Harlow, Essex. CM20 2JE and Associated Companies
throughout the world

pearsonelt.com/expertielts

First published 2017
ISBN 978-1-292-12513-8 (Student's Resource Book with key)
Set in Amasis and Mundo Sans
Printed and bound in Slovakia by Neografia

Acknowledgements

We are grateful to the following for permission to reproduce copyright material:

Illustration Acknowledgements

Illustrated by ROARR Design

Photo Acknowledgements

The publisher would like to thank the following for their kind permission to
reproduce their photographs:

(Key: b-bottom; c-centre; l-left; r-right; t-top)

123RF.com: Franck Camhi 62, Bart Leo Maria de Rijk 67; **Alamy Stock Photo:**
Ammentorp Photography 33, Hera Vintage Ads 37l, 37r; **Fotolia.com:** Alexey
Boldin 41, Dream79 20tl, Steuccio79 71; **Getty Images:** Hulton Deutsch 51;
Shutterstock.com: Peter Bernik 87, Chuyuss 24, Elnür 43tl, Epstock 47tr, Zwola
Fasola 34, Alex Hinds 63, Hurst Photo 22, Charlie Hutton 43tc, Hxdbzxy 28,
Intellistudies 14, Brian A Jackson 26, Sophie James 16, Jcjgphotography 92,
Michael Jung 84, 95tl, Volodymyr Krasyuk 23, Lightpoet 74, Lightspring 30,
Dmitri Maruta 57, Monkey Business Images 72, Ulrich Mueller 42, Ndoeljindoel
93, Nobeastsofierce 61, Ollyy 97, Sari ONeal 6, Pisaphotography 77, Richard
Guijt Photography 12, Pablo Scapinachis 19, Spotmatik 10, Ronald Sumners
43tr, Wavebreakmedia 82, Jamie Wilson 35, Feng Yu 45

All other images © Pearson Education

We are grateful to the following for permission to reproduce copyright material:

Text

Article on page 9 from Neural Integration Underlying a Time-Compensated
Sun Compass in the Migratory Monarch Butterfly, *Cell Reports*, Volume 15, Issue
4, pp.683-691 (Eli Shlizerman, James Phillips-Portillo, Daniel B. Forger, Steven
M. Reppert 2016), with permission from Elsevier, http://www.sciencedirect.
com/science/article/pii/S221112471630328X; Article on page 9 from Monarch
butterflies use internal compass to find their way, *The Telegraph* 27/06/2010
(Richard Gray), Telegraph Media Group Ltd 2010; Article on page 11 from GPS
big data: making cities safer for cyclists, *The Telegraph* 09/05/2014 (Matthew
Sparkes), Telegraph Media Group Ltd 2014; Article on page 18 from Leading the
way to a new kind of city, *The Telegraph* 01/07/2016, Telegraph Media Group
Ltd 2016; Extract on page 22 from How Wikipedia changed the world, *The
Telegraph* 14/01/2016 (Madhumita Murgia), Telegraph Media Group Ltd 2016;
Article on page 27 from Vitamin D – could it stop 'modern' diseases?,
The Telegraph 07/08/2014 (Oliver Gillie), Telegraph Media Group Ltd 2014;
Article on page 37 from The power of advertising: a threat to our way of life,
www.opendemocracy.net, 18/06/2011 (Justin Lewis), Reprinted with kind
permission of Professor Justin Lewis; Article on page 42 from Entrepreneur takes
on plastic packaging, *The Telegraph* 08/07/2014 (Rebecca Burn-Callander,),
Telegraph Media Group Ltd 2014; Article on page 47 from Eco living: the house
of the future?, *The Telegraph* 20/11/2013 (Sarah Lonsdale), Telegraph Media
Group Ltd 2013; Article on page 52 from Many Britons in their 30s doubt they
will ever own their own home, poll reveals, *The Telegraph* 23/03/2016 (Nicola
Harley), Telegraph Media Group Ltd 2016; Article 7. from Will Rotterdam's
Markthal be equivalent of Bilbao's Guggenheim?, *FT.com*, 18/09/2015 (Paul
Miles), © The Financial Times Limited. All Rights Reserved.; Extract on page
69 from https://tfl.gov.uk/modes/emirates-air-line/the-emirates-air-line-
experience?intcmp=1445, Reproduced by kind permission of Transport for
London. © TFL; Article on page 87 from Dame Kelly Holmes on the GSK
Human Performance Lab, *The Telegraph* 07/06/2016 (Louisa Peacock),
Telegraph Media Group Ltd 2016; Article on page 97 from Affective computing:
how 'emotional machines' are about to take over our lives, *The Telegraph*
15/01/2016 (Madhumita Murgia), Telegraph Media Group Ltd 2016